LEFT FOR DEAD

T0356714

Also by
ERIC JAY DOLIN

REBELS AT SEA: PRIVATEERING IN THE
AMERICAN REVOLUTION

A FURIOUS SKY: THE FIVE-HUNDRED-YEAR HISTORY
OF AMERICA'S HURRICANES

BLACK FLAGS, BLUE WATERS: THE EPIC HISTORY
OF AMERICA'S MOST NOTORIOUS PIRATES

BRILLIANT BEACONS: A HISTORY OF THE
AMERICAN LIGHTHOUSE

WHEN AMERICA FIRST MET CHINA: AN EXOTIC HISTORY
OF TEA, DRUGS, AND MONEY IN THE AGE OF SAIL

FUR, FORTUNE, AND EMPIRE: THE EPIC HISTORY
OF THE FUR TRADE IN AMERICA

LEVIATHAN: THE HISTORY OF WHALING IN AMERICA

POLITICAL WATERS

SNAKEHEAD: A FISH OUT OF WATER

SMITHSONIAN BOOK OF
NATIONAL WILDLIFE REFUGES

Left *for* Dead

SHIPWRECK,

TREACHERY,

and SURVIVAL

at the EDGE

of the WORLD

Eric Jay Dolin

Liveright Publishing Corporation

A Division of W. W. Norton & Company
Independent Publishers Since 1923

For information about permission to reproduce selections from this book, write to
Permissions, Liveright Publishing Corporation, a division of W. W. Norton & Company, Inc.,
500 Fifth Avenue, New York, NY 10110

For information about special discounts for bulk purchases, please contact
W. W. Norton Special Sales at specialsales@wwnorton.com or 800-233-4830

Maps on pp. xiv–xv, 81, and 185 by David Cain

Manufacturing by Lakeside Book Company
Book design by Barbara M. Bachman
Production manager: Anna Oler

ISBN 978-1-324-09674-0 pbk.

Liveright Publishing Corporation, 500 Fifth Avenue, New York, N.Y. 10110
www.wwnorton.com

W. W. Norton & Company Ltd., 15 Carlisle Street, London W1D 3BS

10 9 8 7 6 5 4 3 2 1

*To the readers who made
my writing life possible.
Thank you!*

CONTENTS

—

AUTHOR'S NOTE

===

MANY BOOKS TELL STORIES OF FAMOUS INDIVIDUALS AND EVENTS THAT have changed the course of history. This book isn't one of them. While there are a few infamous characters in the following pages, none of the dramatis personae are especially noteworthy. The key events described, while dramatic and compelling, were largely forgotten after they occurred, and very few people today, even avid historians, know anything about them.

So, why did I want to write this book? That's simple. I found the story fascinating. These events, which occurred more than 210 years ago, primarily during the War of 1812, open a small window on the often dangerous and unpredictable world of maritime commerce and transportation during the great Age of Sail. They show individuals under great duress acting nobly, atrociously, and everything in between. As such, the saga reveals both the better angels of human nature and the darker depths to which individuals can sink, tendencies that were only amplified by the violent conflict between the United States and Great Britain. Although one can certainly question the morals of some of the participants, the book is not a morality play. It is, instead, a complex narrative with surprising twists and turns that can stand alongside the most captivating maritime tales ever told. I hope you enjoy reading it.

ONE OF THE CENTRAL elements of this story is the practice of killing seals (sealing) in the South Atlantic during the early 1800s. While a few countries even today allow commercial sealing, the United States does not.

American laws ban the commercial hunting of all marine mammals, including seals. Although many people are repulsed by sealing, and consider it to be cruel and unnecessary in modern society, this book does not debate the merits of sealing, either then or now, nor does it consider whether it is a morally, ethically, or commercially defensible pursuit. Instead, sealing is presented as what it was at the time: a widespread, lucrative, and respectable maritime business that employed many Americans and numerous individuals from other countries.

NOTE THAT ALL ARCHAIC spellings in quotes have been modernized. Also, the place names in the book are those used at the time the story occurs. Their modern-day equivalents are indicated upon first use and in the maps created for the book.

SOME CONTEMPORARY ACCOUNTS DIFFER slightly on the dates when certain events occurred, or the number of people involved in a particular situation. Typically, they are only off by a day or two, or by one or two individuals. In selecting which numbers to rely on, I chose the ones that appeared to be the most accurate and were recorded closest to the time of the event in question. In no case does the difference in dates or the number of people significantly alter the narrative.

LEFT FOR DEAD

Southwest Region
of the
FALKLAND ISLANDS

0   10
Miles

NEW   NORTH
ISLAND   ISLAND

PASSAGE
ISLANDS

Pinch-Gut
Camp

DOANE'S
HEAD

Hook Camp

Sea Lion
Point

States
Bay
(Chatham
Harbor)

LOOP
HEAD

Quaker
Harbor

TUSSAC
POINT
(QUEEN)

BEAVER
ISLAND

Island
Harbor

Canton Harbor
(Gull)

TEA ISLAND

SWAN ISLAND
(WEDDELL)

Cape Orford

SEADOG
ISLAND

FOX ISLAND
(TUSSAC)

BARNARD'S
ISLAND
(DYKE)

Barnard's
Harbor
(Double Creek
West Arm)

McCockling's Lagoon
(Fegen Inlet)

Port Stephens

Arch
Islands
Harbor

BIRD
ISLAND

TWO ISLAND
(TEN SHILLING BAY
ISLAND)

Cape
Meredith

KEY

1813 names first (modern names in parens)

+++++++ Young Nanina (April 12~May 3, 1813)

———→ Overland hike (April 23-25, 1813)

• • • • • Nanina (May 22~June 15, 1813)

– – – – – Hunting party (June 14~July 7, 1813)

— — — Hunting party (July 8-12, 1813)

cain

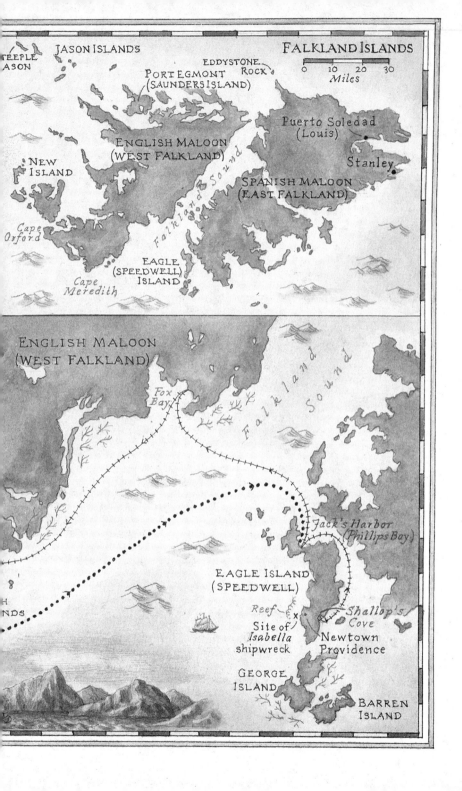

INTRODUCTION

═══

CHARLES H. BARNARD, CAPTAIN OF THE AMERICAN SEALING BRIG *NANINA*, had only the best of intentions. His aim was to ensure the survival of the people under his care. On June 11, 1813, Barnard and four other volunteers disembarked the anchored *Nanina*, climbed into a small boat, and sailed about 10 miles from New Island to Beaver Island, both part of the Falkland Islands archipelago in the South Atlantic. Armed with knives, clubs, lances, and guns, and with the assistance of Barnard's trusty dog, Cent, the five men planned to kill birds and hogs and take them back to the Americans and British who remained on the *Nanina* and were fast running out of fresh provisions. It was a mission of mercy.

The hunt went well, and within a few days the boat was filled to the gunwales with the bloody carcasses of slain animals. But when the men sailed back to New Island late on June 14, they were greeted with an alarming sight. The *Nanina* was gone. Stunned, confused, and angry, the men hauled the boat up onto the beach and, according to Barnard, "awaited the approach of daylight in the most impatient and tormenting anxiety." Sleeping fitfully in the cold night air, they hoped that in the morning light they would find a letter telling them why the *Nanina* had left, and when it was coming back.

A frantic search at dawn turned up nothing: no note either in a bottle or hung conspicuously from a piece of wood or a boulder. They saw only sand, rocks, scrubby vegetation, and birds in the distance, walking on the beach or flying overhead.

Refusing to believe that he and the other four men had been "barbarously deserted," Barnard seized on another explanation. The *Nanina* and her crew must have headed to Beaver Island to pick them up, but they had gone to the opposite side from where the men were hunting, thus missing their comrades. Convinced by Barnard's reasoning, the men's hopes were rekindled. They dragged the boat into the water and sailed off once again. This time they entered the main harbor on the eastern side of Beaver Island.

Upon entering the harbor, as Barnard later recalled, they experienced "the almost insupportable anguish of neither finding the brig, nor discovering any trace that she had been [there]." They had been cruelly abandoned at the beginning of a Falklands winter, with little to sustain them, and no explanation why they had been left in such a horrendous predicament.

THE EVENTS LEADING UP to this abandonment, and what happened afterward, produce a story with so many unlikely threads, and a cast including such exceptionally colorful characters, that one might think that it sprang from the pen of a fiction writer with an overactive imagination. And yet, the story is true. It is a tale involving a shipwreck, British and Americans meeting under the most stressful circumstances in a time of war, kindness and compassion, drunkenness, the birth of a child, treachery, greed, lying, a hostile takeover, stellar leadership, ingenuity, severe privation, the great value of a good dog, perseverance, endurance, threats, bullying, banishment, a perilous thousand-mile open-ocean journey in a 17.5-foot boat, an improbable rescue mission in a rickety ship, and legal battles over a dubious and disgraceful wartime prize. And it all started with two ships—one American, the other British—sailing to the Falklands from different directions.

CHAPTER

1

A-Sealing We Shall Go

==

EARLY IN 1812, CHARLES H. BARNARD MARCHED INTO THE OFFICES OF THE prosperous New York import/export firm John B. Murray and Son and proposed a sealing voyage to the Falkland Islands. The expedition's goal, like all such journeys, was to kill seals to collect their skins and render oil from their blubber. Once the vessel was loaded with "product," it would sail back to New York, while leaving on the islands a small crew of men to continue sealing. Upon the vessel's return to the city, Murray and Son would sell as much of the cargo as possible and then send a larger ship back to the islands to pick up the men who remained there.

The timing of the larger ship's voyage back to the Falklands was contingent upon the likelihood of sealing success. If Barnard believed that a good load of skins and oil could be gathered in short order, the larger ship would sail relatively soon after the first vessel's return to New York. If seals were scarce, the ship might not return to the Falklands for a year or more, giving the men more time to hunt. Regardless of when the ship picked up the men, it would then sail around Cape Horn and into the Pacific, where it would continue sealing at various islands before heading to Canton,* China, to sell the skins and oil. Barnard's proposal made sense economically and personally.

---

* Modern-day Guangzhou.

———

THE SIGNING OF THE Treaty of Paris on September 3, 1783, ended the American Revolution and opened up a whole new world of commercial possibilities to the newly minted United States. Before the Revolution, the hated British Navigation Acts greatly restricted American commerce, essentially requiring that the Americans trade directly with, or route their trade through, England. After the war, the Navigation Acts no longer held sway, and the United States was free to trade with any country it chose.

High on the list of new trading partners was China. Among the Chinese items most cherished by Americans were the teas, silks, and porcelains formerly provided by the British East India Company, which had held the monopoly on the China trade. Now that the Americans had thrown off the shackles of the British Empire, they could go straight to

Oil sketch entitled "American Commissioners of the Preliminary Peace Agreement with Great Britain," by Benjamin West, circa 1783. From left to right are John Jay, John Adams, Benjamin Franklin, Henry Laurens, and William Temple Franklin. The agreement was signed on November 30, 1782. The British delegation refused to pose for the picture, thus leaving it unfinished.

A 1799 engraving of a Chinese furrier hawking his wares in Canton (modern-day Guangzhou), China.

the source to obtain Chinese goods. The pressing issue facing American merchants, therefore, was precisely what should they offer in trade with China?

Ultimately, the Americans assembled a great array of items to entice the Chinese: silver coins and ingots collected through international trade; ginseng from the forests of New England, New York, and farther south; sandalwood from Hawaii and Fiji; opium from the Ottoman Empire; and bêche-de-mer, also called "trepang" or "sea cucumber," from various Pacific islands. Yet another item that proved critical, especially during the first few decades of the America–China trade, was fur.

The king of furs—a sensationally lustrous and soft fur coat that is the densest of any mammal, with as many as a million hairs per square inch— came from sea otters. The Chinese, who treasured furs for their warmth and beauty, were willing to pay exorbitant prices for sea otters' pelts.

To obtain the pelts, the Americans headed to the Pacific Northwest, where the coastal waters were teeming with the creatures. The first American ship to tap into this new and lucrative market was the 84-foot, 212-ton *Columbia Rediviva*. It left from Boston for the Pacific Northwest

A sea otter about to eat a salmon, drawn by John James Audubon,
circa 1845–48. When Audubon visited California in 1843, sea
otter populations were already greatly depleted due to hunting,
so he saw only a single live specimen during his trip.

in September 1787 and returned to the same port in August 1790, after selling its furs in Canton for $21,404.7.* In the process, it became the first American ship to circumnavigate the globe, logging nearly 42,000 miles since leaving Boston three years earlier. Over the next thirty years, sea otters continued to be a staple of the America–China trade. By the early 1820s, however, the American sea otter trade was in its death throes. The root cause was clear—the sea otter had been hunted nearly to extinction, not only in the Pacific Northwest but all along the coast from California to Alaska. Not prolific breeders to begin with, the sea otter didn't have a chance against human avarice.

While the sea otter pelt was the king of furs for many decades, it wasn't the only fur coveted by the Chinese. A year before *Columbia Redi-*

---

* For those who would like to know what this 1790 dollar amount would be worth today, please visit measuringworth.com. As you will see, the question of the present value of a past dollar amount is fraught, and no one calculation is "correct," since it depends on your assumptions and what you would like to measure. Suffice it to say that $21,404.7 in 1790 was a very considerable sum, and certainly the equivalent of many millions of dollars today.

viva sailed, Americans were sending sealskins to China. America's foray into that sealskin trade began with one man's educated guess.

William Rotch Sr., the patriarch of a famed Nantucket whaling family, was in London in 1785 when he read British Captain James Cook's recently published journals detailing his voyages of discovery during the previous decade. During one of those voyages, Cook's men had sold sea otter pelts in Canton for huge sums. One lucky seaman sold his lot of furs for $800, and a few especially prime skins fetched $120 each. The description of sea otter furs selling in Canton for tremendous prices spurred Rotch to think about his family's fleet of whaling ships, which had fallen on hard times due to Britain's decision, in the wake of the American Revolution, to slap a duty of £18.3 per ton on foreign whale oil. Oppressed by this onerous duty, not even sperm whale oil merchants— whose product was the most valuable—could turn a profit. Rotch, seeking another way to make money, thought it might be worthwhile to divert some of the family's ships and men into the sea otter trade off the Pacific Northwest. He urged his younger brother, Francis, to pursue this course. But Francis had yet another idea.

During the Revolution, Francis had briefly relocated some of the family's whaling fleet to the Falkland Islands, in a failed attempt to keep their vessels beyond the tentacles of war. While there, he became quite familiar with the large seal populations that frequented the islands. So, when his brother recommended that he get into the sea otter trade, Francis thought back to the Falklands and decided to pursue sealing instead. He knew that the Russians and the British had successfully sold sealskins to the Chinese, and he was eager to do so as well.* To that end, Francis dispatched the ship *United States* to the Falklands in 1786, where Captain Benjamin Hussey collected thirteen thousand sealskins, as well as ninety tons of whale oil. The skins, sold in New York for fifty cents, were ultimately loaded aboard the New York ship *Eleanora*, captained by Simon Metcalfe, and sent to Canton, where they sold for ten times that amount.

Throughout the remainder of the 1700s, and on into the early 1800s,

---

* The Russians had launched a profitable sealskin trade with the Chinese in the mid-1700s. The British, too, had pursued sealing. In 1775, Alexander Dalrymple, the first hydrographer of the British Admiralty, wrote that, on an expedition to the Falklands, fur seals were found in "such numbers that they killed eight or nine hundred in a day with bludgeons on one small island." Quoted in Robert Cushman Murphy, "The Status of Sealing in the Subantarctic Atlantic," *The Scientific Monthly* (August 1918), 112.

Engraving of a fur seal, or "The Fur Seal of Commerce,"
by W. H. Lizars, 1860.

many more American ships departed on sealing voyages. They went to islands in the South Atlantic, including the Falklands, as well as ones in the Indian Ocean and off the west coast of South America.* The main targets of these voyages were fur seals, the generic name applied to a number of species to distinguish them from the so-called hair seals, including sea lions, whose pelts were not so plush and therefore less desirable and less valuable.† When the opportunity arose, however, sealers also took hair seals. The more costly fur sealskins went to the Chinese, who had developed a process that could separate the coarser outer hairs, leaving the softer undercoat intact, thus enabling the creation of pliable, luxurious, and well-insulated outer garments. While the Chinese typically refused the skins of hair seals, there was a market for them—albeit a less

---

* Many American vessels were solely dedicated to sealing, but some had dual operations, focusing on killing both whales and seals. As Nantucket historian Obed Macy observed, "Sealing was in many respects, nearly allied with whaling. Seals and whales were generally met with on the same coast; it required as large vessels and as many men to engage in taking the former as the latter; the outfits were nearly the same, and the voyages were of like duration." Obed Macy, *The History of Nantucket* (Boston: Hilliard and Gray, 1835), 140.

† The taxonomy of seals is fairly complicated. The two main types of seals that concern us here are earless seals (family Phocidae), including elephant seals; and eared seals (family Otariidae), including fur seals and sea lions.

profitable one—in the United States and Europe, where they were used mainly to make coats and boots.

The scope of the trade in sealskins was almost beyond belief. American ships brought 2.5 million sealskins into Canton alone between 1792 and 1812, according to one estimate, and others claim that the number was considerably higher. The skins sold for anywhere from 35 cents to $5 each. High-quality skins were used to make fur capes, belts, mittens, and caps. The profits were often considerable, as was the case for the *Betsey*, a 90-ton sealing ship, which sailed from New York to the South Pacific in 1797 and returned twenty-three months later with $120,467 worth of China goods. After deducting the cost of the venture, the owners cleared $53,118.

It wasn't only skins that sealers sought. In the South Atlantic, they also targeted elephant seals for their blubber, which was rendered into oil and sold as an illuminant. This high-quality oil burned with a bright flame that produced little smoke, making it nearly as valuable as sperm whale oil, the most sought-after light source of the day. Taking into account all of the financial inducements, it thus became clear that a sealing voyage to the Falklands could be a very lucrative venture indeed for Charles Barnard and Murray and Son.

As for the personal connection to venture, Barnard was intimately familiar with the risks and rewards of such an expedition, having captained earlier sealing voyages to the Falklands, a few in the service of

A male sea lion on New Island, Falkland Islands.

Engraving of an elephant seal by W. H. Lizars, 1860.

Murray and Son. So, when he approached the firm with his proposal, they were confident that he was the right man for the job. But it wasn't only Barnard's sealing experience that prompted the shrewd business-men to have faith in him. Saltwater ran through his veins.

Charles's father, Valentine,* was a seasoned ship's captain born in 1749 on Nantucket, America's whaling capital. Although Charles was born on the island on October 25, 1781, he left a few years later, when Valentine moved his family to Hudson, New York, which proved to be an excellent place for a future mariner to learn his craft.

Despite being located roughly 120 miles from New York City and the open seas, on the banks of the Hudson River, the village of Hudson was intimately tied to the ocean. It was founded in 1783 by an association of whalemen, artisans, and businessmen from Nantucket, Providence, and Martha's Vineyard, who had decided that the time had come for them to relocate. After witnessing the British destroy their ships and ransack their towns during the American Revolution, they wanted to settle in an area that would not be an easy target for foreign invasion, while at the same time provide them with opportunities to earn a living. They reasoned that any location along the eastern coast of America was out of

---

*　Since both Charles and Valentine shared the same last name, I will refer to them by their first names from here onward.

the question, because it would be too exposed. Still, for them to carry on their businesses, especially whaling, and to establish shipping and trade routes, a direct link to the ocean was a necessity. Claverack Landing—Hudson's name until the mid-1780s—appeared to be the perfect choice. Not only did it provide a considerable degree of built-in protection—being so far from the sea—but it also was surrounded by vast stands of large trees excellent for shipbuilding, as well as numerous farms whose produce could be the foundation for a thriving shipborne trade.

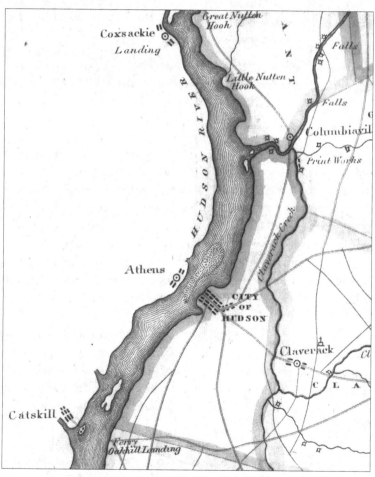

Detail of map by David H. Burr, showing the town
of Hudson along the Hudson River.

View of Hudson, New York, circa 1821.

Hudson quickly grew into a maritime powerhouse. One visitor in 1788 remarked that the town had "emerged from a Dutch farm into a position of a commercial city, with a considerable population, warehouses, wharves and docks, ropewalks, shipping, and the din of industry." Much of Hudson's success was rooted in whaling, as dozens of whaleships left the port and returned with oil and baleen. But sealing voyages also figured prominently. It was in this environment that Charles spent his formative years. From an early age, he took to the sea, rising through the ranks from cabin boy to captain on voyages throughout the Atlantic.

On March 17, 1804, Charles married Mary Ann Paxton. Both Charles and his father were members of the Hudson Quaker Meeting, but Ms. Paxton was not a Quaker, so Charles was promptly booted out of the religion after their marriage. The official reason was his decision to marry outside of the church, but, if that wasn't bad enough, the ceremony had been performed by a "hireling priest." This ouster and Mary's New York City roots were powerful incentives to relocate. So, too, was the fact that New York City was America's premier port, offering many opportunities for ambitious mariners. So Charles and Mary moved to the city in 1805, followed a few years later by his father, Valentine.

CHARLES QUICKLY CAME TO terms with John B. Murray and Son regarding the nature of the Falklands sealing voyage and the responsibilities of the parties. Murray and Son would purchase a vessel, subject to Charles's approval, and fit it out in a manner calculated to ensure its success. Once the vessel was secured, Charles would sign on a skilled crew. For their investment, Murray and Son would receive 52 percent of the net proceeds of the skins and oil procured, while Barnard would control the distribution of the remaining 48 percent to himself and the other men he engaged.

At an auction in New York City on February 12, 1812, Murray and Son bought the 132-ton brig *Nanina*. It was 73 feet long, 20 feet 4 inches wide, and had a draft* of 10 feet 2 inches. With two decks and a hold below, the *Nanina* had enough space to accommodate a small crew and plenty of cargo. Described as "handsome" and "fast-sailing" by contem-

A merchant brig, 1814. The Nanina *would have looked something like this.*

---

* The draft of a vessel is the distance between the waterline and the deepest point of the boat—in this case, the bottom of the hull.

porary chroniclers, the *Nanina* was only eight years old, having been built in Pittsburgh in 1804. After its christening, the *Nanina* was actively engaged as a trader, voyaging to Cuba, Jamaica, and Tenerife in the Canary Islands, and returning with a wide array of goods that included rum, muscovado sugar, coffee, and wine.

Under Charles's supervision, the *Nanina* was loaded for her Falklands voyage with a great array of provisions and supplies, including barrels of salt beef and pork, hardtack biscuits, and water; wood for making fires and for whittling pegs for stretching out and drying the sealskins; extra sails and sailcloth; tents; rope; a forge; iron try-pots for rendering the blubber; broken-down barrels to be put together to hold the oil from rendered blubber; clubs, knives, and lances needed for killing and processing seals; two small boats; and navigational equipment. One of the most crucial pieces of sealing-related cargo was the frame for a 20-ton shallop—a boat with a mainmast and two sails—that would be built after landing in the Falklands. The shallop would enable the men to go on extended hunting cruises far from the brig, and it would also be used to supply sealing crews temporarily stationed on distant islands.

While the *Nanina* was being loaded, Charles also hired the crew—a task made easier courtesy of a European conflict at sea.

The Crew

━━

CHARLES ENJOYED A WIDE CHOICE OF CREWMEN, SINCE 1812 WAS TURNING out to be a dismal year for mariners, due in large part to the ongoing war between Great Britain and France.* In an effort to cripple each other's ability to fight by cutting off supplies, both countries passed draconian laws that clamped down on neutral ships trading with the enemy. American ships trading with Britain were subject to seizure as a prize of war by the French navy, and those trading with France risked being seized by the Royal Navy. As a result, many American merchants kept their ships home to avoid capture, putting numerous mariners out of work. Making matters worse was the ever-present threat of impressment.

The perpetually shorthanded Royal Navy had a long history of impressing American sailors, taking them from their ships and forcing them to serve on British ships. The British claimed that these men were deserters from the Royal Navy, or simply British citizens, but the vast majority were Americans who were seized illegally. The Royal Navy pleaded necessity in pursuing this outrageous practice. Without such reinforcements, it could not adequately man its ships and would have been considerably weakened. Britain's sprawling war with France greatly increased the Royal Navy's need for manpower, causing a rise in impressment in the years leading up to 1812—providing yet another incentive

---

* This war was part of the more expansive Napoleonic Wars (1803–15) that embroiled much of Europe.

British officer looking over group of American seamen on deck of
ship, and evidently planning to impress a few, circa 1810.

for merchants to mothball their ships and further reducing maritime
employment options.

The employment situation for sealers was particularly bad. Years of
relentless seal killing had greatly reduced the mammals' numbers, making it more difficult for expeditions to return with enough skins and oil to
generate a healthy profit. This, plus the dangers of war, kept most sealing
vessels in port. Available records show only two sealing voyages leaving
America's shores between 1805 and early 1812.

Given all this, one wonders why Charles Barnard and Murray and
Son thought a sealing voyage was a good idea. Their calculus was based
on four assumptions. First, the lull in sealing voyages would have given
seal populations in the Falklands a chance to rebound a bit and increase
the prospect of a full load, especially since the *Nanina* was likely to be
the only sealing vessel at the islands. Second, because fewer sealing ships
had gone to Canton in recent years, the Chinese demand for skins would
probably be higher, boosting prices. Third, by trading with China, as
opposed to countries in Europe, the *Nanina* would have a good chance
of avoiding the clutches of either the Royal Navy or the French navy.
And, fourth, with so many mariners out of work, they would have little
difficulty gathering a skilled crew. Beyond these assumptions, it was clear

that Charles as well as Murray and Son were risk takers. In their eyes, it was better to attempt a voyage, despite the potential pitfalls, rather than be idle at home.

Among the unemployed mariners were many ship's captains. Charles tapped three of them—Andrew Hunter, Edmund Fanning, and Barzillai Pease—to become copartners in the expedition. In exchange for putting up a $5,000 bond of performance, each was given a significant stake in the venture. They also agreed to remain on the Falklands with Charles after the *Nanina* was sent back to New York, and then to continue on to China when the larger vessel picked them up.

Almost nothing is known about Captain Hunter, other than that he hailed from Rhode Island and was thirty years old. Captain Fanning is a bit less mysterious. He was a twenty-six-year-old married Nantucketer. He shared the same name as his much more famous uncle, an experienced sealer and explorer who, by the end of his very productive life in 1841, had either led or acted as an agent for more than seventy expeditions throughout the world's oceans, all of which provided the content for his 1833 maritime classic: *Voyages Round the World; With Selected Sketches of Voyages to the South Seas, North and South Pacific Oceans, China, etc.*

About thirty-eight-year-old Captain Barzillai Pease, there is much more to say. Born on Martha's Vineyard on July 27, 1773, as a boy he went on short cod-fishing trips to Nantucket Shoals, but his real introduction to the sea came after his father inherited a riverfront farm in Easton, New York, about 60 miles north of the town of Hudson. In the spring of 1788, the family moved to Easton and began working the land. The young Pease, however, soon tired of farmwork and dreamed of going to sea. So, at the age of sixteen he went to Hudson and signed on as a cabin boy for the brig *Prudence*, master Albertus Swain, fitting out to go sperm whaling off Brazil. Before he boarded, Pease heard from others on the dock that Swain was a "surly master," yet he didn't back out of the trip.

Barely two weeks into the voyage, a violent storm dismasted the *Prudence*, and Swain pulled into Martinique to repair the brig. Rather than continue on to Brazil after the repairs, they went in search of whales around the islands. The whaling was abysmal, a couple of men deserted, and frequent disputes erupted over rations. But the worst part for Pease was his treatment at the hands of Swain. As the situation went downhill, Pease observed that Swain became "morose and petulant, and could scarcely appear pleasant, for at the best he was sour enough. His treatment to me . . . was such that no one would countenance. I was but a lad and wanted instruction and not abuse." But abuse was what he got. Among other things, Swain struck Pease under his ear so that "it was swollen up as big as a hen's eggs and turned both black and blue." He also took Pease by the hair and "pounded" him in the face until he made him "spout [blood] like a whale at the nose." In the end, the entire voyage was a commercial failure, and Pease earned a piddling amount, most of which his father took from him.

Despite this experience, Pease wanted to ship out again, but his father stood in the way. The two men didn't get along, with Pease noting that "in general [his father] was severe in the extreme." When Pease offered his father $100 from his future earnings to buy out his time on the farm, the offer was accepted, with his father setting a date for when Pease could leave. But when that day arrived, his father set a new date—a duplicitous process he repeated multiple times. Frustrated and angry, Pease simply left home with only a blanket and the clothes on his back, and without even saying good-bye. Making his way to Hudson, he signed on to another whaling voyage aboard the *Prudence*, this time with Captain Solomon Bunker.

Though Pease was venturing out on the same ship, his experiences with Bunker and Swain were like night and day. Rather than torment Pease, Bunker treated him like a son and never yelled at him. Pease found the voyage very "agreeable," and, better yet, it was a greasy one, the brig returning with a hold full of oil, Pease's portion of which he sold for a healthy profit.

Pease visited his family, hoping to mend his relationship with his father, but after three days of relative peace, their rapprochement fell apart over money. His father demanded that his son pay the $100 he had earlier promised, but Pease offered only $40, sending his father into a rage. As Pease later recalled, this "opened a complete warfare with me, which I was not able to defend." For a second time, Pease left home bitter and returned to the sea, sailing from Hudson as a common seaman on the brig *Nancy*, bound for a sealing voyage to the Falkland Islands.

This was an entirely new experience for Pease, who had never gone sealing. In short order, he became proficient in killing and skinning the animals and rendering elephant-seal blubber into oil. Nineteen months after departing, the *Nancy* returned home triumphantly, with 8,000 skins and 300 barrels of oil.

Yet Pease's good luck was short-lived. In Hudson, a friend delivered some disquieting news. His father, even more furious about not receiving the $100 he had been promised, announced that the next time he saw his son he "intended to skin" him, just as sealers skinned their prey. A few days later, Pease's father angrily confronted him on the deck of the *Nancy*, whereupon the son handed over a hundred Spanish silver dollars, which considerably brightened the elder Pease's mood.

After returning to Easton, Pease spent about two months with his family, a happy time made more so because his father kept his distance and didn't meddle in his affairs. Then he went back to Hudson and signed on to another sealing voyage. While the ship was fitting out, Barzillai Pease, in his own words, "married me a wife."

Like so many mariners of the era, Pease didn't stay long on dry land. Just two weeks after getting married, he went back to his mistress, the sea. During the balance of the 1790s, and up through his signing on to the *Nanina*, he shipped out ten more times, becoming commander of his first ship in 1802. He had many adventures and misadventures. On another sealing trip to the Falklands, a large wave pushed his jolly boat twelve feet under the water, smashing its sides against the rocky bottom. The men on the boat struggled ashore, hauled in the damaged boat, and survived for two weeks before their brig sighted their signal fire and rescued them. Another time, he was aboard a schooner that overturned during a storm off Sandy Hook, New Jersey. Everyone on board perished, except for Pease and an Indian from Long Island, both of whom were

Jolly boat.

rescued by a passing ship. His most harrowing experience was on the sealing brig *Hero*, which wrecked off South Georgia Island in the South Atlantic, stranding him and the rest of the crew for months before a British ship rescued them.

Despite his many voyages, what Pease wanted most—money—remained out of reach. At one point in 1809, his financial situation was so bleak that he was thrown into debtors' prison. His fervent desire to turn his life around was evident in a comment he inscribed in his journal, right before setting sail on the *Nanina*. "I took my leave," he said, as he left his wife and headed for New York, "with a full determination to make my fortune or never come home."

Aboard the *Nanina* was one other captain: Charles's sixty-three-year-old father, Valentine. Charles wanted a competent person on the trip who could take charge of the brig and navigate it back to New York after it was filled with skins and oil. When finding someone to fill this role proved difficult, Valentine volunteered to take it on, with the understanding that his duty as master would not commence until the brig was ready for its return voyage. Charles eagerly accepted the offer, and, as a nod to his father's seniority, as well as the fact that he would be captaining the *Nanina*'s return voyage, he had Valentine listed on the formal ship's papers as master, even though it was understood that Charles would act as master until the *Nanina* was loaded and sent home. Valentine was quite old for a voyage such as this, and he was not in the best of shape, having to wear two trusses to keep his hernias from getting any worse. Still, he felt healthy enough to support his son in this endeavor.

Having five captains aboard a single ship was unusual, to say the least, and it raised the potential for conflict, since each was used to giving orders, not taking them. Besides the five captains, there were eight more members of the crew. Henry Ingman Defrees,* a twenty-one-year-old from Boston, was mate, and John Wines, a New Yorker, was carpenter. Both of these men were white, while the rest of the crewmembers were Black, including seamen Henry Gilchrist, Jacob Green, Andrew

---

* Early in his life, Henry listed his last name as Ingman, but later he added either DeFreiz or Defreese, with both spellings being used in various documents. During the time he was on the *Nanina*, he went by Defrees, because that is how he spelled his name in the brig's logbook.

Lott, and Havens Tennant, as well as John Spear, the cook, and William Montgomery, the steward. Five of the Black crew hailed from New York City, while Tennant was from Shelter Island, near the tip of Long Island. Last but not least was Charles's dog, Cent. His breed is undetermined, but he was a very tough, powerful, and fearless companion that proved indispensable in the trials to come.

WHILE THE WAR BETWEEN Britain and France helped Charles recruit a crew, the impending war between Britain and the United States made the *Nanina*'s departure a fraught affair.

MEN ON BOARD THE
Nanina

═══════

MASTER
Valentine Barnard

OTHER CAPTAINS AND
COPARTNERS IN THE VENTURE
Charles H. Barnard
Edmund Fanning
Andrew Hunter
Barzillai Pease

MATE
Henry Ingman Defrees

CREW
Henry Gilchrist, seaman
Jacob Green, seaman
Andrew Lott, seaman
William Montgomery, steward
John Spear, cook
Havens Tennant, seaman
John Wines, carpenter

War Intervenes

==

By 1811, ALL SIGNS POINTED TO AN IMMINENT WAR BETWEEN AMERICA and Britain. Many Americans, outraged by Britain's continued violations of American neutrality, regarded three actions as exceptionally odious. The first was Britain's series of Orders in Council, which blockaded all ports that excluded British commerce and also required all neutral vessels, including American ones, to pay transit fees in a British port before continuing to their final destination, or risk capture. The second was the malicious practice of impressment. Since 1800, Britain had seized nearly 900 American ships and impressed roughly 6,000 American seamen. A third flashpoint stemmed from British efforts to arm Indians in the West, via Canada, and to encourage them to resist American expansion along the frontier. At the time, Congress was populated with "war hawks," predominantly from the West and South, who demanded "Free Trade and Sailors' Rights" and also viewed a war with Britain as a prime opportunity to wrest control of Canada from the British and Florida from the Spanish.

Then, in May of 1811, the US frigate *President* fired on the British sloop-of-war *Little Belt* off the coast of Virginia. Although the captain of the *President* insisted that this action was a case of mistaken identity, and apologized, that did not pacify the British. When the British demanded reparations for the damage done to the *Little Belt*, the Americans responded indignantly that first the British should pay reparations for its shelling of the American warship *Chesapeake* in June 1807. But neither side offered up anything. In November 1811, President James

Engraving of the aftermath of the fifteen-minute battle between the
American frigate USS President *and the British sloop-of-war* Little Belt,
by John Hassell, based on a painting by Joseph Cartwright, circa 1811.
While only one sailor was injured on the President, *nine sailors died*
on the Little Belt, *and an additional twenty-three were injured.*

Madison asked Congress to improve the country's military prepared-
ness. A month later, still hoping to avoid conflict, Madison sent the warship *Hornet* to Britain with letters imploring the British to change their
policies toward America or risk war. On April 1, 1812, after failing to
receive a response from Britain, Madison requested that Congress place
a sixty-day embargo on all trade, which was assumed to be enough time
for ships at sea to return safely to port before war was declared.

Charles Barnard and John Murray and Son kept tabs on what was
going on in Congress. When they learned on April 5 that both the House
and the Senate had passed the embargo bill,* they acted quickly. Fearing that the next mail from Washington would bring news that Madison
had signed the bill, which would order New York Customs officials to
shut the port, Charles, with his backer's blessing, immediately sailed the

---

* The embargo bill was actually signed by President Madison on April 4, and it was for
ninety days, not sixty. The news of the signing took a while longer to make it to New York
City.

Nanina out of the harbor and toward the waters just off Sandy Hook, New Jersey. Seventy ships, also hoping to beat the embargo, joined the *Nanina* in its precipitous flight. It was none too soon, because the port closed soon thereafter. Over the next few days, a pilot boat ferried the rest of the *Nanina*'s crew from the harbor to the brig, and everything was readied for the voyage, which commenced on April 12.

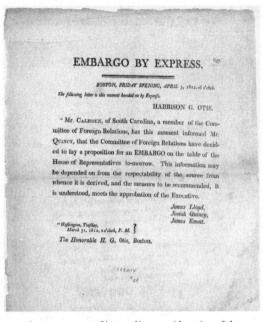

Announcement of impending consideration of the
embargo bill by US House of Representatives.

Voyage to the Falklands

==

THE *NANINA* FIRST STOPPED AT THE CAPE VERDE ARCHIPELAGO, LOCATED roughly 400 to 600 miles off the coast of Senegal, in West Africa. A common waypoint for sealers heading to the South Atlantic, the islands served as an excellent and usually inexpensive place to stock up on water, livestock, vegetables, and fruit. The most important item the islands had to offer was salt, which was essential for preserving the sealskins on a long trip.

It took thirty-four days to reach the Cape Verdean island of Boa Vista, during which time the *Nanina* encountered stretches of fine weather interspersed with squalls, plus a few more intense storms, including one that produced a waterspout. Everyone got along well, with May 7 being "one of the finest" days, according to Barzillai Pease. The deck appeared "almost like . . . a small factory of various sorts of mechanics, all of their different branches, some at carpentering, some at coopering, some at sail making, some at rigging, and others at shoe making, which renders our brig a complete floating mechanical shop."

They spent twelve days at Boa Vista, purchasing salt, beans, potatoes, goats, pigs, hogs, and pumpkins, which Pease pronounced "the best in the known world." The last were especially valued, since they are rich in vitamin C and therefore helpful in warding off scurvy, the notorious mariners' disease that results from a vitamin deficiency, leading to weakness, anemia, bleeding gums, and, in the worst cases, death.

There was yet another item they desperately needed. Because they had left so precipitously to avoid the embargo, everything on board the

Eighteenth-century engraving of a waterspout. Waterspouts typically are not as dangerous as tornadoes on land, but they can damage ships.

Detail of map by John Thompson, circa 1814, showing the islands of Cape Verde. Boa Vista (Bonavista) is at the center right, St. Jago is at the center bottom.

African blue quail, found in sub-Saharan Africa.

Nanina had been stowed in great haste, and the water barrels had been leaking the whole way across the Atlantic. To rectify this, at the end of May they sailed roughly 60 miles to another Cape Verde island, St. Jago,* where they tightened, filled, and re-stowed the barrels. They also picked up more vegetables and fruits, including onions, cabbages, and coconuts.

At one point, when an African blue quail landed on the main deck, Fanning caught it and adopted it as a pet, keeping it in a cage in his cabin. Sadly, the bird did not survive the journey. After being hand-fed by Fanning for weeks, it was released from its cage on the advice of Charles and Hunter, whereupon it promptly flew into a cabin window and "by his temerity lost his life," though "every effort was made to save" it.

The *Nanina* left the Cape Verde Islands on June 2 and headed directly for the Falkland Islands for the next ninety-seven days. The men spent much of the passage making more than 10,000 wooden pegs. Slowly the livestock were sacrificed to feed the crew. To supplement the daily fare, the men caught tuna and cowfish and harpooned nearly a dozen dolphins and porpoises.

On June 22, when the *Nanina* reached the equator, good old King Neptune came "saucily on board" to conduct the line-crossing ceremony,

---

*   Modern-day Santiago.

a time-honored tradition that was an initiation of sorts for sailors who had never before traversed this imaginary line dividing the Northern and Southern Hemispheres. The ceremony involved a crewman dressing up as the ruler of the sea—although who received this honor on the *Nanina* remains unknown—to heartily welcome the few novices to his domain, inducting them into the "Solemn Mysteries of the Ancient Order of the Deep." Typically, Neptune and his assistants dunked the inductees in a barrel of water, gave them a close shave, or put them through some other rituals, which could be quite harrowing, embarrassing, or simply humorous. This time, however, those formalities were dispensed with, Neptune having been bought off with a few bottles of grog. As Charles commented, "Neptune is, indeed, an impudent fellow, but he is such a mighty water-drinker, that he ought to be pardoned for now and then demanding a hearty swig of grog from a novice, as the sea-water might otherwise disturb the tone of his thirsty stomach."

Like the first leg of the voyage, this one was punctuated by numerous storms. But, unlike the passage to Cape Verde, this time there were a few squalls on board as well. On July 4, the men celebrated Independence Day by firing a gun and raising the flag. Pease got carried away by the festivities and fired a shot down the companionway, which unleashed a round of curses from Charles. It also sent smoke into the cabin below, where Captain Fanning was trying to sleep. When Fanning demanded that the cabin skylight be removed to air out the cramped space below, Charles refused, saying he would bolt it down. The two of them had an angry exchange, but finally the skylight was taken off, and tempers cooled.

In subsequent weeks, Charles quarreled with all the other captains, including his father and mate Defrees. It is, of course, hardly unusual for men spending months on ships, enduring close quarters and bad weather, to have disagreements. Add to the mix the presence of five captains aboard, and the potential for conflict rises. But it appears that, other than Pease's errant shot, the only man causing problems was Charles. At one point, for reasons unknown, he even threatened Fanning's life. No doubt contributing to Charles's ill temper was the fact that not long after leaving St. Jago, sores erupted on his legs, causing him great discomfort and keeping him for weeks on end from taking his turn on deck during the night watches.

Charles's problems were not only with his human companions. The *Nanina* left New York with a cat placed on board to help control vermin, specifically rats. How well it performed its exterminator role is not known, but Charles viewed it as a nuisance. He was particularly annoyed with its habit of leaving deposits in his stateroom and shredding some of his belongings. On July 8, having had enough of this bothersome behavior, Charles "committed [the cat] to the deep, alive." Whatever the reason for Charles's combative disposition toward his fellow mariners and the cat, it didn't bode well for the future.

On the morning of September 7, 1812, the tempestuous voyage ended with a cry from the watch: "Land ho!" The men had arrived at the Falkland Islands.

The Windswept Isles

═══

THE FALKLANDS ARE A SPRAWLING ARCHIPELAGO OF MORE THAN 700 ISLANDS located roughly 300 miles from the coast of Argentina, and almost due east, and a bit north, of the Strait of Magellan.* The entire landmass is 4,700 square miles, slightly smaller than Connecticut. The two main islands, and by far the largest, are West Falkland and East Falkland, which in the nineteenth century were called English Maloon and Spanish Maloon, respectively. These islands are separated by Falkland Sound, a sea strait that runs for about 50 miles in a southwest-to-northeasterly direction. The other islands are of varying sizes, some quite diminutive, barely peaking above the waves, and often submerged at high tide. If you eliminate the specks of land that don't seem quite worthy of being called islands, then the number dwindles to a few hundred.

Hundreds of millions of years ago, the Falklands were part of the supercontinent Gondwana. When tectonic forces tore apart this gigantic landmass, the Falklands were left behind on the surface of the ocean like a bunch of geological crumbs, comprising many different kinds of rocks,

---

* Determining the number of islands in the archipelago depends on how they are counted and what one labels an island. Some sources say there are only 200 islands, while others say 700 or slightly more. I opted for 700, since the Falklands Islands Government typically uses that number. It is important to note, however, that some are just bare rock or exposed reef, while others are half-tide islands, accessible from a larger island only during very low tides. Personal communication with Ross Chaloner, Land Surveyor, Falkland Islands Government, January 4, 2023.

Detail of South America map by John Cary, circa 1807,
showing the Falkland Islands and the southern tip of the continent.

the most ancient of which are gneiss and granite more than a billion years old. The islands' geography consists of rugged, often cliff-lined coast-lines, with numerous bays and harbors, open plains, a smattering of lakes, and more than 2,000 small ponds, rivers, and streams. There are also a few relatively short mountains, the highest being East Falkland's Mount Usborne, topping out at 2,312 feet.

Powerful, nearly constant winds blow over the islands, averaging 18 mph, with gusts often exceeding 65 mph. Robert FitzRoy, the Brit-ish naval officer who captained the HMS *Beagle* during Charles Dar-win's famous voyage (1831–36), called wind "the principal evil at the Falklands," an opinion he developed during the time that the *Beagle* spent investigating the islands. "[A] region more exposed to storms, both in summer and winter, it would be difficult to mention. The winds are variable; seldom at rest," and often violent. When the wind is really blowing, spray is lifted off the water and can be felt more than 100 feet from the beach's edge. Walking along the higher elevations in such conditions often requires considerable effort to keep from being knocked down.

The islands are not only windy but also cold. During the South-ern Hemisphere's summer months of December to February, the aver-age monthly temperature is around 49°F. In the winter months of June through August, it falls to around 36°F, and it is a wet cold that chills the bones.* The winds, of course, make the temperatures feel even lower.† Snow is common, but it rarely falls to any great depth, as the winds tend to scour the landscape. The Falklands are not particularly rainy, with annual precipitation of about 24 inches.

WHILE THE GEOGRAPHICAL, GEOLOGICAL, and meteorological history of the Falklands is fairly straightforward, its political history is quite convoluted and contentious.‡ Despite speculation, there is no concrete proof that the islands ever had an indigenous population. Thus, the discovery of the islands is credited to Europeans. Which Europeans deserve the credit, though, is subject to dispute, because the Spanish, Portuguese, English, and Dutch all claimed to have first sighted the islands. These claims, however, are difficult to substantiate. As one historian pointed out, "[T]he records of the early voyages into the South Atlantic are exceedingly meagre; and those that we still possess are often sketchy and inaccurate."

Spain's assertion of ownership of the Falklands rests, in part, on declaration. In 1494, Spain and Portugal signed the Treaty of Tordesillas. The heart of this treaty was a north-to-south geographic line of demarcation drawn on the world map by Pope Alexander VI. Spain was given the right to all lands lying to the west of that line that were not already controlled by a Christian ruler, while Portugal received rights to similar lands to the east of the line. This essentially gave everything in North and South America, minus part of eastern Brazil, to Spain—including the Falklands. Other European countries, which had their own imperial ambitions, rejected the treaty and refused to abide by it. For the Spanish, however, it meant that virtually all of the Americas became rightfully theirs.

As for which explorers actually sighted the Falkland Islands,

---

* The average temperatures for these months were likely slightly lower in the early 1800s.

† For example, if the temperature is 36°F, and the wind is blowing at 18 mph, the air will feel like it is 26°F.

‡ Numerous scholars have written treatises that weigh in on the question of which country first discovered the Falklands, and they have even debated what the term *discovered* means. I will not resolve this debate here, and I am not even sure that it is conclusively resolvable. Thus, please view this discussion in the spirit in which it is offered—to provide a summary background.

there are many threads that are shrouded in the mists of history. Italian explorer Amerigo Vespucci, in the service of Portugal, might have seen the Falklands in 1501/2, but his description is too vague to ascertain exactly where he was at the time. Some claim that an unnamed Portuguese explorer sighted the islands before 1519, and that alleged discovery is reflected on some early maps. Others point to Ferdinand Magellan, in the service of Spain, sighting the Falklands in 1520. English explorer John Davis, who was seeking a passage through the Strait of Magellan, has a claim as well. According to John Lane, who was on Davis's ship *Desire*, on August 14, 1592,* adverse winds drove them "fifty leagues or better" from the mouth of the strait and in among numerous islands "never before discovered by any known relation." While it seems quite likely that Davis did indeed see the Falklands, one problem with this description is the distance he cites. Fifty leagues, at least as measured by the English, is about 150 miles or, at most, 230 miles, but the actual distance from the strait to the Falklands is about 300 miles. Of course, measurements from this early era, when determining longitude was extremely uncertain at best, are often subject to significant error, and Lane did use the phrase "fifty leagues or better," which offers plenty of wiggle room. Two years later, another Englishman, Sir Richard Hawkins, is said to have seen the islands and named them Hawkins Maidenland in honor of both Queen Elizabeth I and his own glory. The earliest largely undisputed sighting of the Falklands is that of the Dutchman Sebald de Weert. In 1600, he spied what are now known as the Jason Islands at the northwest corner of the Falklands and tried to land, but he was thwarted due to stormy weather.

Things are clearer when it comes to the first Europeans to set foot on the Falklands, and that honor goes to Englishman John Strong and his men on the HMS *Welfare*. In late January 1690, they visited the islands, most likely landing at modern-day Port Howard on West Falkland (English Maloon). Richard Simson, one of his crew, provided a humorous perspective on the men's encounter with the locals. "The inhabitants, such as they were, were exceedingly numerous. The penguins (a bird

---

* "August 14th is known as 'Falklands Day' in the Islands and the name of Davis' ship, the *Desire*, is incorporated in the motto on the coat of arms of the Islands: 'Desire the Right.'" Falkland Islands Museum & National Trust, https://falklands-museum.com/early-history, accessed December 10, 2022.

larger than a duck) gave us the first reception. Being mustered in infi-
nite numbers on a rock, upon some of our men's landing . . . they stood,
viewed and seemed to salute them with a great many graceful bows, with
the same gestures equally expressing their curiosity and good breeding."
Strong christened the sound that separates the two main islands Falkland Sound, after Anthony Cary, 5th Viscount Falkland, his patron and
the Royal Navy's treasurer. By the mid-eighteenth century, that name
became the umbrella term for all of the islands in the archipelago, at least
in the eyes of the English.

After Strong's expedition, the Falklands largely exited the international conversation, until Royal Navy officer Lord George Anson voy-
aged around the world in the early 1740s. In the book Anson wrote upon
his return, he said that, in light of the growing importance of the Pacific
Ocean, and the need for British ships to be able to stock up on food and
water before braving Cape Horn, it would be good to have a place in the
South Atlantic where such things could be obtained. He felt the Falklands might "prove extremely convenient for this purpose."

Despite Anson's boosterism, it was the French, not the British, who
first established a settlement. On April 5, 1764, French admiral and
explorer Louis-Antoine, Comte de Bougainville, claimed Port Louis for

A gathering of rockhopper and macaroni penguins on New Island.

*Engraving of Louis-
Antoine, Comte
de Bougainville,
circa 1800s.*

his country. Named for King Louis XV, this outpost was located at the northeastern point of East Falkland (Spanish Maloon). To cement the claim, Bougainville left twenty-eight French settlers behind; when he returned the following year, he dropped off another eighty. Instead of calling the Falklands by that name, the French referred to them as the Îles Malouines, after the French port of Saint-Malo, from which many of the settlers originated.

The Spanish, none too happy at learning of France's land grab, protested immediately. They successfully wrested control of the nascent colony from France for a tidy sum of money. Upon officially taking possession on April 1, 1767, the Spanish renamed Port Louis as Puerto (Port) Soledad (solitude), and they called the Falklands the Islas Malvinas.

But there was yet another international conflict brewing that centered on the islands. Between the time when Bougainville arrived and the Spanish took control, the British landed at West Falkland (English Maloon) and established their own settlement at Port Egmont,* located at the

---

*   Port Egmont was named after the British Lord Egmont, First Lord of the Admiralty. He believed that the Falklands were "undoubtedly the key to the whole Pacific Ocean. This island must command the ports and trade of Chile, Peru, Panama, Acapulco, and in one word, all the Spanish territory upon that sea. It will render all our expeditions to those parts most lucrative to ourselves, most fatal to Spain." Quoted in Lowell Gustafson,

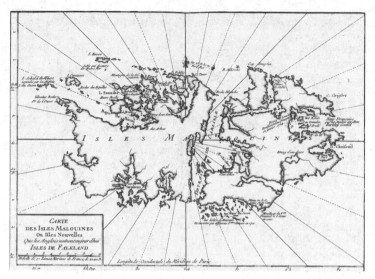

French edition of the Carte des Isles Malouines
by Jacques Nicolas Bellin, 1764.

island's northwest corner. When Captain John Byron* claimed the port
for King George III in early 1765, he knew nothing of the French presence.
But the following year, another British expedition came upon the French
settlement at Port Louis, whereupon the British commander ordered the
French to leave, since he claimed the Falklands were British. The French
commander disagreed, averring that the islands were French, and threatened to attack if the British dared to land any forces. Although the British
did land, no fight erupted, and soon thereafter the British sailed away, not
wanting to create an international incident. But both commanders were
wrong; neither knew about the deal that had already been struck back in
Europe, which transferred the Falklands to Spain.

After an impressive Spanish fleet arrived off Port Egmont in June 1770
and ran off the British forces stationed there, the Spanish and British
almost went to war over the Falklands. Fortunately, cooler heads pre-

---

The Sovereignty Dispute Over the Falkland (Malvinas) Islands (New York: Oxford University Press, 1988), 9.

* John Byron was the grandfather of George Gordon Byron, 6th Baron Byron, better
known as Lord Byron, the famous English poet.

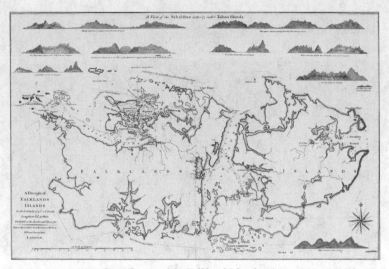

British map of the Falkland Islands, 1770.

A view of Fort St. Louis at Acarron Bay, 1771. A few years later, it was renamed Puerto Soledad by the Spanish. The bay is now known as Berkeley Sound.

vailed, and, through negotiations the following year, the British regained Port Egmont, while the Spanish retained their settlement at Puerto Soledad.* Just four years later, however, the British abandoned Port Egmont. The Spanish remained on the Falklands for a few decades more, but by

---

* In 1771, English critic and essayist Samuel Johnson dismissively commented on the possibility of a war between Britain and Spain over the Falkland Islands, stating, "A war declared for the empty sound of an ancient title to a *Magellanic* rock would raise the indignation of the earth against us." Samuel Johnson, "Thoughts on the Late Transactions Respecting Falkland's Islands [1771], in *The Works of Samuel Johnson, L. L. D.*, vol. VIII (New York: William Durell, 1811), 116.

the time that the *Nanina* arrived in 1812, both the Spanish and the British had left.* Once again, the Falklands were uninhabited.

MANY VISITORS TO THE Falklands in the 1700s and 1800s disparaged them. Royal Navy officer Captain John McBride commented in 1776, "We found . . . a mass of islands and broken lands, of which the soil was nothing but a bog, with no better prospect than that of barren mountains, beaten by storms almost perpetual." Bougainville, writing about the first time he landed on the Falklands, observed:

> [N]o inviting objects came in sight, and excepting the beauty of
> the port in which we lay, we knew not what could prevail upon us
> to stay on this apparently barren ground: The horizon terminated
> by bald mountains, the land lacerated by the sea, which seems to
> claim empire over it; the fields bearing a dead aspect . . . no woods
> to comfort those who intended to be the first settlers, a vast silence,
> now and then interrupted by the howls of marine monsters; and
> lastly, the sad uniformity which reigned throughout.

Darwin labeled the islands "miserable" in his journal, describing them as "An undulating land, with a desolate and wretched aspect, . . . [which] is everywhere covered by a peaty soil and wiry grass, of one monotonous brown color." And a travel writer in the 1890s proclaimed: "The Falkland Islands are not quite the place one would choose for a honeymoon trip, or for driving away depression."

But not all observers were so critical. Amasa Delano, an American mariner who visited the Falklands in 1800, found much to his liking: "It appeared to me that something handsome might be made of these islands,

---

* The incredibly contentious and debatable history of European discovery and settlement reverberates to the present day. The dueling claims of Britain and Spain would later morph into dueling claims between the British and the Argentines, since the latter argued that they took control of the Falklands in 1820, four years after declaring independence from Spain, while Britain also claims possession of the islands as a result of earlier settlement, as well as colonization of the islands in the mid-1800s. Continuing debates over which country owned the Falklands provided the fuel that led to the relatively short and bloody undeclared Falklands War in 1982, pitting Britain against Argentina. Britain won, yet that conflict did not resolve the territorial dispute. Both sides still claim sovereignty, but the Falklands currently operate as a self-governing British overseas territory.

Drawing of tussac grass and penguins, Falkland Islands, 1843.

were due attention to be paid to them. The soil is very good and clear of rocks, and capable of easy tillage. There are plenty of good fish to be caught amongst them[.] . . . The climate is very healthy; but the weather is dreary and misty the greatest part of the time." A British mariner who lived on the Falklands for six months in the late 1830s also rejected earlier negative characterizations: "With regard to the climate of the Falklands, it is a singular fact that this archipelago has always been characterized as barren, desolate, and tempestuous. Nothing can be more erroneous." And American sealer Ebenezer Townsend Jr. simply said, "[T]he Falkland Islands are beautiful."

However dreary and desolate the archipelago appeared to many early travelers, the Falklands do indeed have a stark beauty. The rugged landscape is undeniably spectacular, as are the flora and fauna. While the Falklands have no native trees,* at lower altitudes there are extensive areas of majestic tussac grass, which can live as long as 200 years or more,

---

* Although there were no trees on the islands in the early 1800s, later in that century Falklanders began planting shelterbelts close to settlements for a number of reasons, including the protection of crops and newly shorn sheep from high winds. The main species planted are Monterey cypress, Alaskan lodgepole pine, and radiata pine. See

The "Falkland Strawberry."   *Scurvy grass.*

and grow in large, dense clumps reaching 9 feet tall, and sometimes even higher.* They are so tall that early explorers thought they were trees when seen at a distance. To a mid-nineteenth-century observer, it appeared as if the tussac grass covered the islands "like a forest of miniature palm-trees." The islands also boast a great variety of smaller plants, including wild celery, parsley, Falkland strawberry,† red crowberry, numerous ferns and mosses, and so-called scurvy grass.

Offshore, there is an equally impressive display of vegetation. Surrounding the islands are vast forests of kelp, including giant kelp and bull kelp. Held down by a sturdy stipe that grips onto rocks or other hard sub-

---

Alan Low and Jim McAdam, *Guidelines for Shelterbelt Planting in the Falkland Islands* (Stanley: Stanley and United Kingdom Falkland Islands Trust, 1999).

* Early whalers and sealers often referred to the grass as *tushooks* rather than *tussac*.

† They are not real strawberries, but rather a member of the rose family that has a small red fruit.

A variety of hogs and boars depicted in Johnson's Household Book
of Nature, *1880. It remains unclear which of any of these—or even
some other species of hog—lived on the Falklands in the early 1800s.*

strates on the bottom, kelp grows upward toward the sun. Giant kelp, the
largest of all the species, can reach astonishing lengths of more than 200
feet. The profusion of kelp—its many blades often blanketing the surface
of the water like an undulating verdant carpet—created a potentially dangerous situation, as particularly dense patches could camouflage rocks
just beneath the surface and lead vessels to founder. As a result, *The Nautical Magazine* in 1832 urged seamen to "avoid kelp everywhere." There
was, however, one good thing that kelp did for mariners. By dampening

Engraving of a warrah titled "The Wolf Fox of Faulkland's Islands,"
1773. While some observers, such as Byron's men, viewed the warrah
as vicious, others saw it more as curious, and skilled at snatching
food and other items from those who visited or lived on the islands.

the impact of waves, it helped calm the waters in harbors and bays where ships anchored.

The waters around the Falklands are home to many animals, including dusky dolphins, squid, rock cod, scallops, assorted crabs, mullet, and Southern right, sperm, and humpback whales. Birds are numerous, including a few penguin species, Johnny Rooks (striated caracaras), stinkers (turkey vultures), black-browed albatross, and a variety of geese and petrels. When the *Nanina* was there, there was also an abundance of wild hogs, the descendants of porcine cargo brought ashore by earlier expeditions. These hogs, however, were nothing like the ones you might see on a farm, where the animals are well fed and quite meaty. Instead, Falkland hogs were wiry and very tough. They used their sharp tusks (actually lower and upper canines) to root around for food and to defend themselves. Other introduced animals included horses, cattle, rabbits, and goats. The only quadruped native to the Falklands was the warrah, a small wolf that was also called the Falkland Islands fox or dog. Not plentiful to begin with, the warrah was mercilessly hunted, and by 1876 it was extinct.

The most important animals on the Falklands in the eyes of sealers were, of course, the fur, hair, and elephant seals. South American fur seals, sometimes referred to as Southern fur seals or Falkland fur seals,

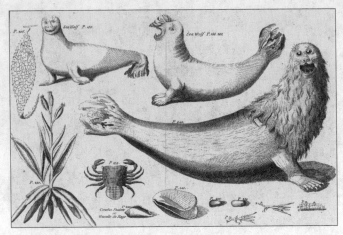

Antoine-Joseph Pernety accompanied Bougainville on his voyage to the Falkland Islands in 1764 and later published a book detailing the trip. This engraving from his book depicts a sea lion—looking very much like a lion with a shaggy mane—and a male elephant seal with its proboscis. The other seal is likely a female elephant seal. Although Pernety labels the elephant seal a sea wolf, veteran sealers usually applied that name to sea lions. Other animals and plants of the Falklands are also depicted in this engraving, including a kelp frond at the upper left.

were also often called sea bears or sea dogs by the sealers. They have a dark gray, black, or brown coat that is particularly lush, with a soft, dense underlayer and a slightly coarser outer layer, which is composed of guard hairs and most prominent toward the head. Males reach about 6 feet in length and weigh more than 400 pounds, while females top out at nearly 5 feet and about 110 pounds. Sealers referred to mature male fur seals as bulls or wigs, the latter because of the curly hair on the head. Females were called clapmatches, because their movements when excited were very rapid, "like the flash of a gun on touching a match."

South American sea lions, which sealers labeled as hair seals, are much larger than fur seals, with males exceeding 9 feet and 700 pounds, and females coming in at more than 7 feet and 300 pounds. The male, in particular, has a massive head of regal bearing, covered with a healthy mane, the characteristic that led to its appellation of *lion*. Sealers also called them sea wolves. As with fur seals, males were wigs, and females were clapmatches. Their fur, ranging from light yellow-brown to orangish-brown, is less plush than that of fur seals, lacking the dense

From top to bottom: fur seal, sea lion, and elephant seal.
Engraving from Johnson's Household Book of Nature, *1880.*

undercoat. A member of the Zoological Society of London who visited the Falklands in the late 1860s spent some time observing sea lions, noting that they congregate on headlands or isthmuses, where one of the old males stands guard "with outstretched neck and upraised head, as if sniffing around for the slightest ominous warning. The signal of a grunt or growl sets the others on the alert; and on any real approach of danger they rush all helter-skelter towards the water." Sea lions and fur seals kept to their own kind, with the former preferring sandy beaches, while the latter gravitated to rockbound shorelines.

Southern elephant seals, or sea elephants, are the largest of all seals, with mature males being up to 16 feet long and 11,000 pounds, and

Engraving of a sea lion by W. H. Lizars, 1860.

Female Southern elephant seals amid the marram/sand grass.
They are molting—shedding their outer layers of fur and skin
so they can be replaced with new layers. This is evident most
clearly around the head and flipper of the closest seal.

females reaching a very imposing 10 feet and 2,000 pounds. Its name derives not from its great size but from the fleshy protuberance at the end of the male's snout, which reminded Europeans of an elephant's trunk. Gray to brown in color, elephant seals can have blubber as thick as 6 inches, accounting for roughly a third of the animal's bulk.

EARLY IN THE AFTERNOON of September 7, 1812, the brig *Nanina* arrived at New Island, at the westernmost reaches of the Falklands archipelago, and anchored in a few fathoms of water in Hooker's Harbor.* This was a very common base of operations for sealing ventures, serving as a prime jumping-off point for hunting forays farther afield.

Now, the real work could begin.

---

* Modern-day Settlement Harbor.

The Killing Begins

==

AFTER SO MUCH TIME AT SEA, THE MEN WERE HAPPY TO GO ASHORE. WHILE A
few who were suffering from scurvy remained on board, the rest got busy
erecting tents, ferrying supplies to the beach, cleaning the brig, shooting
dozens of geese to add variety to the daily fare, gathering local plants to
help the sick, filling water casks, and starting to build the shallop.

The men hoped that building the shallop would go quickly, since the
vessel was essential to the smooth operation of their sealing ambitions.
But it dragged on for more than two months, hampered by numerous
bouts of stormy weather and the carpenter's severe hand injury. In the
meantime, the men used the brig's smaller boats to visit nearby islands
and begin sealing.

When sealers visited islands that had yet to be used as hunting
grounds, "A man might walk in . . . [the] midst [of the fur and hair seals]
without giving the smallest alarm," as James Fenimore Cooper related in
his classic *The Sea Lions; or, The Lost Sealers*. All the men had to do to
kill the seals, therefore, was approach and hit them over the head with a
wooden club. "It would be," Cooper observed, "like picking up dollars
on a sea-beach."

The Falklands, however, had long been a destination for sealers, so
the hunting methods used by the *Nanina* crew were different because the
seals knew to fear humans. First, the men positioned themselves between
the seals and the water. Sensing danger, the seals huddled together, barking wildly, as the men advanced. Sometimes the men rushed in, wooden
clubs and lances at the ready, giving the seals a blow to the head or a

Female upland goose. Five types of geese are found on the Falkland Islands, and the men from the Nanina *likely shot or captured a variety of species, including the upland goose.*

Sealers on Beauchene Island (southernmost of the Falkland Islands) clubbing seals, circa early 1800s.

thrust to the body. Other times they formed a lane with men on either side, then drove the seals through this bloody gauntlet, clubbing and lancing them as they fled toward the water.

Once dead, the seals were skinned, which involved cutting the skin from the animal and then scraping off blubber, meat, and sinew with a two-handled beaming knife. Although this was a laborious process, one veteran sealer claimed that he knew a man who could skin an almost unbelievable sixty fur seals in an hour. Next the flipper holes were stitched up, and the entire skin was rinsed in saltwater and slathered with salt on the inner, hairless side before being stretched on wooden pegs and left to dry. A relatively warm summer's day with a good breeze often allowed enough time for the skins to be taken from the pegs, but the drying process could last many days under less ideal conditions. Whether the skins were dried quickly or slowly, the men repeatedly dragged their beaming knives over them, aiming to make them as clean as possible. Once the drying process was complete, any remaining salt was scraped off, and the now-rigid skins were stacked like salted cod. Since the piled-up skins released sweat, the crew would occasionally shift and separate them to be

Early nineteenth-century sealers on the beach of an unidentified South Atlantic island, quite likely in the Falklands. The men in the foreground are preparing a supper of upland geese and loggerhead ducks. In the background, on the opposite beach, are some small hair seal (sea lion) rookeries.

sure they were dry. At the same time, the men would beat the skins to get rid of worms. Well-prepared skins, whether stored in a hut on an island or stowed in the ship's hold, could keep for years.

Although fur and hair seals were usually killed fairly easily, there were instances in which they fought back, sometimes biting their attackers or knocking them off rock ledges to their deaths. But the greatest danger came when hunting elephant seals. Despite being not very fast on land, elephant seals can rear up and come down upon their attackers like, well, a few tons of blubber. Their teeth, too, are potent weapons. The men of the *Nanina* approached elephant seals warily, but they did not hesitate to kill them, lancing and clubbing them to death. Then they cut off their blubber and boiled it in small iron try-pots fed by fires made of wood they had brought with them or driftwood found on the beaches. The resultant oil was then sealed in casks for transport home.

WHILE THE SEALING WAS going well—albeit a bit limited because the shallop was not ready—relations among the men of the *Nanina* were getting worse. Most of the blame for that continued to rest with Charles Barnard. On September 22, 1812, he nearly came to blows with Fanning when the two argued about loading the boats. Both men stripped off their shirts to fight, but the rest of the crew intervened. At about the same time, Charles got into a verbal row with Hunter, over what is not clear, but, according to Defrees, Charles threatened to burn all of Hunter's belongings and pitch his trunks overboard.

Charles's most serious flare-up, involving both Pease and Fanning, occurred a little more than a week later. As a sealing crew was preparing to leave Beaver Island, Pease asked Charles to take some of the elephant seal blubber onto his boat, because Pease's boat was overloaded. Charles refused. Stymied, Pease then ordered one of the men to place the blubber on his boat. At this point, Charles reconsidered his refusal and told another man to take a few pieces from Pease's boat and bring it to his boat. When Pease, still angry over Charles's initial refusal, prevented the crewman from doing so, Charles flew into a rage. Charles hurled insults at Pease, and threatened him, saying at one point that he would "have his heart's blood."

When the boats returned to the brig on New Island, Charles went below, loaded a pistol, and returned to the main deck, brandishing the

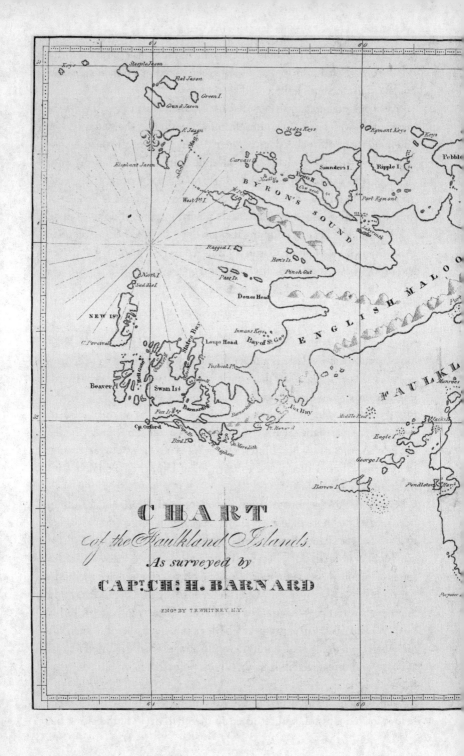

CHART
of the Faukland Islands.
As surveyed by
CAPT. CH. H. BARNARD

ENGD BY T.R.WHITNEY N.Y.

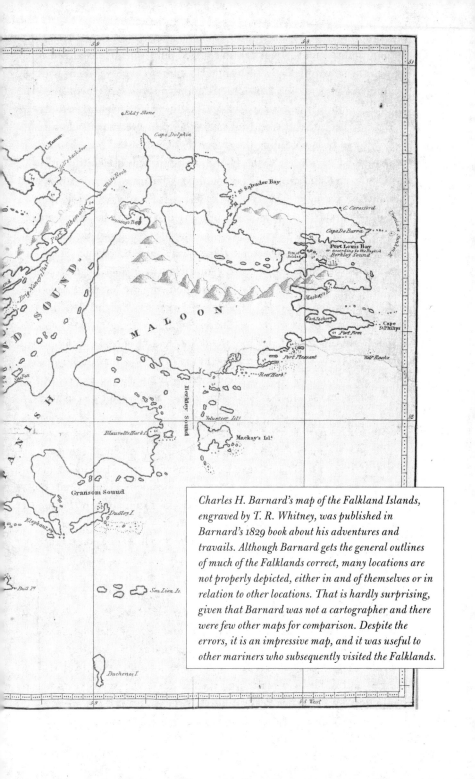

Charles H. Barnard's map of the Falkland Islands, engraved by T. R. Whitney, was published in Barnard's 1829 book about his adventures and travails. Although Barnard gets the general outlines of much of the Falklands correct, many locations are not properly depicted, either in and of themselves or in relation to other locations. That is hardly surprising, given that Barnard was not a cartographer and there were few other maps for comparison. Despite the errors, it is an impressive map, and it was useful to other mariners who subsequently visited the Falklands.

weapon and stomping about like an enraged bull. Valentine, alarmed at his son's aggressive behavior, demanded to know what he was doing with the gun. Charles said he was not only going to shoot Pease but also to "blow [Fanning's] brains out." Charles was angry with Fanning because of their earlier altercation as well as another perceived slight. He said Fanning had been spreading the rumor that Charles had been banned from New York's Tontine Coffee House, a place heavily used by the city's merchants and ship's captains for conducting business and socializing. Equally infuriating to Charles was the fact that Fanning would not tell him who had started the rumor. Valentine tried to wrench the pistol from his son's hands, but he failed. Instead of following through on his threats, however, Charles shot the pistol in the air and then stormed off.

Charles's eruption rattled Pease so much that he confided in his journal that it caused him "to lay awake many hours in fear" of being visited by Charles, whom he labeled "a midnight (or rather daylight) assassin." Pease also said he was tired of Charles acting as "mate, master, and owner," and that he and many of the others had "resolved not to have him any more on our sealing cruises [in the Falklands] for fear of being shot or rather murdered." Pease even wrote in his journal a "protest" against Charles, in which he said that he had "a disposition to quarrel and a want of stability, continually insulting directly or indirectly one or the other of his partners."

There were many other instances when Pease got into arguments with Charles—or the "Collossean," as he often referred to him, using his own quirky spelling to highlight Charles's imposing physique. Some of the friction between the two could have been due to animosity on Pease's part. On three voyages earlier in Pease's career, Valentine had been the first mate, and the two of them had gotten along well. At one point, Pease confided in his journal that Valentine "had always been good to me and knew me well." Pease was especially fond of Valentine for having stepped in to stop the "surly" master of the *Prudence*, Albertus Swain, from continuing a reign of terror over him. Always in search of a father figure, Pease clearly viewed Valentine in that light, and he might have been jealous of Charles's good fortune in having Valentine as his real father. Furthermore, Pease no doubt chafed at having to answer to the 31-year-old Charles as the de facto master, given that Pease was seven years his senior. Finally, in reading Pease's journal of the voyage of the *Nanina*, as well as some of his other journals and reflections, it becomes clear that he held many grievances with people in his life, and that might have been the result of his personality, as much as it was a byproduct of the actions of those around him.

Defrees also complained mightily about Charles. In early October, Defrees confided in the official logbook, which he maintained, the following bitter observations:

> I am sorry to say it but the whole passage has been one continual term of quarreling which in my opinion was entirely from the disposition of Capt. Barnard Junior—the treatment I have received from him has been such as I should be ashamed to give a dog. He has abused me shamefully, and even threatened to kick me over the bows so that I considered my life in danger. I have endeavored to conduct myself in such a manner as to demand the treatment and respect that is due to a chief officer.

Defrees's anger toward Charles was no doubt nurtured when Charles recommended that Defrees's lay for the trip be significantly reduced because of what Charles claimed to be his habit of "hanging on his eyelids doing nothing." When the other captains took up that suggestion, they agreed with Charles, and not only was Defrees's lay, or share of the voyage, nearly cut in half, from 1/22 to 1/40, but he was also relieved of his position as mate.

On at least one occasion, Charles even had a fight with his father, over what is not clear. As a result of this, and the other affronts he thought had come from his fellow captains, Charles told his father that he planned to return home on the first ship that arrived at the islands.

Unfortunately, we do not have Charles's view on what transpired. He did not commit to paper anything about these various disputes, either with other captains or with Defrees. Perhaps there were extenuating circumstances that would paint Charles's behavior in a better light, or, at least, not make him appear so incredibly hostile and combative.

Of course, whether the captain was a despot or a benevolent ruler was almost beside the point. A ship's captain or master was truly the monarch of all he surveyed, his opinions law, and his control over the crew nearly absolute. Nevertheless, disputes between masters and their crews during the Age of Sail were not rare events. Shipboard life was often quite volatile. Even if some of the friction and fights between Charles and the other

*Landscape on Swan (modern-day Weddell) Island. The flowering plant
in the foreground is common gorse. The accumulations of rocks and
boulders in the distance, on the hillside, are called stone runs.*

captains, as well as the crew, could be attributed to these dynamics, that
hardly lessens Charles's culpability for his seemingly rash and aggressive
behavior. In light of the complaints lodged against him by both Pease and
Defrees, Charles doesn't appear to have been an effective leader, at least
for some of the time, and his actions showed a distinct lack of emotional
and physical control.

The combustible situation on the brig came to a head on October 31
during breakfast. Given that Charles had vowed to go home, Valentine
announced to the assembled company that he, and not his son, would
now be the acting master of the expedition. Blindsided by this, Charles
released a fusillade of curses, rescinded his vow to leave, and said that
he intended to head up the sealing business from there on out. This
caused Fanning, Pease, and Hunter to exclaim that they would not follow Charles's lead as long as they lived.

To keep things from getting totally out of control, Valentine invited
Fanning, Pease, and Hunter on shore for a conference, during which he
discussed their grievances and "promised that he would be responsible
for his son's conduct in the future, and that his son should make atone-

ment for everything that has passed." Assuaged, the other captains ended their protest. Charles even showed some contrition, promising to behave better. As a result, he was allowed to take the lead on sealing operations. Apparently Charles stayed true to his word, because from there on out, Pease and Defrees stopped complaining about his behavior.

Valentine's confab had another effect. A few days after it was held, Fanning told Defrees that the captains had agreed to increase his lay from 1/40 to 1/38. Even though that was a minor increase, Fanning urged Defrees not only to accept it but also to resume his position as mate, both of which he did.

A little more than three weeks later, on November 25, the shallop was launched to the firing of muskets and christened the *Young Nanina*. Sealing could now begin in earnest. In the following weeks, the shallop transported crews to islands farther away, including Swan Island* and the Jason Islands, the latter of which were located about 50 miles northeast of New Island and considered the best sealing grounds in the Falklands. During one particularly good stretch on Steeple Jason, the men killed and skinned 500 seals in a couple of days.

But just as things were finally getting on track with the *Nanina*'s sealing operations, events back home forced the Americans to alter their plans dramatically.

---

* Modern-day Weddell Island.

Ripples of War

=

SINCE ARRIVING IN THE FALKLANDS IN SEPTEMBER 1812, THE MEN OF THE *NANINA* had not seen another ship. That was a bit surprising, given that both American and British whaling vessels regularly used New Island and others nearby as a stopping-off point for water, hogs, and wildfowl during their long trips chasing leviathans of the deep throughout the South Atlantic and the Pacific. If Charles thought anything was amiss, he didn't share his concern with anyone. But, perhaps, in the back of his mind, he was second-guessing the choice he and Murray and Son had made: to depart for the Falklands on the eve of the embargo. It was a risky decision. In the months before the *Nanina* set out, the drumbeat for war with Britain had become ever louder, and the embargo clearly meant that America was laying the groundwork for a potential conflict. Charles knew that if war had broken out after the *Nanina* set sail, that could have reduced maritime traffic to the Falklands. The coming of war would also upend the *Nanina*'s sealing expedition. On January 3, 1813, when a ship finally arrived at New Island, everything changed.

That afternoon, Charles was returning to the island from a trip to Steeple Jason to resupply the sealing crew. Entering Hooker's Harbor, he saw an unfamiliar ship moored near the *Nanina*. It was the sealer *Hope*, out of New York, and it brought disturbing news. The *Hope*'s master, Obed Chase, told Barnard that the United States had declared war against Great Britain back in June. Chase also handed over letters from Charles's friends and family, as well as a letter from the Murrays,

Cliffs on the western side of New Island.

instructing Barnard to return immediately to the closest and most convenient American port. This last order came as no surprise to Charles. The contract he had signed with Murray and Son included a clause that declared the terms of the voyage "null and void" in the event of the outbreak of war.

After summoning the crew from Steeple Jason, the captains considered this new information and came up with a plan of action, which they presented to the others. Rather than leave right away, they proposed staying at the Falklands for at least twelve months. Since the *Hope* had brought word that Britain's odious Orders in Council had been rescinded, the captains surmised that peace would soon be concluded, and then they could sail back home in safety after a year had elapsed. And if peace didn't come quickly, they figured it would be better to collect a full cargo, since their chances of getting back to the United States

Steeple Jason Island, the Falkland Islands.

without being captured by a British ship would be the same whether the *Nanina* was full or only partly so. Finally, as Charles observed, "[T]he time in collecting a full freight would pass much more pleasantly than in the walls of an English prison; and if in completing it, the war should not have terminated, and we should have the misfortune to be captured on the passage, we would not have so long a time to spend in confinement, as if we now made the effort and became prisoners of war." All of the men assented to the new plan.

But that still left the question of the *Nanina*'s location. The captains knew they couldn't stay on New Island because it was frequented by British whaleships, which were often commissioned as privateers during times of war.* If one should arrive, the *Nanina* would likely be taken as a prize, and an easy prize it would be, since the brig was lightly armed. Therefore, they took the *Nanina* to a well-protected harbor about 40 miles distant, on the southwestern side of English Maloon. Charles had spotted the harbor on an earlier sealing foray, and he believed it had never been visited by any other Americans or Europeans. Thus, he dubbed it

---

* For background on privateering and its role during times of war, see Eric Jay Dolin, *Rebels at Sea: Privateering in the American Revolution* (New York: Liveright, 2022).

Barnard's Harbor.* The harbor's entrance was "protected by four small islands, and its sides by vast and lofty hills," features that Charles thought made it one of the finest harbors in the South Atlantic.

Once there, the *Nanina* was stripped of its spars and rigging to reduce the strain on the masts and lessen the chance of damage. The men also built small huts, planning to settle in for a years-long stay. From this base, they launched the *Young Nanina* on two multiweek cruises—one in February, the other in March—which returned with thousands of sealskins. During the March cruise, the weather was particularly fierce, and the men were pelted with rain, hail, or snow nearly every day. With the passage of time, their fears of being discovered by a British ship began to fade. As far as they could tell, they were alone in the Falklands. But they were not. A British ship was also there.

---

* The harbor was, for years after Barnard's ordeal, named Barnard's Harbor, but today it is known as either Double Creek West Arm or Double Creek East Arm—which one it was is not exactly clear from Barnard's description, but, more than likely, it was the West Arm.

The *Isabella*

===

O<small>N A VERY HOT FRIDAY MORNING, DECEMBER 4, 1812, THE 193-TON BRIG</small> *Isabella* was preparing to depart from Port Jackson Harbor* in the British convict colony of New South Wales.† The brig's destination was London, via Cape Horn. The fifth governor of the British colony, Lieutenant Colonel Lachlan Macquarie, along with various military officers, were there to wish everyone a safe voyage. The *Isabella* had ten small cannons on board, and its considerable cargo consisted primarily of ninety-one casks of whale oil, 19,000 sealskins, and seventeen tons of mother-of-pearl shells, which were used to make high-quality buttons. There were also five pipes‡ of Madeira wine, a few casks of rum, and fifty-four people on board, including twenty crewmen and thirty-four passengers, fourteen of whom were Royal Marines.

A few of the passengers were somewhat notable, while others were notorious. Among them were Scottish Captain Robert Durie of His Majesty's 73rd Regiment of Foot, his very pregnant wife, Joanna-Ann Durie, and their 18-month-old daughter, Agnes. Durie was the senior military official on board, in charge of the Royal Marines. Another Scottish officer in the 73rd, Lieutenant Richard Lundin, was carrying diplomatic dispatches for the new prime minister of Great Britain, Robert Banks

---

*   Modern-day Sydney Harbor.

†   Modern-day State of New South Wales in Australia.

‡   A pipe is a large barrel or cask, and a pipe of Madeira wine can vary in size, but typically contains around 126 gallons.

*View of the port of Sydney (Port Jackson Harbor, Australia) and
the mouth of the Parramatta River, by François Péron, 1811.*

*Miniature
of Captain
Robert Durie,
circa early
1800s.*

Jenkinson, 2nd Earl of Liverpool. Both Durie and Lundin were going
home for well-deserved breaks from their service abroad.

Another passenger was forty-seven-year-old Captain Richard Brooks,
who hailed from Devon, England. A merchant mariner, he had had considerable experience on ships, but he had a checkered reputation because
of his trials with the *Atlas*, a convict transport he had led to New South
Wales in 1801–2. An alarming sixty-five people died during the seven-
month voyage, roughly a third of the convicts on board. That was a death
rate far greater than any other convict ship to date, some of which had
lost only a single individual. Another four convicts on the *Atlas* died soon
after landing, and those who were still alive were, in the words of Governor Philip Gidley King, "in a dreadfully emaciated and dying state."

Late nineteenth-century
engraving of Richard Brooks.

The horrific conditions on the *Atlas* resulted in a near-mutiny among the passengers, soldiers, and convicts.

A committee appointed by Governor King laid most of the blame at Brooks's feet, claiming that "the want of proper attention to cleanliness, the want of free circulation of air, and the lumbered state of the prison and hospital"—which were filled with Brooks's personal trade goods that he hoped to sell in Australia—had caused the astonishing death rate. Brooks was censured by Governor King, but he received no formal punishment. Amazingly enough, he went on to helm another convict transport a few years later, this time landing healthy prisoners and partially restoring his reputation. He followed that with the commands of a few trading vessels doing business with the colony. He was returning home on the *Isabella* to collect his wife and children and bring them back to settle in Australia in a new ship that he would captain.

Ten of the *Isabella*'s passengers were former convicts who had either served out their time or been pardoned. Like the vast majority of the citizens of New South Wales, the convicts had been transported there courtesy of Britain's twenty-five-year-old policy of dealing with prison overcrowding in the mother country, one that was born of necessity. Between 1718 and 1775, Britain had sent roughly 50,000 to 70,000 convicted criminals to its American colonies, where they were sold into indentured servitude—really a form of slavery—for periods of up to fourteen years. While many welcomed them for the cheap labor they provided, other Americans were upset with the policy, including Benjamin

Mezzotint, A Fleet of Transports under Convoy, *by Carington Bowles, 1788.*

Franklin, who referred to these convicts as "venomous reptiles we call RATTLE-SNAKES."

Once the Americans rebelled in 1775, this pipeline for offloading convicts was cut off, and British prisons were soon bursting at the seams. The initial response was to place excess prisoners on retired warships and transports, or prison hulks, permanently moored in the River Thames. But even these were soon overloaded, becoming eyesores, breeding grounds for disease, and the source of olfactory distress. Because the influx of prisoners showed no signs of abating, a new place for them had to be found, and the solution was New South Wales. By late 1812, when the *Isabella* was preparing for departure, many thousands of convicts had already been transported Down Under.

One well-known convict on the *Isabella* was fifty-six-year-old Joseph Holt, who was accompanied by his wife, Hester, his thirteen-year-old son, Joseph, and three of their ex-convict servants. Holt, a prosperous Irish farmer and businessman in the late 1700s, was, he said, "contented with my lot" when the Irish Rebellion of 1798 broke out. He did not support the rebels, who wanted to break free of Britain, and he had a track record of supporting the Crown. Indeed, he had even been appointed to

The first fleet of convict transports entering Port Jackson,
January 26, 1788. Drawn by E. Le Bihan, 1888.

Drawing by Thomas Rowlandson, 1797, showing convicts
embarking for Botany Bay in New South Wales.

Drawing of two convicts in New South Wales, 1793.

a few notable government positions. But that didn't spare him. One of Holt's disgruntled business associates, who wanted "revenge," swore to British soldiers sweeping through the country that Holt was a member of the Society of United Irishmen, a rebel. With that false information, the soldiers marched to Holt's farm to arrest him.

When Holt saw the soldiers approaching, he hastily bade good-bye to his family and bolted, taking with him his "sword, cane, a brace of pistols, and some money." Since the soldiers were pursuing him, Holt believed they would leave his family and property alone. He was wrong. The soldiers ushered his family out of the house and burned it to the ground. And it wasn't over. When Holt later reunited with Hester, she told him the British were still intent on capturing him.

Enraged by what the soldiers had done after he had been such a loyal subject, and having no faith that his protestation of innocence would clear him should he turn himself in, Holt felt he had no choice, so he joined the rebels and fought against the Crown. His success as a rebel leader earned him the informal title of "General Holt." Despite his heroic efforts, the rebellion quickly fizzled in the face of superior forces, and

*Engraving of Joseph Holt, after an original 1798 painting
by an anonymous artist. The introduction to Holt's
memoir includes the following description of the man:*

*"Of Holt's personal appearance, the portrait prefixed to this volume will
convey a correct idea. His height was about five feet ten inches; he was
extremely well made, of compact muscle, and remarkably athletic and
vigorous. Holt's hair was black, and his eye-brows heavy and bushy; his
eyes were dark and penetrating, but rather small. His nose was of that
class usually termed Roman, his forehead was finely developed, and his
face well-proportioned and intellectual. He wore his beard under his
chin, shaving only the prominent parts. . . . Holt had the power of readily assuming a commanding or determined look, but there was nothing
ferocious in it or in his appearance; and his smile was one beaming with
benevolence. His whole appearance was likely to gain submission, as
determined resolution was stamped on his countenance. In his manners
he was simple and unaffected."*

a £300 reward was offered for his capture. Realizing that he might be
treated more leniently if he turned himself in, he surrendered. His sterling pre-Rebellion record, plus his revelation of critical intelligence to
the British government, was enough to save him from a trial and public
humiliation. But a price still had to be exacted. In early 1799, he agreed to
be labeled a convicted felon and transported to New South Wales.

Once there, Holt settled into his new life, becoming a farm manager. His rebellious reputation, however, made local authorities wary, and he was arrested three times for allegedly conspiring to foment an Irish uprising in the colony. In each instance, he was exonerated. Holt was later accused of participating in the failed Castle Hill convict rebellion of 1804, a charge that he vehemently denied, arguing that he was the object of false accusations. Nevertheless, he was found guilty and sent to Norfolk Island, another penal colony established by Britain in the Tasman Sea. Eighteen months later, having served his time, he returned to his steadfast wife and family in New South Wales and eventually purchased his own farm, where he raised cattle and sheep.

Keeping out of trouble, and becoming a respected and prosperous citizen, Holt applied for and received a pardon from the governor in 1811. This cleared the way for him and his family to return to Ireland. Holt sold his farm, liquidated his holdings, and purchased space on the *Isabella*. To ensure that his party had some measure of comfort on the voyage, Holt had paid £180, which procured a small cabin in steerage, with

The Castle Hill Rebellion was the first convict uprising in Australia. The rebels were Irish convicts whose goal was to overthrow British rule in New South Wales. After that had been achieved, the rebels hoped to return to Ireland and continue to fight for independence. About thirty-nine convicts died. This painting was done in 1804 by an unidentified artist.

*Miniature of
Sir Henry Browne
Hayes, circa 1820s.*

enough space for Joseph to set up his cot and for his three servants to hang their hammocks.

Another infamous ex-convict on board was fifty-year-old Irishman Sir Henry Browne Hayes. A former captain of the local militia, and then sheriff in the City of Cork, Hayes was a popular, if peculiar, man-about-town who had received a knighthood in 1790 for performing some relatively minor task for the Crown. After his wife died in the mid-1790s, leaving him with several children to raise, he took a pecuniary interest in a twenty-one-year-old Quaker heiress, Miss Mary Pike, who was worth more than £20,000.

Upset with Henry's eccentric and oftentimes irresponsible behavior, his wealthy father, who owned a brewery, cut him out of his will. Although Henry had become quite comfortable, thanks to his own employment and prior paternal support, he desired a much brighter financial future, so he set his sights on wooing Mary. There was only one problem: He had not yet met her. Conniving to get himself invited to the residence where she was staying, he was introduced to her during a group dinner. After failing to make inroads for her affection during that soiree, he concocted a bold and dastardly plan. He sent a letter, penned by him but ostensibly written by the doctor who was treating Mary's mother, which said that her mother had fallen ill and Mary needed to get there as soon as possible. Mary summoned a carriage, and, along with her aunt and another woman, she raced to her mother's house, exactly as Hayes had hoped.

Along the way, Hayes and a few men he had hired—all of whom covered their faces—stopped the carriage at gunpoint, grabbed Mary, and threw her into another waiting carriage, which took her to Hayes's house. There, Hayes told Mary that he was going to marry her, and when she protested, he threatened to shoot himself. Although Mary didn't consent, Hayes proceeded nonetheless, forcing a ring onto her finger and having a man dressed as a priest, but clearly an imposter, "marry" them.

This outlandish gambit was not out of character for Hayes, much of his life having been marked by truly odd and disturbing behavior. However, Miss Pike would have none of it. When Hayes unwisely, at least for him, gave her a pen and paper the morning after their sham marriage, she wrote to her friends, imploring them to rescue her from the clutches of

Drawing captioned "Miss Pike was seized by the muffled man and lifted into a waiting coach," from a magazine article on Hayes published in 1910.

her new "husband." And they did, with no opposition from Hayes other than verbal attacks.

Foiled, Hayes immediately took off, and there followed two rewards for his arrest and capture: one of £500, offered by Mary Pike's father, and the other of £200, put up by the Lord Lieutenant of Ireland. After two years on the lam, Hayes was feeling remorseful. He wrote to Mary, saying he was willing to stand trial, then he turned himself in.

The sensational trial took place in Cork in April 1801. Found guilty of abduction, Hayes was at first sentenced to death by hanging, but then he was given mercy, with an alternative sentence of banishment for life to New South Wales. Without his children, he sailed to the penal colony aboard a convict ship, departing England on November 29, 1801. The ship was the *Atlas*, where he became intimately familiar with its captain, Richard Brooks.

Hayes paid a sizable sum—some called it a bribe—to Brooks to receive preferential treatment on board. Not only did Hayes have his own cabin, but he also was allowed to carry with him £5,000 worth of goods and personal items, which took up a lot of the storage space that had been promised to other paying customers, and which certainly contributed to the eventual problems aboard the *Atlas*.

True to form, Hayes caused trouble on the voyage. He took a particular dislike to fellow passenger Thomas Jamison, who was to be the colony's new surgeon general. Hayes enjoyed ridiculing Jamison, whom he later said was "stupid when sober and when drunk outrageous." When Jamison drank too much and caused a disturbance one night while the *Atlas* was on a stopover in Rio de Janeiro, Brooks confronted him. Angry words turned to punches, with Hayes egging on Brooks to keep pummeling the surgeon. Fearing for his life, Jamison transferred to the convict ship *Hercules*, which was traveling to New South Wales in convoy with the *Atlas*.

Brooks's and Hayes's ill-treatment of Jamison came back to haunt them when they reached New South Wales. Jamison turned out to be a friend and colleague of Governor Philip King, who encouraged Jamison to take legal action against the two. Brooks successfully defended himself, but Hayes was convicted and thrown into jail for six months. In subsequent years, Hayes, locally referred to as "Sir Harry," got into many other scrapes with powerful people in the government, which earned him

Drawing depicting the fight aboard the Atlas *between Captain Richard Brooks and the surgeon Thomas Jamison, from a 1910 magazine article on Sir Henry Browne Hayes.*

other prison terms and two stretches of hard labor in the Newcastle coal mines, in between which he managed to pursue a rather grand lifestyle at his splendid cottage, Vaucluse House. Ever the operator, he wangled a pardon from Governor Macquarie in early 1812. Accompanying Hayes on the *Isabella* was another pardoned convict named Samuel Breakwell.

About the remaining passengers, very little is known. Two were the wives of marines. Four others were unattached women, quite likely prostitutes, who had served their sentences. There was also a shadowy fellow named William Mattinson. One contemporary claimed he was a stowaway, although that was certainly not the case. Mattinson even took out an ad in the *Sydney Gazette and New South Wales Advertiser* a month before the *Isabella* sailed, identifying himself and inviting all of his creditors to come forward and present their claims for payment before he left Australia on the brig. There were also whispers that Mattinson had been a Royal Navy sailing master or gunner who had been dismissed for bad conduct, although an assiduous search of the Royal Navy archives could not verify that claim.

Vaucluse Bay, Port Jackson, circa 1820. Sir Henry Browne Hayes built his cottage, Vaucluse House, at the head of this bay (which is just barely visible in the image). In the years after Hayes left, the cottage was expanded and the grounds were transformed, creating an impressive estate. In 1915, Vaucluse House became Australia's first official house museum.

The decision to have the *Isabella* sail on a Friday is surprising, particularly in light of the common superstition among sailors at the time that sailing on a Friday brought bad luck. As one old couplet goes, "The ship what on a Friday sails, is sure to meet with stormy gales." However, it was not superstition that threatened the voyage. It was the *Isabella* itself and its leadership. As Lieutenant Richard Lundin observed, "[O]ur vessel was exceedingly ill provided, both as to rigging and crew. The captain and mate at the same time possessing those dangerous propensities in seamen—drunkenness and laziness. The ship was also much overloaded." George Higton was the captain, and George Davis the mate. The owners of the brig and its passengers put their faith in them, which turned out to be a very bad decision indeed.

OFFICERS, CREW, AND
PASSENGERS ON THE *Isabella*

MASTER
George Higton

MATE
George Davis

CREW
*Joseph Albrook; Samuel Ansell;
Jose Antonio; John Babtist;
Hans Brockner; John Brown;
Joseph Ellis; Daniel Elrict;
Ford [first name unknown];
James Hubbard; John Gordon;
Charles Lewis; James Louder;
Angus McCoy; James Moss;
James Read; William Robarts;
John Servester*

ROYAL MARINES
*Sergeant William Bean;
Corporal Richard Sargent;
Privates Robert Andrews, John
Bellingham, William Catford,
Thomas Green, William
Johnson, James Rea, Richard
Rowell, James Spooner, Richard
Walton, and Joseph Wooley;
and Drummers John Brind and
William Hughes*

DURIE PARTY
*Captain Robert Durie
Mrs. Joanna-Ann Durie
Agnes Durie (18 months)*

HOLT PARTY
*Joseph Holt
Mrs. Hester Holt
Joseph Harrison Holt
Family servants: John Burns;
Philip Harney; Edward
Kilbride*

HAYES PARTY
*Sir Henry Browne Hayes
Samuel Breakwell*

OTHER FEMALE PASSENGERS
*Mrs. Elizabeth Bean
(wife of Royal Marine)
Mary Bindell
Ms. Connolly
Elizabeth Davis
Mrs. Hughes
(wife of Royal Marine)
Mary Ann Spencer*

OTHER MALE PASSENGERS
*[Captain] Richard Brooks
Lieutenant Richard Lundin
William Mattinson*

CHAPTER

9

On the Edge of Disaster

=

TWELVE DAYS AFTER LEAVING PORT JACKSON HARBOR ON A SOUTHERLY COURSE, the *Isabella* had passed far beyond Van Diemen's Land* and was now heading east toward Cape Horn, nearly 5,000 miles away. This stretch of the southwestern Pacific Ocean had rarely been traversed by humans. It was only a few years earlier that two of the islands in this region— Macquarie and Campbell—had been discovered by Frederick Has- selborough, a sealer out of Port Jackson searching for new territory to plunder. So new were these discoveries that they did not appear on any of the *Isabella*'s charts. Aware of that, Higton had spoken to a merchant in Sydney before sailing to obtain information about their locations. By his calculations, the *Isabella* was well clear of both of them.

Around midnight on December 15, Lieutenant Lundin was awak- ened by a Royal Marine running into his cabin screaming that the brig was going to crash. Lundin rushed to the main deck, where he saw the crew and passengers huddled together, panic-stricken and immobilized with fear. Directly leeward of the *Isabella*, visible in the darkness, was an unbroken line of towering cliffs as far as the eye could see. It was Camp- bell Island, and it was looming closer by the minute.

As Lundin was to learn later, a few hours before this horrific scene greeted the crewman on watch, he had rushed to Higton's cabin, warn- ing him of land in the offing, but Higton, who was drinking, smoking, and chatting with some of the other seamen, appeared not to care, and

---

* Modern-day Tasmania.

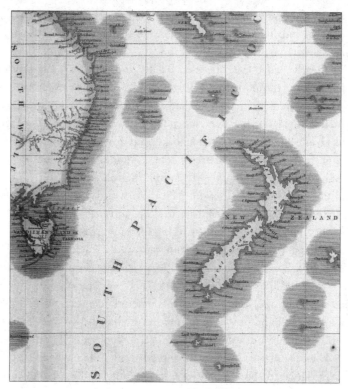

The small island to the south of New Zealand, and closest to the edge of the image, is Campbell Island, upon which the Isabella *almost foundered. Detail of map by Daniel Lizars, 1831. Part of New South Wales and the island of Tasmania are visible at the upper left.*

ignored him. The watchman returned to the captain's cabin two more times, each time with more urgency, only to be met with the same reaction.

Finally, after Captain Brooks arrived topside and took command, the crew, the Royal Marines, and Lundin jumped-to, bracing the yards and setting sails in a frantic attempt to haul off and avoid the shore. The whipping winds shredded the main staysail, and with no possibility of replacing it, the crew had to depend on the main-topsail and the foresail for propulsion. "Nothing could now be done," observed Lundin, "but to watch the progress we made along the shore, and in the momentary dread and expectation of the masts or sails giving way, when further exertion would have been in vain. If we had struck, not a soul would have been saved, owing both to the intenseness of the cold, and the shore being quite inaccessible."

For nearly two hours, the men fought the wind and waves, until finally, at two in the morning, the brig cleared the last promontory, reaching open water. The immediate danger was over, and Higton's standing on board was left in tatters, much like the main staysail. Afterward, Brooks confronted Higton, yelling that he and his men "were very much to blame, for not keeping a better lookout, . . . and that five minutes more would have made an end of the voyage, for then all the men in the world could not have saved the *Isabella*." Pleading with Higton to take more care in the future, Brooks went back to sleep, still worrying that the captain's apparent ineptitude and shirking of responsibility might in the future endanger all of them once again.

The *Isabella* continued onward, experiencing baffling winds and finally reaching Cape Horn just before Christmas. As expected, when rounding the Cape, the *Isabella* encountered tempestuous weather. A gale forced the brig to lie-to for fifty-six hours, and the crewmen on board, Holt observed, were "very hard set to cook our Christmas dinner." Worse, four of the sails were shredded, and the mainsail and the jib were damaged. Fortunately, pleasant weather followed the storm, enabling the *Isabella* to clear the Cape.

In the Atlantic now, Higton wanted to stop at the Falkland Islands, having heard that whalers often did so to trade old clothes with Spaniards on the islands, for which they received food and water in return. (He was unaware that the Falklands had no settlements at that moment.) Brooks, who by now had no trust in Higton, urged him to reconsider, since there were no charts of the islands on board, and Higton didn't even know the name of the port the whalers used. Higton relented, but his passengers and crew still desperately needed food and water. Realizing that he didn't have enough of either on board to make it to St. Helena, the usual stopping-off point on the way back to England, Higton decided to sail for Rio de Janeiro instead.

The *Isabella* changed to a more westerly course in order to pass between the Falklands and the South American continent. At about 6 p.m. on February 7, 1813, Higton was surprised to see land off to port, a few miles away. With darkness coming on, and doubts mounting about the ship's location, Brooks advised Higton to put the ship about in an

Engraving titled A Squall off Cape Horn, *by Currier & Ives, circa mid-1800s. The waters off Cape Horn are notorious for rough weather, and the* Isabella *experienced a bit of this during its passage from the Pacific to the Atlantic.*

attempt to pass by the eastern side of the Falklands rather than continue on their current path. The course was changed.

Lundin reported that he and some of the other passengers walked "the deck to a late hour, congratulating each other upon having got over the worst part of the voyage; and making calculations on the probable time of our arrival in England, anticipating the pleasure of so soon seeing our friends and country." Then they retired to their respective cabins.

At the same time, Higton began drinking. A short while later, he barreled into Holt's cabin three sheets to the wind, gesticulating wildly, saying he would not let anyone on board know what harbor he planned to enter, and adding, "[I]f the ship should sink, and all on board perish, who was to be responsible but him?" Holt stood and stared at the deranged captain, calmly telling him that "it did not matter much, if all perished, where the responsibility rested, as no one would be alive to prosecute." Then Higton, too, retired, but not to his cabin. Instead, he went to visit Mary Bindell, one of the former prostitutes and ex-convicts, and he was welcomed into her bed.

Grief

=

AROUND ONE IN THE MORNING OF FEBRUARY 8, 1813, IN A SICKENING REPLAY of the earlier alarm off Campbell Island, Lundin was aroused by yelling and scurrying on the main deck. Through the gloom of a moonless night, land was visible very close by. With Higton drunk and otherwise occupied, Brooks had once again taken command and was trying his best to steer the *Isabella* clear of the danger. Finally, believing that he had gained a moment of reprieve, and that the brig would pass by the land, Brooks went below to don warmer clothes. No sooner had he descended to his cabin, though, than cries rang out: "[R]ocks on one side and breakers on the other!" Lundin rushed to get Brooks, but at the moment he reached the main deck, the *Isabella* crashed into a rocky reef "with dreadful force." This collision unshipped the rudder, leaving the *Isabella* unable to steer, and thus at the mercy of wind and waves. A following swell lifted the brig off the rocks for a few moments, only to launch it into other ones as soon as the next trough arrived, forcing everyone on board to grab hold of something to avoid being thrown about or pitched into the water.

Down below, Holt had roused his family members, who promptly sank to their knees to pray for "God's mercy and assistance." When the brig crashed into the rocks a second time, Holt's wife, Hester, placed Joseph in between them, saying, "Let us all, linked in each other's arms go to our watery graves together."

Meanwhile, the *Isabella* floated free of the rocks but was still being propelled rapidly toward the looming shore into increasingly shallow waters, with massive waves crashing all around. The sea was cov-

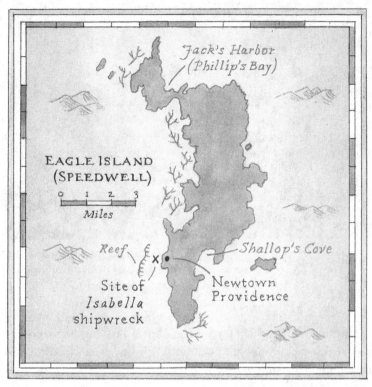

Determining the exact site of the wreck of the Isabella, *and the location of Newtown*
Providence was not easy, in part because the descriptions of the British castaways
and the American sealers are not determinative. However, a deep reading of their
comments, and valuable historical and photographic information provided by Chris
May, the current co-owner of Eagle/Speedwell Island (along with his wife, Lindsey),
made it very clear that the locations on the map—where the Isabella *came to rest,*
Newtown Providence, and the offshore reef that the Isabella *first struck—are correct.*
In discussing the wreck of the Isabella, *the castaways talk about the rocky reef offshore,*
rock ledge leading up to the beach, and rocks on the beach, all of which are present in
the locations indicated. Furthermore, numerous artifacts—including an anchor,
nails, wood, pearl shells, and pottery and glass shards—have all been found at the
sites. Images of some of these items can been seen on pages 82, 84, 85, 86, and 87.
Determining the location of Shallop's Cove was more difficult. But, again, a deep
reading of the primary materials, help from Chris May, and artifacts on the
ground, point to the location indicated being the most likely site of Shallop's Cove.

ered with foam as far as the eye could see. The few sailors who were
responding to Brooks's commands climbed aloft to square the yards

A view of the reef offshore upon which the Isabella *crashed during the early morning hours of February 8, 1813. It is the thin, dark line in the distance near the horizon. A close look reveals a wave breaking on the reef.*

so that the brig could run toward land. Finally, the *Isabella* struck fast on a rock ledge. It was high tide, so the brig was much closer to shore than if the tide had been out, and the tip of the bowsprit reached the beach. Brooks then yelled over the din, "[T]here is now no danger of our lives," and he ordered the men to cut away the mainmast, which fell toward the land.

At this point, the true nature of some of the crew and passengers came to the fore. Abandoning all sense of order or control, a few of the sailors careened through the brig demanding liquor from the frightened passengers. Foremast hand Samuel Ansell appeared to be leading the pack. According to the prostitute Mary Ann Spencer, he entered her berth, grabbed a glass of rum from her hand, emptied it, and dashed it upon the deck, exclaiming, "[W]e shall have no more use for glasses, for this is the last time, either at sea or on shore, that we shall ever drink."

Lundin and Brooks meanwhile were trying to organize the crew and passengers and get out the small boat so it could be rowed to shore, with women and children going first. Once the boat was in the water and tied off with a towrope, however, Hayes, Breakwell, Mattinson, and two Royal Marines pushed the other passengers aside and commandeered the boat, jumping in and taking with them three of the *Isabella*'s four oars. Then the scoundrels noticed that the boat's plughole was open and the boat was taking on water at a rapid rate, slowly sinking. While they frantically searched for the plug, Lundin learned its location from the carpenter and told those in the boat, an act he later much regretted. Rather than reconsider their action, the deserters plugged the hole and released the towrope, leaving all of those aboard the *Isabella* to their fate and filling them with "rage and disappointment" after this "unexampled treachery."

All hands who were not drunk now focused on launching the *Isabella*'s longboat, which required great effort, being a very bulky and heavy vessel designed to carry lumber and water. It was loaded with supplies, including flour, biscuits, and other provisions quickly brought up from below. Once the longboat was filled, Brooks and a few of the marines attempted to set out for the beach, but they were finding it nearly impossible to maneuver the vessel with only one oar. Suddenly, Lundin remembered the beautifully carved paddles he had acquired from South Sea Islanders, which he was taking home as souvenirs. Retrieving them from his cabin, he pitched them into the longboat, which was still alongside the brig.

Doing their best, the marines managed to use the one oar and the souvenir paddles to muscle the boat along the shore and around a small promontory, on the other side of which they landed, secured the boat, and carried the provisions ashore. They had wanted to return to the brig, but they would not have had a chance of making way against the wind with such a poorly propelled vessel.

Who soon joined them but the five deserters, having landed a little way down the beach. Brooks harangued Hayes, the apparent ringleader of this despicable bunch, telling him that what he had done was disgraceful. Hayes parried the verbal blow, expressing great "effrontery, pleading self-preservation," which, Lundin later commented, was the "first law of nature, which, to persons of his selfish and despicable principles, will indeed ever be a primary consideration."

Walking back toward the stricken *Isabella*, Brooks and the marines were cheered by the sight of passengers making it ashore. A hawser, or thick rope, was strung to the wreck and equipped with a jury-rigged bosun's chair, allowing the women and children to escape first, and then the others. Despite her very pregnant state, Joanna-Ann Durie "supported herself with great fortitude" during this ordeal. Holt helped see

Photo of the upper rocky beach where the Isabella's *castaways came ashore.*

An iron anchor resting on the rock ledge at low tide on the beach where the Isabella *wrecked. It is 11 feet long, with the one remaining fluke measuring 4 feet from tip to shank. It is almost certainly one of the* Isabella's *anchors.*

Close-up of the fluke of the iron anchor at the Isabella *wreck site.*

that his wife and son made it to the beach, but when he asked two of his servants to help him gather his belongings to take them off the brig, they ignored him and joined the marines and sailors in their bacchanalian debauchery. Only Holt's third servant, an old and infirm man, lent a hand. By the time the dawn light illuminated the scene, everyone had disembarked. "Never," Lundin mused to himself, "did a weary traveler reach his destined rest with more heartfelt joy than we did, now cast upon this desert shore."

Soon after Holt and Durie made it to the beach, they searched for their wives, who had been separated from them in the confusion. They found the women sitting together on a gentle rise, which Holt dubbed "sorrowful bank." Joanna-Ann held out a bottle of rum and urged Holt to take a swig. "I will, Madam," he responded warmly, "for it is wanted to me, as I have not broken my fast this day." Thus began the stay of the *Isabella*'s crew and passengers on Eagle Island,* located about 110 miles from where the *Nanina* was holed up.

---

* Modern-day Speedwell Island.

Forlorn

===

O<small>N THE DAY AFTER THE DISASTROUS WRECK OF THE *ISABELLA*, THE MOST</small> urgent need was to unload the ship onto Eagle Island. This was accomplished only with great difficulty, because most of the sailors and marines were drunk and of little help. They had begun drinking even before making it to shore, and their imbibing continued apace once off the ship. To keep them from further inebriation, Brooks and Lundin smashed all of

Artifacts collected by Chris and Lindsey May, owners of Speedwell Island (formerly Eagle Island), at the site of Newtown Providence. They include pearl shells, shards of pottery and glass, copper sheathing, iron nails and fastenings, balls from muskets, and, possibly, a small swivel gun. Not shown are copper nails and additional pieces of iron and glass also found at the site.

This turned stanchion with a copper cap and the attached
swivel deck railing were found at the site of the wreck
of the Isabella *and are now displayed at the*
Charles H. Barnard Museum on New Island.

the remaining casks of rum, the mariner's liquor of choice. A few bottles
of rum, however, were saved from destruction.

By nightfall, an assortment of clothes, coal, wood, provisions, guns,
and gunpowder had been retrieved. Spars and small sails had been carried ashore and some were used to set up makeshift tents about 60 feet
from the water's edge. The castaways christened their small community
of woe "Newtown Providence."

Exhausted and on edge, the survivors fell into a disturbed sleep, only
to be awakened by screams in the middle of the night. Some of the fires
set to cook dinner had not been fully stamped out, and nearby patches of
tussac grass were ablaze. The flames, carried on the wind, spread fast.
To arrest the conflagration, the men employed a variation of the tactic
used by urban firemen, who level any buildings in the path of a fire, thus
starving it of fuel and halting its advance. In this case, the men chopped
away the tussac grass downwind of the fire. According to Lundin, "had
it been allowed to continue much longer, our efforts to extinguish it must
have been unavailing."

The following morning, Holt and Brooks called a meeting of all
the crew and passengers. To be a functioning community, rules were
needed, they announced, and the task of determining those rules was
assigned to an appointed council. Durie nominated Brooks as a member, and both Durie and Brooks nominated Lundin and Holt. The Royal
Marines named Hayes, "for he was a favorite with them." Despite Higton's abysmal performance leading up to the wreck, he was added to the

A dense growth of tussac grass along the edge of Eagle Island (modern-day Speedwell), very similar to what the castaways from the Isabella *would have seen on the island when they arrived. Extensive sheep farming on the island, going back to the late 1800s, has killed much of the tussac grass, since sheep love eating it.*

group, along with his mate, Davis. The council then drew up the following articles, which everyone assented to and signed:

> FIRST—That no man should be exempt from work, till our provisions were all landed.
>
> SECOND—Any man found guilty of stealing or robbing was to be punished according to his offence.
>
> THIRD—Every man should attend roll-call in the morning.
>
> FOURTH—That no man should have more provisions than another.
>
> FIFTH—That all private stores should belong to the general store.
>
> SIXTH—That nothing should be done without the voice of the majority.
>
> SEVENTH—That the provisions should be served out twice a week, to prevent waste in the first part of the week.

After the meeting, having established a loose form of government, everyone turned to unloading more items from the *Isabella*—even the sailors and marines, who were still shaking off their hangovers. This task was aided by another high tide that floated the brig so far onto the shore that it was possible to walk out to the wreck at low water and use a human chain to speed the process.

Over the next couple of weeks, the castaways kept quite busy. They explored the island, which is shaped like an upside-down "L" and is about 11 miles long and 4 miles across at its widest point. It is relatively flat throughout, with the highest point being only 150 feet. The nature of the beach adjoining the settlement, of course, varied with the tides. At high tide, it was covered with sand and mud and numerous rocks and pebbles. Low tide, however, exposed broad reaches of fractured rock shelving, the edges of which had been worn down and rounded due to the ceaseless pounding of waves. The perimeter of the island was covered in a dense mat of tussac grass, and the interior was described by one of the survivors as "bleak and barren, with scarcely any trace of vegetation." The numerous penguins and wildfowl on the island appeared totally unafraid of humans. Of critical importance, the castaways found small ponds with an abundance of brackish but palatable water.

The men built a storehouse with walls made of turf "bricks," while spars from the *Isabella* overlaid with the brig's sails provided the ceiling. Food was guarded and distributed according to a set schedule established by a committee, the goal being to have the supplies last for up to a year. Weekly rations were set at one pound of beef or pork, half a pound of flour or rice, two pounds of bread, and a pint of wine. Additionally, Indian corn was used to make ersatz coffee by charring the kernels and then boiling them in water.

Within relatively short order, not surprisingly, a problem arose with the wine. Although a sentry was posted to keep an eye on the food and drink, many of the crewmen and marines repeatedly got drunk, even though the allowed daily pint was not sufficient to cause such a state. The storehouse was reinforced, and security increased, to no avail. When called out on their deception, the inebriates professed their innocence. The reprobates' behavior led Holt to observe, "[Y]ou may rest assured you might as well expect to squeeze honey out of a smith's anvil, as to make an old marine or sailor honest." A meeting was held, and the majority decided to bury the pipes, or casks, three feet below ground, so that the wine could be extracted only when they were uncovered and a hand pump was attached to draw the rations out. Finally, the daily intoxication came to a halt.

The best marksman would be tasked with hunting for the group, so he was chosen through a competition. Ten candidates shot at a paper target, marked with a circle, a hundred yards off. The results were so abysmal, with only a couple of the soldiers being able to place a shot within the ring, that Holt joked that he had "good reason for knowing all soldiers to be bad marksmen, as they had missed me so often in [the rebellion of] 1798; for that probably more shots were aimed at me, with the intention of killing me, than had ever been aimed at any man alive and able to tell the story." Nevertheless, John Bellingham, in the end the most accurate shooter, was selected; for encouragement, he was given an extra allowance of spirits during bad weather. Very soon, steady streams of geese and other dead birds were making their way into camp.

While many of the birds were shot, others were simply clubbed to death. Their tameness made the killing easier, since Bellingham could walk right up to a flock on the ground and, with a single shot, kill six or more birds. The rest of the birds, instead of taking flight, would gather around their fallen peers, giving Bellingham time to reload and shoot again, or simply to dispatch them with a few quick swings of his club. Even birds hovering overhead could be brought to ground with a well-placed blow. The castaways supplemented their meaty fare with bunches of wild celery that Holt pronounced to be "as fine indeed as I ever saw in Dublin market, which was very useful to us for cooking and making soup."

The tight rations forced Holt to part with something very dear to him—exotic birds. In Australia, he had collected quite a menagerie, and onto the *Isabella* he had brought twenty-one parrots and one cockatoo, all housed in a large cage. Fifteen of the parrots "spoke, and whistled, in a very remarkable manner," and they seemed to be able to repeat any tune. The cockatoo was no slouch, being able to speak, bark like a dog, and imitate other animals, including sheep. Holt felt he could not spare any food for his aviary, so he released the birds into the wild and let them fend for themselves. They didn't stand a chance. No sooner had the birds flown out, than some rather large native birds—which Holt called "eagles"—swooped in, captured them in their talons, and greedily consumed most of them. Four parrots, however, quickly sought protection in the hut, where they did their best to ingratiate themselves with Joanna-Ann, perching on her lap and crying out "pretty dear" and "pretty polly."

It worked. The Holts put the four back in the cage and fed them from their rations.

Inevitably, tensions arose among the castaways, so they peeled off into small groups, each with their own shelters, where they ate, slept, and tried to avoid each other. Higton, almost universally reviled for the execrable performance of his duties while the *Isabella* was afloat, repaired to his own hut, along with Mary Bindell. He acted in a mercurial manner, often berating others or defending his actions. At one point, he got into a fight with Ansell, already known to be a mean drunk with a violent temper who suffered from recurring "black rages." It started after a storm hit the island, pounding the *Isabella* against the rocks and bilging it, a dénouement that spurred Ansell to shove his fist in Higton's face and yell, "Where's your quarterdeck now?" Intimidated, Higton reared back, but then James Hubbard, an American seaman who had signed onto the *Isabella*'s crew, intervened to keep the two men from coming to blows. Ansell next transferred his anger to the peacemaker and waited until Hubbard had let down his guard, then hit him on the side of his head, sending Hubbard sprawling onto the ground, where he lay "in the agonies of death." Hubbard finally got up and had his wound dressed, but thereafter he suffered from erratic behavior, likely due to a skull fracture or a serious concussion. As for Higton and Ansell, not long after their altercation, the two of them were getting along famously once again.

ABOUT A WEEK AFTER the crash, Joanna-Ann Durie, on the verge of giving birth, became nearly inconsolable when the roof of her hut fell in after a deluge, leaving her soaked. She bewailed "her hard lot, and gave many evil wishes to Higton, whose drunkenness had caused all our misfortunes." Holt stepped forward and "endeavored to comfort her, and told her that God had already been gracious, and saved all our lives, and was able, and would provide for her in her necessity." With Holt taking the lead, the men rallied and built Joanna-Ann a brand-new hut made out of sod bricks and stones. It was 20 feet long, 10 feet wide, and 7 feet high. To create the roof, a spar from the brig was used to make a ridgepole held up by deck planks that were placed on end and nailed to the spar. Three sails were then draped on top of the structure. They sloped toward the wall, allowing rain to drain off. Deck planks were also used to make a floor, and the stove from the ship was placed inside the hut, with a funnel rising through a hole in the sails to let the smoke escape. A table, chairs, and bedding from the wreck made the lodging a bit more comfortable.

The new shelter was timely. On February 21, at dinner, Holt noticed that Joanna-Ann appeared to be in some distress. He grabbed his glass of wine and said to Brooks and Durie, who were also there, "a safe passage to all on their journey," and with that the three men promptly took their leave and went for a walk. About an hour-and-a-half later, with Hester Holt's assistance, Joanna-Ann gave birth to a healthy girl, hopefully named Eliza Providence Durie. It is quite likely that she was the first European born on the Falklands. The entire camp, in honor of the event, "drank very heartily that night."

The day after Eliza's arrival turned out to be yet another momentous one. Almost immediately after coming ashore, the survivors had begun trying to devise a means to save themselves. They finally settled on a plan to send six men off in the 17.5-foot longboat to explore the islands and see whether they could reach Port Egmont. There they hoped to get help, and possibly procure a larger vessel they could use to transport the rest of the survivors to safety. The help they expected to get, however, would come not from the English but from the Spanish. The *Isabella*'s castaways knew that England had abandoned Port Egmont decades earlier, but they hoped that the Spanish would have taken up residence in their stead. (Unbeknown to the castaways, though, the Spanish had never settled in Port Egmont, and they had left the islands in 1811.) If the men in the longboat failed to get help at Port Egmont, they would plan to sail to Montevideo (in modern-day Uruguay), and then on to Rio de Janeiro, where relief might be found. Richard Lundin was fatalistic about the prospects for this ambitious expedition. If they did not succeed, "it was only exchanging one death for another; as so many people could not be supposed to exist for a very long period, the provisions every day decreasing."

To make the open longboat ready for such a perilous journey, the men built a deck about 13 feet long, starting at the bow and going aft. A small hatchway was placed in the center to allow the men to get in and out of the makeshift cabin, which was barely big enough for the supplies and for the men to sleep in shifts. Near the stern, they constructed a platform where they could sit while sailing the vessel. Another strake was added all around the boat, raising her sides by about 4 inches. The longboat was also rigged with a mast, from which hung a lug foresail, a jib, and a small mizzen.

Richard Brooks, being the best navigator and having proved his mettle on the voyage from Port Jackson, was selected by vote to lead the mission. When Lundin volunteered, Brooks eagerly welcomed him, because he had stepped forward for one very practical and important reason. If the voyagers made it to Rio de Janeiro, they hoped to encounter the British admiral commanding that post. If they did, Lundin believed that he, as a British officer applying for assistance on behalf of British subjects, would receive a warmer welcome than a group of sailors. To that end, he packed his grenadier's uniform, which included a scarlet jacket and epaulets. Lundin also carried with him a letter penned by Captain Durie to be handed over to British Vice Admiral Michael De Courcy.

To round out the crew, Brooks chose George Davis, a marine named Joseph Wooley, an American named Ford, and a Portuguese seaman named Jose Antonio. By February 22, the longboat had been loaded with salt beef and pork, chocolate, and biscuits, along with 3 gallons of rum and 40 gallons of Madeira wine—enough, it was thought, to last them three months, should their journey take that long. Also carried along were a navigation chart, a compass, a quadrant, a large iron pot for cooking, and some extra clothes. To signify the critical nature of the voyage, and the launch itself, a bottle of rum was taken out to christen the longboat *Faith and Hope*. After saying good-bye, and receiving many heartfelt wishes for a successful trip, Brooks and his tiny crew shoved off at four in the afternoon and soon were out of sight.

Searching for Salvation

═══

U NFORTUNATELY, THE LONGBOAT PROVED TO BE A DULL SAILER, AND
Brooks had to use all of his skills to get it to bend to his will. Over the
next two weeks, the men traveled many miles throughout the Falklands,
exploring numerous inlets and bays in hopes of finding signs of humanity. Most nights they stopped on an island, sometimes staying for a few
days if the weather was too rough to proceed. At each place they stopped,
they climbed to the highest point to see whether they could detect any
settlements or derive some sense of where they were in the archipelago.
Before departing their temporary camps, they set fire to the tussac grass
so that the extensive burned areas provided evidence of where they had
been, should they return.

Along the way, the men encountered some of the Falklands' wildlife.
On February 23, while wandering among the mounds of tussac grass,
they suddenly came upon eight immense sea elephants, each "as large as
a whale," which "growled like thunder" upon being disturbed from their
slumber. The men tried to kill one of them, to procure its tongue, which
they knew to be quite tasty, but firing lead balls into the animal was fruit-
less, as they failed to penetrate its thick coat of blubber.

Another day they were visited by a warrah. The creature was quite
curious, not scared of humans, and it almost made off with Wooley's
knapsack before it was yanked from the creature's mouth.* This meeting

---

* Another indication of how little the warrahs feared humans comes from the story of
an interaction Barzillai Pease experienced with one of the creatures. While he was sitting

Engraving of a warrah from The Zoology of the Voyage of the H.M.S.
Beagle, Part II, Mammalia *(London: Smith, Elder, and Co., 1839).*

took place in what later was dubbed Fox Bay because of all the warrahs in the area.

The men also had some traumatic experiences that nearly ended the expedition. At one island, the line from the boat to shore broke. The kedge anchor held, but the boat drifted farther offshore, until the anchor rope stopped its progress. Luckily, one of the men was a strong swimmer—unusual for seamen at that time—and he launched himself into the surf and fought his way to the longboat, which was soon once again tethered to land.

About a week later, the boat came around a promontory and became caught in a race,* with waves crashing in every direction and the water exhibiting "the appearance of a boiling pot." Lundin was so unnerved by the sight that he shut his eyes, while Brooks steered the longboat. When

---

on a tussac mound on English Maloon, a warrah approached him and began sniffing his feet, and then moved up to his knees and hands. Pease took a thin rope snare from his pocket and laid it out about 10 feet from where he was sitting. When the curious warrah examined the snare, Pease waited until it stepped in the snare's looped end, then he pulled the rope tight, grabbing one of the animal's feet. Pease then clubbed the warrah to death. See Barzillai Pease Journals, Special Collections Research Center, Syracuse University Libraries, Journal 13, insert p. 11, near the entry for March 28, 1813.

* A strong current flowing through a narrow channel.

Brooks cast a glance at Lundin, he thought he was napping, and yelled, "How can you sleep at this awful moment?" They made it through into calmer water, but it was far from their last narrow escape.

The following day, the seas were again boiling, and the shoreline for as far as the eye could see was a jumble of shelving rocks being pounded by a thunderous surf. Anchored just a few hundred feet from the island, the men had to make a decision. Should they attempt to land, the boat surely would be destroyed, so if they managed to struggle to shore, they would be stranded. If, on the other hand, they headed out to sea, they would face the angry ocean, with the outcome in doubt. Ultimately, they agreed to take their chances at sea, raised the anchor, and sailed off.

Waves battered the boat, forcing the men to bail continuously to avoid swamping. At around midnight, while they were still struggling to keep clear of the coast, the boat's progress was suddenly arrested by a thick bed of kelp, which seemed to grab hold of the hull. This gave them only a few minutes' reprieve from being violently tossed about before the strong current pushed the boat back into open water. Over the next six hours, the men were repeatedly forced to take down the sails and lie-to while squalls accompanied by tremendous rains rolled through. That night "was the most dreadful and tedious of my life," Lundin later recalled, "as during eleven hours we had reason to expect every moment would be our last."

Come dawn, they had sailed through the worst of it, intact but weary. The longboat's impressive performance in this and other rough passages caused the men to look more admiringly on their vessel, despite the fact that it was neither fast nor agile. But they were far out to sea and next to a small, barren island erupting from the ocean's depths. Like its lonely namesake off the coast of England, it had been named Eddystone Rock by British sealers who had encountered it years earlier.

The crew turned about and sailed onward for many hours, finally coming upon a large landmass that they hoped was English Maloon, but it was actually Spanish Maloon. They continued along the coastline looking for a sheltered place to land, and late in the day they entered a broad inlet. In their eagerness to get ashore, they crashed into some rocks, nearly bilging the longboat. Only some dexterous maneuvering avoided disaster and got the boat back out into deeper water. A short while later, they landed in a safer place and were greeted with a heartening sight—horses and cattle grazing on a nearby hill. Thinking that they must be near Port Egmont, the men's spirits lifted.

The next day, however, their explorations of the island turned up nothing, other than more horses. Having little faith in the success of further searching, the men agreed they had to strike out for Montevideo, since the weather would only become stormier and colder as they headed into late March and early April. While most of the crew worked to make the longboat more seaworthy, packing its seams with oakum and pitch, Lundin and Ford made one last, wider circuit of the area to see whether they had missed anything. They had.

As they came over a rise, they saw a long-abandoned hut, which Lundin assumed had been occupied by Spaniards. One of its walls had collapsed, and inside were three beds made of bullock hides and a few skeletons of horses and cattle. The great prize, however, was the still-intact wooden roof, a few planks of which Lundin and Ford used to start a small fire for warmth. After lingering a while, the two men hurried back to the rest of the party to share the exciting news.

The next morning, the whole crew visited the hut and collected most of the wood to use for cooking on their onward voyage. While the other five were thus engaged, Lundin wrote a note and hung it from a beam in the center of the hut, in case any of the former inhabitants should return:

> Spaniards and Christians, should this ever meet your eye, know that fifty-four British subjects have been shipwrecked upon one of these desert islands . . . six of whom, in order to obtain relief, have endeavored to reach the mainland in a boat. If they fail in this undertaking, their companions will, in all probability, be left to perish. If you find them there, the boat has been lost: If not, we have brought them relief. March 8, 1813.

While Lundin was leaving his note, Ford spotted what looked like a road or path in the distance. Curious to see where it might lead, Ford and Lundin headed in that direction, while the rest of the men went back to the longboat. A few hours later, the two wanderers passed a large number of horses and cows before coming upon a group of buildings and what appeared to be the mast of a ship. At the sight, they "literally leapt for joy, and hurried with renewed ardor, anticipating the pleasure of passing a comfortable night with a friendly Spaniard, and returning to our friends in the morning with such agreeable tidings."

As Lundin and Ford moved in closer, the number of horses and cows increased, but the men's spirits sank. The buildings, including a small stone chapel, appeared to be deserted. Just before the men reached what looked to be a settlement, a herd of about eighty cattle—which, according to Lundin, "seemed to regard us with the greatest surprise"—decided to charge, and they came thundering down a hill. Running did not appear to be a winning option, so the men stood their ground, staring down the stampede. It worked. The cattle came to stop a few hundred yards away, looked at them, and then retreated.

Some minutes later, as the two men wandered through the settlement, their fears were confirmed. Nobody responded to their calls, and every structure was empty. A sign on the side of a building proclaimed that these islands belonged to King Ferdinand VII, bearing the date of February 1811. The mast they had thought they saw was a signal post on the edge of an old, turf-walled fort. There was, however, a vessel in the harbor, a large barge that had beached, its hull smashed. In one of the settlement's storehouses, they found a few knives and pikes. Although the men didn't know it, they were standing in the abandoned Spanish settlement of Puerto Soledad.

The hour being late, and darkness descending, Lundin and Ford looked for a place to spend the night. In one of the buildings, they found empty wooden casks, knocked the tops off of two of them, put them on their sides, and crawled in. Hours later, as the temperature fell, Ford reluctantly joined Lundin in his cask, with hardly any room to spare.

After a night of fitful sleep, constantly shifting their positions to try to keep each other warm, they rose early and "breakfasted very heartily upon" the cabbages they found growing in a nearby garden. Corralling an old, one-eyed horse—Rosinante,* as they called it—they loaded it up with their found "treasures," including cabbages, an iron pot for cooking, and some shoes, and headed back to the longboat.

The reunion was joyous, for their companions had thought they were lost or, perhaps, had been gored or trampled to death by wild cattle, or maybe even had been taken hostage by "savages." They loaded up the longboat, and the next day, March 10, 1813, before the sun rose, they hoisted the longboat's anchor and headed into the open ocean.

---

* Spanish slang for a broken-down nag.

———

THE FIRST DECISION RICHARD BROOKS and the crew had to make was which course to take. They could either hug the continent or go in more of a straight line, farther out to sea. On the one hand, there was some comfort in being close to shore in case a storm threatened to overwhelm the boat and force them to land. But the possibility of being driven onto the Patagonian shore by contrary winds was deemed to be the graver danger, so they plotted a route almost due north, hoping to reach Montevideo, nearly 1,200 miles away.

The men sailed onward, constantly chilled and often wet, battling to keep the sails properly oriented in the face of strong and variable winds. During the first week, little light came from the new moon, which was often hidden by passing clouds. In those dark hours, a lantern and candles provided enough illumination to read the compass so that they could maintain their course. When the skies allowed, Brooks used celestial navigation to track their progress.

They quickly fell into a cooking routine. In fine weather, they lit a wood fire in the large iron pot brought from the *Isabella* and placed the other, smaller pot within, loaded with two days' worth of food. That way, if rough weather intervened, they might have enough cooked provisions to see it through. The usual fare was as follows: When the ocean was calm, the breakfast, prepared by the men on watch, consisted of tea or heated chocolate, fried salt pork, and a biscuit. When conditions were rough, however, breakfast was pared down to half a pint of wine and a biscuit. They always skipped lunch, and dinner consisted of soup made from salt beef, the geese that had been shot on Eagle Island, and the cabbages the men had collected at the abandoned settlement. To that was added a pint of wine. For a nightcap, they treated themselves to a splash of rum diluted in a cupful of water. This routine was altered after one of the men, fumbling about in the dark, spilled some of the water, reducing the store of this precious commodity. After that, tea was eliminated from the menu. Despite the lack of exercise, other than moving about on the cramped boat, and the monotony of the food, the men maintained good appetites and remained healthy throughout the voyage.

The sleeping quarters on board were extremely uncomfortable. Squeezing in and out of them required great contortions of the body and a considerable amount of time. Once below, the men were relegated to a thin mattress that was bumpily layered over their trunks and supplies. So confined was the space that, when lying on their backs, they could not bend their arms or legs, and their faces were right up against the decking overhead. Although going below got them out of the wind, they could not escape the cold. And when the waves were high, or it was raining, water seeped through the spaces between the decking planks, leaving the men "generally well soaked."

The voyage nearly ended one evening. The three men above were chatting, including Davis, who was steering the boat. The conversation was so engrossing that they failed to pay close attention to what lay ahead. Luckily, at one point, Ford casually glanced over the bow, and, without uttering a word, he violently twisted the helm from Davis's grasp and brought the boat about. In doing so, they avoided the lash of a whale's tail, as it "darted like lightning across our bow." This was the crew's closest call with the mighty leviathans, but throughout their trip, the men could hear and see whales nearby.

Finally, on March 23, the tired, weather-beaten crew sighted Cabo Lobos,* and, two days later, they sailed into the Río de la Plata, a large, muddy estuary formed by the confluence of the Paraná and Uruguay Rivers. They steered directly for Montevideo on the northern shore. So excited were they to have nearly attained their goal, that one night, while anchored, they celebrated with a variation on fondue—fried salt pork dipped in the last of the chocolate. As they waited for the pork to cook, a wave caused the boat to lurch, which sent the man holding the pot of molten chocolate careening into Lundin and spilling the scalding liquid on his feet. Not only had they lost their chance to savor the chocolate, but now the lieutenant's feet were seriously burned, leaving him in great pain. Soothing spermaceti oil† was quickly applied, which seemed to reduce the inflammation a bit.

His feet still swollen and throbbing, Lundin fell into an unsettled sleep. Then, his situation worsened. A large wave rolled entirely over the bow, flooding the deck. The three men sleeping below, including Lundin, were rudely awakened, gasping for air and fearing the worst, as the water surged down through the hatchway and enveloped them in a bone-chilling embrace.

---

*   Present-day Cabo Corrientes.

†   This comes from the head or case of a sperm whale.

Detail of a map of South America by Conrad Malte-Brun, 1812,
showing the Río de la Plata and Buenos Aires. Cabo Lobos,
which can be seen below the mouth of the river, was the early
nineteenth-century name for modern-day Cabo Corrientes.

The next morning, after that miserable night, the men sailed the longboat across the mouth of the estuary, with Montevideo now in sight. But
adverse winds prevented a landing there. Eager to get ashore, Brooks
steered the boat to a nearby river and onto one of its banks. Filled with
pride at having made it this far, and to proclaim their arrival, the men
hoisted the British colors on the mainmast of the *Faith and Hope*. Thus
began the next stage of their fraught journey.

Getting Help

=

SHORTLY AFTER THE SIX WEARY TRAVELERS LANDED NEAR MONTEVIDEO, A FEW men on horseback rode by, barely glanced at the new arrivals, and soon disappeared from view. Brooks and one companion left the boat and headed inland to get help, having little idea of whom they would find, or whether they would have a peaceful encounter. Peaceful it wasn't. They had arrived at a turbulent time, when the whole area was in rebellion. Various Spanish factions were fighting for control in a war that was part of a much larger tableau of South and Central American independence movements rupturing Spain's colonial empire and leaving behind a chain of newly independent countries. The men's greatest fear was that they would get caught in the crossfire and possibly be imprisoned.

It wasn't long before the exploratory party returned, but they were not alone. In their wake rode a few dozen "ragged and fierce-looking people," some armed with fusils.* They pointed menacingly to the British flag, whereupon Brooks "very dejectedly" told the men on the boat to haul it down. Lundin used his rudimentary Spanish to ask, "Aren't the British and the Spaniards friends?" This elicited a sharp "no" from the group, one of whom told Lundin that the local soldiers had been alerted and would arrive soon. With that, most of the Spaniards surrounded the six men, while the rest jumped onto the boat and helped themselves to clothes that caught their fancy. They even grabbed the cap off Wooley's head.

"Our appearance was indeed little calculated to command respect,"

---

* English guns with overall lengths between 52 and 55 inches.

*José Casimiro
Rondeau Pereyra,
painted by Gaetano
Gallino, circa 1820.*

Lundin later wrote. "We were dirty, ragged, and miserable looking creatures." Nevertheless, he was so angered by this insolent treatment that,
in an attempt to awe the impudent thieves, he donned his old regimental
jacket, with its impressive red wool body, blue facings, and paired brass
buttons. This produced a seismic shift in the behavior of the Spaniards,
who suddenly became very solicitous of their honored "guests."

Over the next few days, the *Isabella*'s men were feted and passed up
the chain of command—first to General José Gervasio Artigas, and then
to General José Casimiro Rondeau Pereyra, both of whom were leaders
of the rebel army of the Banda Oriental, which later became Uruguay. At
that very moment, the rebels were laying siege to Spanish Royalist forces
in Montevideo.

Rondeau gave the six men a choice. They could either be sent into
Montevideo under a flag of truce, or they could go to Buenos Aires,
where there was a British warship on station. Brooks wanted to go to
Montevideo, from which he thought they could get passage on a ship to

Rio de Janeiro, but after much discussion and debate, the party finally agreed to go to Buenos Aires, about 120 miles away by water.

Rondeau gave the men passports and horses, and, a few hours later, they were back at their boat, which was being guarded by soldiers sent by General Artigas. Early on March 29, the men shoved off, with a fine wind at their back, but, at three o'clock the next morning, about a mile from shore, they ran aground. According to Lundin, "had we not almost instantly got off, our boat must have soon gone to pieces."

In the early afternoon, the men saw two vessels tucked into a creek along the shore and went to investigate, in hopes of learning how far they were from Buenos Aires. The vessels turned out to be American merchant ships, which were hiding out for fear of being made prizes by the British. The Americans told Lundin and his companions that their destination was still 30 miles off. Before reaching Buenos Aires, they would pass a fort a few miles upriver, where permission to proceed would have to be granted by the local commandant.

Following the Americans' advice, the longboat landed beneath the fort and Brooks went to find the commandant, while Lundin and the others remained at the home of the local customs officer, who appeared quite suspicious of the visitors. With an American from the local village acting as interpreter, Lundin told the officer their story, and his demeanor quickly changed. The officer welcomed Lundin and the others "very cordially, and appeared greatly interested in the fate of the people left behind, regretting that we should be a moment detained from hastening to their relief." Brooks soon returned with the commandant's blessing. The following day at around four in the afternoon, when the wind shifted in their favor, the men got back onto their boat and set sail. An hour after sunset on March 31, they arrived at Buenos Aires.

The sudden appearance of such a bedraggled group of mariners in the capital city elicited a considerable amount of local interest, but the story was almost entirely ignored in the press. Indeed, the only article about the tremendous voyage appeared in the British *Edinburgh Annual Register*, and it was merely an extract of a letter sent from Buenos Aires by a correspondent. "Nothing but the protection of the Almighty," the article proclaimed, "could have preserved them from the inclemency of the weather, considering the great fatigue they must have endured, both in mind and body, and so long a navigation in seas almost proverbial for storms."

HOBBLING, WITH HIS FEET still bandaged, Richard Lundin boarded the HMS *Nereus* on the evening of March 31, accompanied by Richard Brooks. They were ushered into Captain Peter Heywood's cabin, whereupon Lundin handed Heywood the letter from Robert Durie:

FALKLAND ISLANDS, FEB. 22, 1813

Sir, I beg leave to acquaint you that a merchant ship, the *Isabella*, bound to Europe from Port Jackson, Higton master, whence she sailed fourth December last, struck upon a rock the eighth instant. There were fifty-four souls on board, including fourteen marines placed under my command by his Excellency, Governor Macquarie. The ship's boat, which was immediately fitted out, has this day sailed to endeavor to find out a settlement, as the island we were cast upon, one of the most Eastern, is uninhabited; and, should she fail in the attempt, will proceed to Montevideo. Lieutenant Lundin, of the 73d regiment, accompanies a

Captain Peter Heywood, by John Simpson, 1822.

Mr. Brooks in the boat, . . . they will be able to give every further information respecting our present state.

To add to my personal afflictions, I have a wife and child, and Mrs. Durie expects to be confined immediately. Confident that you will have the goodness to order a vessel for our preservation, I have the honor to remain, &c., yours,

Robert Durie, Capt.

Heywood listened intently to Lundin and Brooks as they related the harrowing tale of the wreck of the *Isabella* and their subsequent courageous journey in the longboat. He was greatly affected by their story. In fact, because of Heywood's own story, they couldn't have found a better man to respond with compassion and alacrity to the plight of the *Isabella*'s passengers.

Heywood, at age fifteen, had sailed as a midshipman on the HMS *Bounty* on a mission to Tahiti to gather breadfruit trees and transport

Lieutenant William Bligh and eighteen of his loyal men being set adrift from the Bounty *on April 28, 1789, as depicted in a color engraving by Robert Dodd, circa 1790.*

them to the British possessions in the West Indies to use as food for slaves. The ship, commanded by Lieutenant William Bligh, became infamous when the first mate, Fletcher Christian, led a mutiny on April 28, 1789, setting Bligh and eighteen men who remained loyal to him adrift in a 23-foot launch, which Bligh masterfully navigated more than 3,600 miles to safety at Timor, in the Dutch East Indies. From there, he and the other survivors were transported back to England. Heywood was not aboard that launch, and he later claimed that he did not participate in the mutiny and intended to join Bligh, but he was prevented from doing so.

Although there is still some question as to whether Heywood was in on the mutiny, or just a victim of circumstances, his trajectory after the mutiny is clear. He and some of the others who remained on the *Bounty* parted ways, staying in Tahiti, while the *Bounty* continued on to Pitcairn Island. In 1791, the HMS *Pandora*, sent from England to retrieve the mutineers for trial, arrived in Tahiti and placed thirteen men in chains, Heywood among them, since Bligh had implicated him as one of Christian's supporters. On the voyage back to England, the *Pandora* wrecked on the Great Barrier Reef, killing thirty-five men, including four of the prisoners, but not Heywood. The survivors used the *Pandora*'s boats first to get to a nearby uninhabited cay, and then they embarked on an impressive open-water voyage that ultimately took them to Batavia, the capital of the Dutch East Indies, from which they returned to England.

Despite his claim of innocence, Heywood was court-martialed in September 1792 and sentenced to be hanged. However, the court recommended mercy, and King George III subsequently granted him a pardon. After this ordeal, Heywood resumed his naval career, his conviction apparently having little effect on his rise through the ranks. When Lundin and Brooks appeared before him, Heywood was in the midst of a three-year stint protecting British merchant ships trading in South America.

After hearing their saga in his cabin on the *Nereus*, Heywood wanted to launch a rescue mission immediately and relieve the *Isabella*'s passengers from further suffering, but he wasn't sure how to do so. There were no readily available merchant vessels to be chartered, and he couldn't send the *Nereus*, owing to its important role protecting British trade, and the need to protect the large amount of specie it had on board, which would be placed in jeopardy on such a dangerous voyage. But there was one option, although not a particularly encouraging one.

Under Heywood's command was the HMS *Nancy*, an 80-foot, 200-ton brig, with a beam of 25 feet and eight 6-pound cannons on the main deck. A former merchant vessel, it had been drafted into naval employ in 1808. Years of service in South America had taken a toll on the brig's seaworthiness, no single event more destructive than a violent storm that pummeled the *Nancy* in early February 1813, essentially leveling its masts and rigging and breaking its bowsprit. After the *Nancy* limped into Buenos Aires a few days later, Heywood ordered a review of the damage. The bottom line—that it would cost far more to fix the brig than it was worth—convinced Heywood to recommend that the *Nancy* be sold, a move that was ultimately endorsed by the Admiralty. In the meantime, however, Heywood still planned to use the *Nancy* for some minor local trips. To that end, he ordered some repairs to the brig, which took about a month to complete.

Heywood ordered the *Nancy*'s commander, Lieutenant William Peter D'Aranda, to report to his cabin on the *Nereus*. D'Aranda was briefed on the outlines of the situation and ordered to proceed to the Falklands to rescue the castaways and bring them and all of their belongings back to Buenos Aires without delay.

This urgent mission resuscitated the brig's naval career and postponed its sale indefinitely. Lundin volunteered to go along, since he was familiar with the location of the wreck and could help guide the *Nancy* to the site. There was likely yet another reason for Lundin's keen interest in returning to the Falklands. Aboard the *Isabella*, he had struck up a very close relationship with Mary Ann Spencer, one of the prostitutes and ex-convicts. Thus, his eagerness to join the expedition was perhaps as much personal as it was professional.

Still not convinced that the *Nancy* was up to the task, Heywood ordered additional repairs. This included mending the bulwarks, caulking the decks and hull, preparing new rigging and sails, and replacing missing, broken, and rotted planks. All of this work was done, D'Aranda wrote in his log, with the "utmost dispatch." The *Nancy* was also loaded with supplies—not only to sustain the forty-six men who manned the vessel, plus passenger Lundin, but also all of the *Isabella*'s survivors. Among the items boarded were roughly 11,000 pounds of hardtack, 1,000 pounds of flour and rice, 6,500 pounds of salt beef, 600 gallons of rum, and 650 pounds of coffee.

While the brig was being repaired and loaded, Lundin stayed in the same inn where Heywood resided. The landlady was so moved by Lundin's travails that she would not allow him to pay for his room. Finally able to rest a bit, Lundin had his filthy bandages replaced with new ones, lessening his pain and furthering his recuperation.

Lundin's five companions all found lodging and pursued their own paths. Richard Brooks and George Davis made their way back to England, while Jose Antonio and Ford found employment in Buenos Aires, reportedly for high wages. Joseph Wooley signed on to the *Nereus*, "where in three days his appearance changed wonderfully for the better." One day, after Wooley had joined the *Nereus*, Lundin played a joke on him. He asked Wooley if he was ready to head back to the Falklands on the *Nancy*. Upon hearing this, Wooley "put on a very piteous face, and earnestly entreated" Lundin not to make him go. He truly enjoyed being on the *Nereus*, and never wanted to go back to the Falklands. Lundin was quiet for a moment, to keep Wooley in a state of anguished suspense, but then told him he was kidding. Relieved, Wooley "became all smiles and good humor."

ON APRIL 16, THE *Nancy* was ready to sail. Heywood gave Captain D'Aranda a letter to deliver to Durie:

> As misfortune was one of my earliest acquaintances, and having more than once borne myself the painful privations incident to shipwreck, I can, therefore, by experience and fellow-feeling, judge of and sincerely commiserate the distressing situation to which you have been reduced by the loss of the *Isabella* on the Falkland Islands.
>
> Your misfortune is the more deplorable, from the peculiar circumstances of a family nature, deprived as your lady perhaps is of every comfort and convenience her situation so much requires.
>
> I was extremely sorry I had it not in my power to send any vessel immediately to your relief, on the 31st ult., when Lieutenant Lundin providentially arrived in the boat, and delivered to me your letter addressed, on the king's service, to Admiral De Courcy, acquainting him with your disaster, and requesting a vessel might be sent for your preservation. The only vessel of his Majesty's at the moment, or now, under my orders, was the

Nancy, a small armed brig, and she had recently arrived here
with the loss of masts and bowsprit. . . .

Every possible exertion has, however, been used to put the
Nancy in a fit condition to proceed; and as Lieutenant Lundin
and Mr. Brooks tell me, that the greater part of the provisions,
and other necessaries, was saved from the wreck, I shall cher-
ish the hope that Lieut. D'Aranda, who commands the *Nancy*,
will arrive at the island you exist on, in sufficient time still, (if it
please God,) to deliver you and all your fellow-sufferers, more
particularly before the pain of hunger, and the severities of the
approaching winter, are felt by your little babes and their afflicted
mother.

I wish the vessel and her accommodations were more suit-
able, but the Lieutenant will, I am sure, do everything in his
power for their comfort, that you desire and the brig can afford. I
can only further express my regret that the nature of my orders,
and the particular service on which I am employed in this river,
put it entirely out of my power, under present existing circumstances, to hasten myself to your relief in the *Nereus*, as I could
have wished.

I beg you to be assured, Sir, that I shall pray for your happy
deliverance, a favorable passage, and a safe arrival here. I remain,
in the meantime, with truth, your sincere and faithful servant.

Peter Heywood

About two weeks before the *Nancy* left Buenos Aires, the situation in the
Falklands had changed dramatically for both the survivors of the *Isabella*
and the American sealers, and it would greatly affect the trajectory of the
rescue mission.

Discovery

====

THE CREW OF THE *YOUNG NANINA*, AMONG THEM CHARLES BARNARD AND
Captains Fanning and Hunter, as well as eight other men, slowly made
their way along the eastern side of English Maloon in late March 1813,
stopping wherever the prospects for sealing looked promising. Then, on
March 30, while anchored at the mouth of Fox Bay, they beheld a puz-
zling sight. About 25 miles away, on the other side of Falkland Sound,
a large column of smoke was rising into the sky from one of the Anacan
Islands, which comprised Eagle, George, and Barren Islands.

Charles initially assumed that the fire might have been set by the
Spanish, specifically the *Guardas Costas*, or the Spanish coast guard,
who were known to travel occasionally from Buenos Aires to run off foreign vessels in order to maintain Spain's sovereignty over the Falklands.
With the same goal in mind, the Spanish sometimes set fire to the tussac
grass to make areas less welcoming for seals, which used the clumps of
vegetation as shelter for breeding and hauling out. No seals meant no vis-
its from foreign sealers. But the one problem with this theory was that the
Anacans were not a usual haunt of sealers, as they were rather desolate
and surrounded by rocky reefs that threatened to sink large vessels that
neared the islands.

Smoke was still visible during the following days, leading Charles to
reevaluate his assumption. Now he thought it more likely that the fires
were set by unfortunate mariners who had been wrecked and were possibly signaling for help. With the consent of his men, Barnard led his crew
to the Anacans to investigate.

Upon reaching Eagle Island, the most northerly of the Anacans, the Americans slowly made their way down its eastern side, sealing along the way. Meanwhile, they were becoming increasingly curious about the continuing plumes of smoke, to which was soon added the sound of small arms firing. On April 3, in the early afternoon, Charles raised his spyglass and saw what appeared to be a flagpole, or the topgallant mast of a ship, toward the opposite side of the island. This convinced him that his new theory was correct, a view that was given further support when Captain Fanning returned from a walk along the beach carrying a new sealskin moccasin, and a report of a recently killed, and partially skinned, seal.

Around six, Tenant Havens, manning the helm of the *Young Nanina*, called out that he saw a man walking down a hill from the direction of the flagstaff toward the shallop. The rest of the crew got up from their dinner and rushed to the main deck, where they witnessed a most unusual sight. Within a few moments, about ten people were on the beach, waving wildly, and more were hurrying down the hill to join them. "Among the latter party, to our great surprise," observed Charles, "we noticed a female, whose exertions and fleetness were not surpassed by many of her male companions." It had been 209 days since the Americans had arrived in the Falklands, and these were the first other people they had seen.

To reveal their identity, the Americans aboard the *Young Nanina* hoisted the Stars and Stripes, prompting shouts of joy from the crowd, who embraced one another "with as much ardor as though their deliverance were already effected." Charles yelled across the water, inquiring as to what ship or nation they belonged. "The *Isabella* of London, wrecked on her passage from Port Jackson!" came the reply. The fact that two of the men on shore wore British military uniforms gave Charles confidence that they were telling the truth, and he immediately sent the boat ashore to bring some of the people back to the shallop. So many tried to clamber aboard that, after eight succeeded, the boat's crew was forced to shove off for fear of sinking. As the boat pulled away, others followed, wading far into the water in the hope of getting on.

As soon as the British climbed onto the deck of the *Young Nanina*, Charles asked them about the people he saw gathered farther down along the shore. Hearing that the captain of the *Isabella* was among them, Charles sent the boat to bring him aboard as well. George Higton soon arrived, accompanied by Durie and Holt, and the three of them proceeded to share their tale of woe, beginning with the departure from

Port Jackson and ending with their increasingly desperate situation these past few months, when they were living, as Holt said, "between hope and despair."

Charles was shocked when he learned about the longboat *Faith and Hope*'s desperate gambit. Given the treacherous waters that girdle the Falkland Islands—especially the many tide rips*—he didn't think that a boat that size, and helmed by men unfamiliar with local conditions, could have survived its search for a settlement. And if the boat had some-how managed to leave the Falklands, Charles didn't hold out any hope that it would reach Montevideo.

Higton told the Americans that he was working on a backup plan in the event that the longboat never returned. He proposed to build a boat out of the *Isabella*'s remains, in which he hoped to transport everyone to the mainland of South America. Charles marveled at the captain's ambi-tion but thought it to be "the most visionary scheme which had ever been attempted," since Higton admitted that the *Isabella*'s carpenter was not very skilled, and key items needed for such a task—such as a forge, tar, pitch, and good timber or planking—were not available. Nevertheless, persisting in his chimerical quest, Higton asked whether the Americans could provide these items so he could build the boat. Wanting to help, Charles said he was willing to lend Higton the services of his carpenter, in return for another man to take his place on the sealing crew. Charles could also supply a forge, tar, and pitch. But, lacking timber or plank-ing, Charles said that, in the end, he couldn't provide all the assistance Higton wanted.

The Americans also heard about another rescue effort. A few days before the shallop arrived, the British had manned the *Isabella*'s jolly boat and sent it off to look for settlements in the area. The boat had four passengers: William Mattinson, the head of the expedition, plus a marine and two cabin boys. The boat had yet to return, and fears were mounting that it never would.

With the hour getting late, Durie and Holt expressed their desire to be landed so they could tell their families about the "change in their prospects, [thereby] elevating them from the abyss to the summit of

---

*   A tide rip is an area of turbulent water created when two opposing currents meet, or when a rapid current flows over rocks or an uneven terrain submerged just below the surface.

hope." They also wanted to share the wonderful news with the rest of the *Isabella*'s crew and passengers. To that end, the boat was readied to shuttle all of the British back to the shore. As they were leaving, Durie and Holt invited the captains to visit Newtown Providence and stay the night. Captain Hunter and Charles said they would be honored, and after everyone had been returned to the beach, the shallop proceeded to tack along the shore, arriving at Shallop's Cove, the anchorage located across the island from the encampment, at around 9 p.m.

Before Charles and Hunter left the shallop, the captains called a meeting of everyone on board the *Young Nanina*. It was clear, they said, that the *Isabella* castaways knew nothing about the war. Since there was no telling how they might react to that information, the captains thought it best not to inform them until they had a better idea of how this situation was going to play out. Once the crew agreed to keep the secret, Charles and Hunter went ashore.

The two captains were escorted across the island to the Duries' hut, where they were presented with the best dinner that could be cobbled together from the provisions on hand, including plenty to drink. When

The wreck of the Isabella *and Newtown Providence camp,*
engraved by T. R. Whitney, included in Charles H. Barnard's
narrative of his experience in the Falklands, 1829.

In some ways, this image does not accurately reflect the text in Barnard's book. For example, he states that the camp was roughly 600 feet from the edge of the water, and that the boat being built (and seen on the left side of the image) was even farther away from the shore. Also, the huts were not nearly as well designed and built as those depicted. They would have been more makeshift and rough, built primarily out of tussac-turf bricks.

Charles asked whether Higton would be joining them, Durie replied that it was not likely, since the captain had retreated to his hut and was enjoying the comforts of his lady friend.

The food and wine loosened Joanna-Ann's tongue, and she freely shared her observations on the other passengers, as well as the captain and the crew of the *Isabella*. She gave most of them good reports, but some, according to Charles, were discussed in a very unfavorable light. The character portraits "of Captain Higton and Samuel Ansell . . . were very dark; and Sir Henry Brown Hayes and William Mattinson's were notoriously black, for their departure from those principles that distinguish the honest man and the gentleman from the felon and the depraved." Joanna-Ann no doubt also shared another story that supported her opinions of Mattinson and Higton. Not long after the longboat left, Mattinson, Higton, and one other man had volunteered to take the *Isabella*'s jolly boat and sail across Falkland Sound in search of help. They carried with them provisions to last for eight to ten days, including plenty of wine. But instead of searching for help, they repaired to one of the neighboring islands, where they stayed for two days, eating and drinking to their hearts' content. When they returned to Eagle Island, they were still quite drunk. Joanna-Ann's unsavory assessments, however, could not dampen the spirits of the gathering. According to Joseph Holt, "We were so much delighted at the prospect of being released from our confinement to Eagle Island, that we were very merry, and kept it up jovially with our new friends, until past twelve o'clock that night."

Deal

=

EARLY THE NEXT MORNING, CHARLES AND HUNTER SURVEYED THE CAMP. Its arrangement was quite different from the way it had been in the early weeks after the wreck. Nearly all the real and makeshift tents had been replaced with sod-walled huts located on a bluff nearly 600 feet from the water. They were arranged roughly in a large square, with the storehouse in the center. The huts' ceilings were made of spars and other pieces of the wreck, covered by sails or sealskins. As they walked around, the Americans were repeatedly stopped by people who wanted to share "the history of their misfortunes" and express their excitement at the prospect of returning home.

Since first constructing his hut, Holt had made great improvements to it, the most impressive of which was the new "kitchen," comprising a small basin, a cutting surface, and some compartments for storage. Made of wood, it was sheathed in copper from the brig. He also made a handsome stone chimney, inside of which he had placed a stone shelf for keeping food warm.

Not far from the huts, and even farther from the beach, Charles and Hunter visited Higton's boatbuilding operation. The men had made barely any progress, and one of them admitted to Charles that even if they managed to finish the boat, they had no idea how they would transport it the great distance to the water. Thinking that they had convinced Higton that his goal was unattainable, Charles and Hunter accepted an invitation to visit his hut. Upon entering, Charles was scandalized to see Mary Bindell, Higton's "*chère amie*," lying on a bed, "perfectly at her ease."

Everything went downhill from there. Higton did not broach the subject of his crew or the passengers, and when Charles inquired about Higton's intentions with respect to them, Higton's monosyllabic answers, yes or no, were "distant and reserved." It seemed apparent to Charles that Mrs. Durie's estimation of Higton's character was squarely on the mark. "After wasting a few minutes in his *too agreeable society*," Charles later recalled that Higton "graciously told me that he suspected breakfast was waiting for me at Capt. Durie's. After so delicate an intimation to weigh anchor, I retired with all the respect due to *so important* a personage, and [Hunter and I] went to Capt. Durie's."

At breakfast, Charles told the Duries and the Holts of their chilly reception from Higton, noting "that as far as it respected the future fate of his passengers and crew, he appeared to be as unconcerned as if they were all at home, enjoying the comforts of life in the bosom of their families." Now feeling unsure how best to help the *Isabella*'s crew and passengers, Charles played for time. He informed his hosts that he and his crew intended to leave for a few days of sealing, and when they returned, he would endeavor to ascertain whether Higton felt disposed to make arrangements to return to Europe, "assuring them, at the same time, that it would afford me pleasure to exert all my abilities to forward their departure from these desolate shores." Upon their return, if Higton were to persist in his fanciful attempt to build a boat to take everyone to the Continent, Charles would, against his better judgment, lend Higton the services of the *Nanina*'s carpenter while the Americans continued sealing. Charles also offered to give Higton a few tools from the shallop, and then gather additional tools and supplies from the *Nanina* and bring them back to Eagle Island.

As Charles and Hunter rose to head back to the shallop, Joanna-Ann expressed great regret that they were leaving, and she appeared quite stricken. Before the two captains had gotten very far, General Holt and Captain Durie came rushing up. Durie told them that as soon as they had departed, Joanna-Ann started sobbing, and she implored him to ask the captains to take their entire family with them, adding that she would prefer to face any dangers and hardships on board the *Young Nanina* than to remain on Eagle Island. Furthermore, she feared that the rude treatment the captains had received from Higton might induce them to not come back at all, and instead return to the *Nanina*, forswearing their earlier offers of assistance.

Alarmed by this turn of events, Charles and Hunter quickly doubled back, only to find Joanna-Ann still in tears. So moved was Charles by her distress that he consented to her request, promising to welcome them on board the shallop, and then, after some more sealing, take them to the *Nanina*. When the Americans headed home, the Duries would go along. Upon reaching the United States, they would book passage to some British port.

Unsurprisingly, this somewhat rash and limited offer elicited a similar request from Holt for his family and servants. Charles now had a real problem. He couldn't also take on the Holts, and even if he could, what about the rest of the *Isabella*'s passengers and crew?

Charles and Hunter briefly excused themselves to consider the situation in private, where they decided that if Higton simply communicated his plans in a candid manner right now, they had no doubt that they could devise a plan of action for getting everyone transported to a South American port, from which they could get a ship to England.

Holt was in favor of this, but he told the Americans that he had already "conversed with Capt. Higton on the subject, but his only answer was, we must not appear too anxious to get off, for in that case the Americans might take advantage of us." Charles, angered by Higton's paranoia, told Holt that the captain "had formed a wrong opinion of us; that our motive in coming to them was not to take advantage of their distress, but to relieve it to the full extent of our power." In fact, both Charles and Hunter said that they felt it was their responsibility as mariners, and fellow human beings, to help the British out of their predicament. With winter fast approaching, their situation would only become more dire.

To convince them of this, Charles and Hunter offered a deal. In return for accepting everyone from the *Isabella* on board the *Nanina*, and taking them to a port in South America—or even the United States—from which they could sail to a British port, the Americans wanted to be given all that remained of the *Isabella* and the *Isabella*'s cargo, individual property excepted. This was eminently fair, Charles argued; by saving the castaways, the Americans were cutting short their sealing expedition and losing an opportunity for profit. And that profit might have been substantial indeed. The Americans had already gathered roughly 1,800 fur seal skins, 3,500 hair seal skins, 120 salted hog skins, and 8 tons of elephant seal oil, along with another 50 barrels of elephant seal blubber, which would make even more oil. Another condition was that the castaways help load the *Nanina* with the *Isabella*'s cargo. Finally, the master of the *Nanina* would be in charge. The castaways had to do what they were instructed and accept the master's decisions regarding the allowance of provisions until the brig reached a port in South or North America.

While the Americans were presenting the terms, Higton was standing off to the side, a bit out of earshot, since he had had a fight with Durie and wanted to keep his distance. When Holt went over to inform Higton of the deal that had been offered, he "appeared surprised at the liberality" of the Americans' demands. Having finally been convinced of the impracticability of building a rescue boat, Higton agreed to the terms. In addition, Durie threw in a sweetener, which was verbalized but not put in writing. He told the Americans that once he made it back to London, he "would use his influence with the British government to procure additional compensation" for the captains, crew, and owners of the *Nanina*.

Once the agreement was written down, it was read aloud to the *Isabella*'s passengers and crew, and they all verbally assented. To make the agreement binding, Charles wanted everyone to sign it, but before doing so, he felt he had to tell them about the war. He worried that, if he didn't let them know, they might find out anyway if one of the *Nanina*'s crew let the secret slip. In that event, the British would know that the Americans had kept critical information from them, and they could feel justified in overpowering the Americans at sea, which they clearly could do, given their superior numbers.

Pulling aside Durie, Higton, and Holt, Charles delivered the news. He then asked that Durie inform the marines, Higton the sailors, and Holt the passengers. Not only did the three men do so, but they also asked their respective audiences to continue the verbal agreement they had already made, and act as though there were no state of war between the two governments. The castaways seemed nonplussed by the startling revelation, and it appeared that all of them were still in favor of signing the agreement—except for Henry Hayes, who, in light of the new circumstances, advocated forcing the Americans to take the castaways to South America or England.

At this juncture, Holt sought to avoid a general debate, saying, "Now you all have heard the generous offer. . . . Let all those who are inclined to accept it follow me, and step over on this side, and those who wish to remain on the island let them stand by Sir Henry Hayes." Everyone, except for Hayes, his associate Breakwell, Higton, and Miss

Photo of Jack's Harbor, now known as Phillip's Bay.

Bindell, lined up next to Holt. Higton quickly reconsidered, saying that, despite the state of war, he would go with the consensus. Both he and Bindell then switched sides. Charles threatened to leave Hayes and Breakwell on the island if they did not sign, but they refused to budge. Rather than try to overcome their intransigence, Charles decided to drop the issue for the moment. He would deal with it later.

With the agreement signed by all but Hayes and Breakwell, the cast-aways' weekly rations were increased from two-and-a-half pounds to four pounds of bread, and from one to three pounds of pork and beef. The amount of food on the *Nanina* and *Young Nanina*, plus that which had been saved from the *Isabella*, justified such largesse. In addition, each day one goose was to be split among three people.

Charles then prepared to take the shallop back to the *Nanina* and ready it for the voyage. Meanwhile, Fanning, Hunter, and four seamen from the *Nanina* were to remain on Eagle Island, with the *Young Nanina*'s boat, to help gather together the *Isabella*'s cargo and oversee preparations for departure.

With six men left behind, Barnard was shorthanded, so he asked to take along six sailors and five marines from the *Isabella* to help rerig the

Nanina. Others joined the party, including the Duries, Mrs. Durie's attendant, and a drummer and his wife. When adding Charles and the four Americans who remained on board the *Young Nanina*, the shallop would be transporting a total of twenty-one adults and two children. To make room for all his guests, Charles emptied the *Young Nanina*'s hold of its sealskins and other articles, all of which were placed on Eagle Island, to be picked up later. The shallop's cabin was also prepared to make the Duries as comfortable as possible.

It took a number of days to unload the shallop and then bring aboard the personal effects that the British wanted to take along. Finally, with everyone crowded aboard the *Young Nanina* in the early afternoon of April 12, the journey began. As they sailed out of Shallop's Cove, the winds soon became too strong to proceed, so they anchored in Eagle Island's Jack's Harbor* for the night. The next morning, when the winds moderated, the shallop began its 110-mile voyage back to Barnard's Harbor, where the *Nanina* awaited them.

---

* Modern-day Phillip's Bay.

Rough Passage

===

WHILE THE *YOUNG NANINA* WAS BATTLING CHOPPY SEAS TO MAKE HEAD-way across Falkland Sound toward English Maloon, a mystery was solved. The men on board saw a small boat in the distance, bobbing among the waves and barely afloat. Upon closer inspection, it was found to be the *Isabella*'s jolly boat, flooded nearly to the gunwales. The *Young Nanina* gingerly pulled alongside and took the small boat aboard, along with its drenched and shivering passengers, saving them "from a watery grave."

William Mattinson, apparently dumbfounded by his deliverance, sat on the shallop's deck for a while, staring into the distance with a puzzled gaze, while the marine and two boys who had shared his trial went below to warm up. When a large wave crashed into the shallop, causing her to roll sharply and sending a wall of spray onto the main deck, Charles looked down upon the still-shocked Mattinson, asking him what he thought would have happened had the shallop not saved them. "God only knows," he replied, "but who are you, and what am I aboard of?" Charles told him, whereupon Mattinson said that he had been amazed when he first sighted the shallop—"it appeared as though she had risen from out of the sea" to save him. Regaining his senses a bit, Mattinson then went below to get out of the weather.

Charles recalled the dark portrait that Joanna-Ann had painted of Mattinson, and, as if to confirm her characterization, once belowdecks, he broke into a cask of wine that had been set aside for use by the ladies on board, and then began drinking. By the time the shallop anchored in

Fox Bay that night, about 25 miles across the sound from Eagle Island, Mattinson was rip-roaring drunk.

The gale continued the next day, forcing the *Young Nanina* to remain anchored. At one point, Mattinson, who by now had learned of the war and was continuing to swill wine, posed an ominous and threatening question to Charles. He asked "how American prize money would drink?"—implying that if he and the other castaways forcibly took control of the *Nanina* as a prize of war, they would receive a windfall in the form of prize money. Charles viewed this as a grave insult and provocation, having just saved this "ungrateful wretch," as he called him, from a "premature grave."

Realizing that Mattinson was likely to be nothing but trouble, Charles wanted to be rid of him. With Robert Durie's support, he told Mattinson that when the weather cleared, he should take the jolly boat back across the sound to the *Isabella* wreck. However, the marine and two boys who had accompanied Mattinson, and who would also have to go, pleaded with the Americans to allow them to stay. Charles relented, and all of them, including Mattinson, remained.

For many days, gales kept the *Young Nanina* from making much headway, a situation that was made more precarious still by the overcrowding on the shallop, which kept the boat low in the water and in danger of swamping. Twice Charles attempted to round the perilous Cape Meredith, but each time he was forced to turn back to Arch Island Harbor, which was on the opposite side of English Maloon from Barnard's Harbor, where the *Nanina* lay.

With the continued likelihood of nasty weather, and no good prospect of rounding the two treacherous capes that lay ahead on the journey (Meredith and Orford), Charles determined there was only one viable option: He had to take most of the men with him and hike across English Maloon to Barnard's Harbor. Then he and a few of his men would hike back to the *Young Nanina* to wait for better weather and bring it around.

Charles selected eighteen men, along with the two cabin boys, to accompany him across the island. This left behind on the shallop one of his crewmen (Henry Gilchrist), the Duries, Mrs. Durie's attendant, and the drummer and his wife. The traveling party packed a change of clothes and sufficient bread for two days' travel. They left early on the morning of April 23, arriving in the late afternoon at Barnard's Harbor, a distance of about 13 miles.

Only Valentine Barnard was there to greet them, since Barzillai Pease was off on another one of his lone sealing cruises. Charles briefed his father on all that had transpired and gained his consent for the actions taken—not that he had much choice at that point. The following day, the Americans, assisted by the British, began the task of preparing the *Nanina* for its upcoming voyage, replacing the spars and rigging and loading her with cargo.

In the afternoon, when Pease returned from his trip with plenty of sealskins and a good quantity of driftwood, he was shocked at what he saw. Having left behind only Valentine on board the brig, now he could see more people than the *Nanina*'s entire crew. Even more alarming was the sight of an armed British marine standing sentry on the main deck.

Nevertheless, Pease pulled alongside the brig and asked Charles what was going on. Wanting to have a little fun at his nemesis's expense, Charles made up some fanciful, but unrecorded, story about why the *Nanina* was crawling with British. Pease grew increasingly angry about this "farce," as he dubbed it in his diary, but, just before things got out of hand, Charles told him the truth. Once Pease calmed down, he, like Valentine, consented to the new arrangement.

On April 25, Charles, accompanied by three men—including one of his crewmen, Havens Tennant—hiked back to the *Young Nanina*, where they were received like conquering heroes. While they all wanted to head off right away, strong winds kept them in place for a little more than three days. Finally, in the early morning hours on April 29, with light breezes helping them along the way, the *Young Nanina* headed out to sea. By two that afternoon, they had rounded Cape Meredith and landed at Two Island Harbor,* near the entrance to Port Stephens Harbor.

Charles and a few of the men accompanied the two women to shore to stretch their legs and get some exercise. Ever the sealers, Charles and Tennant were ready for action. When the party came across a large male sea lion, they clubbed him about the head multiple times, and then Charles delivered the coup de grâce, plunging a lance deep into the animal's breast. Around another bend, Barnard and Tennant used their clubs to kill a few clapmatches, or female sea lions. Believing that the women were too delicate to witness the skinning process, Charles escorted them back

---

* Modern-day Ten Shilling Bay Islands.

to the shallop and then joined Tennant to cut off the pelts. Adding to
their haul, they killed a few geese and collected some driftwood.

The next day, the shallop ran the gauntlet around Cape Orford and
anchored in a sheltered bay with a sandy beach, called Canton Harbor,*
on Swan Island. Awaiting the party in this sheltered place was one of
the *Nanina*'s boats, along with a few guns, which had been placed there
by earlier arrangement so that Charles and Tennant could kill hogs and
geese. Given the numerous mouths to feed, this was critical. Charles
hoped to rely on fresh meat as much as possible while still in the Falklands, saving the salted provisions, which had a very long shelf life, for
the voyage. After killing a number of animals, the Americans reboarded
the *Young Nanina*. At midnight on May 3, the shallop sailed into Barnard's Harbor.

---

* Modern-day Gull Harbor.

Preparations

==

RIGHT AFTER THE *YOUNG NANINA* DEPARTED EAGLE ISLAND ON APRIL 12, Hunter and Fanning had taken charge of the situation. Their goal was to collect everything of value aboard the *Isabella* and transport it to Shallop's Cove. When the shallop returned, it would then deliver all of those items to the *Nanina*, which was to be anchored farther up the coast in Jack's Harbor. So the work proceeded in two directions simultaneously.

One group stripped the remains of the wreck and gathered in a single staging location what needed to be moved. The main cargo left on the *Isabella* consisted of sealskins, casks of whale oil, and pearl shells, all of which were taken off. The hull's copper sheathing and the ship's anchors, cables, and ironwork, including nails pulled from the wood, were also landed. It took several weeks to cannibalize the brig.

Then, getting everything across the island to Shallop's Cove posed a problem. The ground between the camp and the cove was uneven and dotted with rocks, bumps, hollows, and numerous patches of tussac grass and other low vegetation, making it virtually impossible to simply roll the casks and drag the other cargo and supplies to their final destination. The solution was to build a road, and that is what engaged the second group's attention.

Holt, experienced in roadbuilding, volunteered his services. He employed the ship's lethal boarding pikes to help keep the road's course running true, and then he split his crew into two teams of two. One team used adzes to cut down the rounded banks of sod and the clumps of vegetation, while the other used the pikes to cut up pieces of sod to fill the hollows. Both groups flung or rolled rocks out of the way. After about a week, the road was finished and immediately put to good use.

In addition to stripping the wreck, building the road, and hauling cargo and supplies to Shallop's Cove, there was plenty of sealing. Holt often walked along the perimeter of the island, and whenever he came upon seals, he informed Fanning and Hunter, who soon arrived with their crewmen to dispatch the animals. Many sea lions met their end this way, and they were duly skinned. The Americans also killed numerous elephant seals, once eight within half an hour. With no try-pots available, they left the blubber behind but cut out the tongues, which were deemed a great delicacy and shared throughout the camp. Holt claimed to have forty-five of the salted tongues hanging in his chimney at one time, where they dried out, creating what qualified as tongue-jerky. When Holt told his wife about the tremendous sizes of the elephant seals, she found it hard to believe him. To prove he was not lying, he took her on a few occasions to witness the Americans at work, and she was amazed. The Americans added to the gustatory options by shooting countless geese, and when their numbers thinned on Eagle Island, Fanning repeatedly took the shallop's boat to George Island to hunt, bringing back nearly two hundred birds.

During this time, Hunter and Fanning bunked with the Holts. By all accounts, they "lived merrily together." No doubt, their moods were improved by the liberal drinking of spirits, the distribution of which was controlled by the two captains. The only note of discord came from Higton and Hayes, who kept pretty much to themselves, and with whom neither of the American captains socialized.

BARNARD'S HARBOR WAS ALSO a hive of activity. Ever since May 3, when Charles and his expeditionary force from the *Young Nanina* arrived in Barnard's Harbor, the Americans, aided by the British, spent their time loading the *Nanina* and fitting her out so that she would be as "staunch as possible." That was critical, since the brig would have to withstand the rigors of sailing among the Falklands and beyond during the late fall and early winter months, when temperatures dropped and stormy weather prevailed. Oil casks, sealskins, and supplies were stowed on board, the rigging and spars were set, the sails were hung and unbended, and ballast was placed in the lower hold. Hunting expeditions were sent out to kill hogs and shoot geese, to feed everyone and add to the brig's larder.

As was the case on Eagle Island, the Americans and the British were getting along well, anticipating their ultimate departure from the Falklands in furtherance of the agreement they had reached. By May 16, both the shallop and the *Nanina* were ready to set sail.

At that very same moment, the *Nancy* had almost reached Eagle Island. Its arrival dramatically altered the Americans' and the Britons' plans.

D'Aranda's Surprise

═══

ON APRIL 17, 1813, THE *NANCY* LEFT BUENOS AIRES AND HEADED OUT INTO the Río de la Plata Estuary. Three days later, it exited these relatively protected waters for the open ocean, sailing south. The *Nancy*'s commander, Lieutenant William Peter D'Aranda, was only twenty-five, but he had already been in the Royal Navy for eleven years. Starting out as a midshipman, he had risen through the ranks, gaining proficiency on multiple vessels that saw action in major battles, on blockade duty, and in small-scale engagements. His postings had ranged from the North Sea to the Mediterranean to the coast of South America, and he was considered a knowledgeable and capable officer. Although his Spanish-sounding name puzzled some, he was British through and through, his ancestors having first settled in England in 1619. Now, as commander of the *Nancy*, he hoped to burnish his reputation by successfully rescuing his countrymen from the desolate shores of the Falkland Islands.

Even though Richard Lundin and Richard Brooks had benefited from fairly good weather on their perilous journey in the longboat, D'Aranda and the *Nancy* did not have such luck. According to Lundin, "the weather was extremely bad," and there were "tremendous seas" and nearly continuous gales and squalls. One wave swept the jolly boat off the main deck and into the sea, and powerful wind gusts split a number of sails. While the repairs in Buenos Aires had tightened the vessel, apparently that was not enough, for the pump was in nearly constant use. To make matters worse, the temperatures dropped, and, on May 6, they experienced their first snowstorm. Whereas it took the longboat fifteen days to sail from the Falklands to the mouth of the Río de la Plata, the *Nancy*'s voyage in the reverse direction took twenty-seven. "Sometimes the wind blew so strong," said Lundin, "that D'Aranda feared he must return; and every day was so tempestuous, that had we experienced the like in the [long]boat, we must inevitably have been lost."

With Britain at war with the United States, the men on the *Nancy* had to be prepared for any eventuality. In the Falklands, they might encounter an American warship or a privateer lurking about or replenishing their provisions. They might also find an American sealer or whaleship in the area. Should any of these things occur, they had to know how to respond. Thus, on May 9, each division of the ship's crew was summoned, one at a time, and read the Articles of War, the regulations governing their conduct if they confronted the enemy.

The *Nancy* sighted Cape Orford on May 14 and then rounded Cape Meredith the next day. With Lundin helping to guide the way, the *Nancy* approached Eagle Island on May 17. Just before noon, the remains of the wrecked *Isabella*, its flagstaff flying the Union Jack, the camp's huts, and people on shore came into view. Finding it impossible to get close to the beach because of the dangerous reefs, D'Aranda anchored the *Nancy* about a half-mile offshore in five fathoms of water, and then announced the brig's arrival with a fourteen-gun salute.

Nobody aboard the *Nancy* was more excited than Lundin. "Nothing could exceed my joy and exultation at having now accomplished our dangerous undertaking, and brought the long wished for relief to so many people; and I anticipated, with the greatest delight, the sincere happiness and heartfelt satisfaction I should experience at meeting them all again under such happy circumstances." Lundin, D'Aranda, and a few of his men then hopped into a boat and went ashore. Eighty-five days had elapsed since the men on the longboat had left Newtown Providence to seek help.

The *Nancy*'s arrival was indeed sweet for the castaways, but not for the Americans. When D'Aranda landed, Captain Andrew Hunter was the only American present, as Fanning and the four other Americans were on a hunting trip to a neighboring island. Joseph Holt introduced Hunter to D'Aranda and told him a little about the *Nanina* and the agreement that had been reached. With this intelligence, D'Aranda immediately pronounced Hunter a prisoner of war. The stoic American captain replied, "Very well. Many a good man has been a prisoner." D'Aranda also took the written agreement from Holt.

It was already apparent to Holt that it was D'Aranda's intention to make the *Nanina* a prize and declare all the Americans his prisoners. D'Aranda's opinion of the Americans only worsened when a few of the other castaways spoke ill of them, although what they said is unknown. And when Lundin saw his servant in a sling, and learned that he had been stabbed in the hand by one of the Americans during a fight, he and the others had yet another reason to view the Americans in an unfavorable light.

Holt was dismayed by this turn of events. "I regretted that anything unfortunate should happen to those [Americans] who had so well treated us, and who had acted in every respect like men and Christians. . . . [T]his is a hard case, considering their conduct to distressed British subjects." But, rather than stand up for the Americans, and argue with D'Aranda, Holt invited the commander and Lundin to his hut for tea with his wife. When she departed, the men toasted each other with wine.

D'Aranda knew he could not remain anchored in such an exposed spot—the very same place where the *Isabella* had wrecked—so the following day he sailed the *Nancy* to Jack's Harbor. Captain Higton had come on board, offering to assist in the relocation, but D'Aranda soon got the measure of the man and turned the helm over to his own second master, who had no knowledge of the area. D'Aranda later commented, "[H]ad I attempted the entry into Jack's Harbor under [Higton's] . . . guidance we must inevitably have perished."

When Fanning and his crew finally returned on May 19, they received the same treatment that Hunter did. Holt, still feeling poorly about the situation, volunteered to have the two American captains stay with him. The rest were held in a different part of Newtown Providence. During the day, the Americans were allowed to walk about, but only within the confines of the camp.

Having dealt with the Americans, D'Aranda now had to contend with a problem coming from his own ranks. Marine Sergeant Joshua Nightingale had been drunk on numerous occasions in recent weeks, causing him to neglect his duties. While D'Aranda had let most of those instances slide with only reprimands, he finally had had enough of this insubordination. On May 20, after Nightingale had another bout of inebriation, D'Aranda demoted him to private. The following day, Nightingale was punished with thirty-six lashes from a cat-o'-nine-tails. And no sooner was Nightingale carried away than British seaman Robert Williams was subjected to twelve lashes for neglecting his duties.

Ever since the *Nancy* arrived on Eagle Island and D'Aranda had learned about the American brig, he had been waiting eagerly for it to arrive. But first came the shallop.

AT 5 A.M. ON MAY 16, the *Young Nanina* left Barnard's Harbor with a north wind blowing under cloudy skies. Henry Defrees, in charge of the shallop, was joined by another American, Henry Gilchrist, and two British marines. His mission was to sail to Eagle Island to help Hunter and Fanning with any tasks they might have, and also to be ready to load the *Nanina* when it arrived. Over the next nine days, the men stopped off in various bays and harbors along the way to wait out stormy weather and kill seals and hogs.

On May 25, while the shallop was luffing around the northern reach of Eagle Island, a stunning sight greeted them: a brig anchored in Jack's Harbor. Defrees initially assumed it was the *Nanina*. As he got closer, however, he quickly realized his mistake. Not only did this vessel look different from the *Nanina*, but a boat full of British marines soon came alongside, ordering Defrees to make sail and anchor under the brig's stern.

As soon as the shallop dropped anchor, Defrees and Gilchrist were escorted on board the *Nancy*. D'Aranda met them on the main deck and unceremoniously informed them that the *Young Nanina* was a prize, and they were now prisoners of war. He then led them to his cabin for interrogation, where most of his questions focused on the *Nanina* and its whereabouts. He was quite pleased when he heard that the brig had planned to leave Barnard's Harbor not long after the shallop, and, as a result, was expected to arrive in a couple of days.

Understandably, Defrees was concerned about what had happened to Hunter, Fanning, and the other Americans, and he asked D'Aranda whether he could see them. "No!" D'Aranda barked, and then he sent Defrees and Gilchrist below, to be guarded by armed marines.

The next day, D'Aranda demanded that Defrees turn over his chart of the Falklands. When Defrees replied that it was on the shallop, D'Aranda called him a "damned rascal," and ordered him to retrieve it. Defrees did as he was told, but upon returning to the main deck of the *Nancy*, he found all of his clothes, bedding, and other personal items strewn about. Instead of letting Defrees gather his personal effects, D'Aranda sent him below once again, but not before letting loose a verbal barrage against the American, which Defrees felt was "unbecoming any officer, or gentleman."

While waiting for the *Nanina* to arrive, D'Aranda ordered his men to keep a sharp lookout for the brig. In the meantime, his crew hunted for geese, took some of the *Isabella*'s cargo on board, and made various repairs to the *Nancy* to fix the damage sustained on the difficult journey south. On June 4, work was briefly halted to honor King George III's seventy-fifth birthday. The sickly though still-popular monarch was granted a twenty-one-gun salute, no doubt greatly annoying the Americans, who viewed him as a tyrant.

D'Aranda continued to have disciplinary problems with his crew. On two more occasions, he resorted to corporal punishment: once for drunkenness (thirty-six lashes), and another time for neglect of duty (forty lashes).

As the days turned into weeks, and the *Nanina* failed to appear, D'Aranda grew concerned, wondering whether his prize would ever arrive. Given the stormy weather, fear rose that the brig had foundered. It hadn't, but something quite troubling had occurred.

Treachery

=

CHARLES'S PLAN TO SAIL THE *NANINA* OUT OF BARNARD'S HARBOR LATE IN the day on May 16 was stymied by calm winds blowing in the wrong direction, so he turned back. Conditions failed to improve over the next few days, and when Charles attempted to leave the harbor on May 18, he was forced to run in again. Infuriated by this delay, Mattinson told Barnard that he could easily sail the brig to the wreck himself, and the two of them hurled insults at one another. Suddenly, Charles became acutely aware of the tenuousness of his position. The Americans on board were greatly outnumbered by the British, and now Mattinson, plus the few British marines who backed him, appeared to have a "mutinous disposition." This made Charles quite uneasy, "for I felt assured that, if instigated and led by this ruffian, they should attempt to capture the brig, and deprive me of the command," and the Americans would be powerless to stop them.

To keep things from deteriorating further, and to avoid another challenge to his leadership on the trip, Charles called a meeting of everyone on board. He presented three options: Mattinson could be placed under guard or set on shore, or the brig could be stripped and laid up. Despite Mattinson's unruly behavior, nobody was in favor of marooning him, even temporarily. Nor were they willing to halt their journey to Eagle Island, as relieving those castaways was part of the agreement. Therefore, Mattinson was confined belowdecks and guarded by a sentry.

The calm weather persisted, but finally, when the *Nanina* beat out of the harbor on May 22, strong winds began to blow, followed by gales accompanied by snow and hail. This would be hopeless for heading southwest toward Cape Orford, as Charles wanted to do. Instead, he sailed around Loop Head, the northeast point of Swan Island, ultimately reaching Coffin Harbor, on New Island, the following day. With the gale continuing, three of the *Nanina*'s anchors were deployed, and nearly the entire length of the cables were run out, placing the brig perilously close to the rocks. Charles ordered the lower yards taken down and the topmasts secured. That evening, the temperature dropped even more, and snow and hail fell even harder, creating misery on board. Many of the crewmen were sick, and there was not enough warm clothing to go around, so many had to fight to keep from freezing to death, and few were available for any type of duty.

This atrocious weather continued virtually unabated until early June. However, during short stretches of calmer, though still unsettled, conditions, parties went ashore to hunt geese, hogs, rabbits, and goats—and they even found a few seals. On one of those brief excursions, Pease was severely injured by a rock carelessly thrown off a cliff by one of the British passengers. The injury forced him to remain in his berth a few days to recuperate. Another time ashore, Charles visited a small plot of potatoes that he had discovered when the *Nanina* first arrived at New Island the previous year. He dug up fifteen "fine ones" and presented them to Joanna-Ann Durie and Mary Ann Spencer in order to lift their spirits. From that point on, the potatoes were reserved for their use.

On June 3, with the storms still showing no signs of letting up, Charles came to a decision. Greatly concerned about the survival of the *Nanina*, and well aware that the brig provided the only means of ensuring everyone's safety so they could leave the Falklands, Charles thought it foolish to risk pressing on in such dangerous weather. To that end, he recommended to his father, Pease, and Durie that they move the *Nanina* to a more protected anchorage, strip its sails, and wait for better weather before proceeding to Eagle Island. They all agreed that was the prudent course, with Durie stating that he "would rather wait three months than encounter such a series of bad weather" as they had met with recently. When this plan was presented to all on board, the majority gave their assent.

As soon as it was safe, the *Nanina* was moved to a safer spot in nearby Hooker's Harbor and moored close to shore. Everything on board the brig was made secure, and everyone settled in for a stay that was anticipated to last a few weeks, when Charles believed the weather would be much improved.

Just over a week later, during another break in the wretched weather, Charles proposed taking a small hunting party to neighboring Beaver Island to replenish the provisions.* Although the island had no beaver, it did have plenty of game, and, most important, hogs. Charles also hoped to collect some driftwood.

The *Nanina*'s boat, which would transport the hunting party, was well designed for this task. It was modeled after the whaleboats of the day, which served whalemen so capably in pursuing the leviathans of the deep. Twenty-two feet long, clinker-built,† and made of cedar clapboards, the boat was a double-ender, with a V-shaped bow and a V-shaped stern, making it equally nimble at moving forward or aft. It was so light that two men could easily maneuver it on land, and that lightness, combined with a shallow draft, allowed the boat to move swiftly over the water. The boat could be rowed or sailed, using a removable mast. Quite stable, the boat could carry a heavy load while only minimally compromising its seaworthiness.

Just minutes after proposing the hunting trip, all of the British—including Mattinson, whose confinement had been relaxed—came forward and demanded that the *Nanina* proceed immediately to Eagle Island so as to fulfill the terms of the agreement. Charles, backed up by Valentine, told them the time was still not right, but he assured them they would leave soon. Placated for the moment, the British dropped their demand.

Believing that things were under control, Charles asked for volunteers to join his hunting party. Four stepped forward. Three were former members of the *Isabella*'s crew: Samuel Ansell, Joseph Albrook, and James Louder. The fourth was Jacob Green, a foremast hand from the *Nanina*, a former whaleman who was, in Barnard's estimation, "the most

---

*   Beaver Island was named after the Nantucket whaleship *Beaver*, the first (or one of the first) of the American whaleships to round Cape Horn and enter the Pacific Ocean. The *Beaver* stopped off at Beaver Island during its voyage. https://nha.org/research/nantucket-history/history-topics/the-falkland-gambit-part/, accessed December 4, 2022; and "History and Heritage," Falklands Conservation, https://www.newislandtrust.com/history/, accessed December 4, 2022.

†   A method of boatbuilding in which the edges of the hull planks overlap one another. This is also referred to as lapstrake planking.

experienced black man I ever knew." Taking only minimal supplies and food, the hunting party left for Beaver Island.

On June 13, Valentine and Pease took stock of the provisions and reduced the weekly allowance of biscuits from seven to six, in order to make the food last longer. This incensed the British, who feared that even after adding all the provisions that were saved from the *Isabella*, they would run out of food in a few months' time. They urged the Americans to press on for Eagle Island so they could all leave the Falklands as soon as possible.

Later that day, the British, with Mattinson leading the angry chorus, renewed their demand that the *Nanina* set sail without delay now that fair weather had returned. Valentine vehemently protested such a move, since his son and the other four men were still on Beaver Island. Once they came back, the older captain promised, they would leave immediately.

Mattinson and the marines wouldn't have it, and they stood fast. Growing more alarmed, Valentine appealed to Captain Durie to intervene. Surely, this officer who commanded the marines would take charge and halt what could accurately be characterized as a mutiny, or, if not that, at least a heartless proposal. Durie, however, far from being sympathetic to the American's plight, sided with Mattinson's group, stating that he "had no objection to the brig proceeding." Shocked by this answer, Valentine responded, "[Y]our marines are under your charge, and I demand of you assistance, and if you do not assist me, I conclude that you take charge and you shall be accountable for whatever happens."

Unfortunately for Valentine and the missing men, Durie lacked a spine of steel. He ignored Valentine's plea. Lundin, who knew Durie quite well, commented on his seeming inability to stand up for what was right, by saying that he was "without sufficient determination of character to quell . . . acts of misconduct" such as this one, and others that had occurred in the aftermath of the *Isabella* wreck.

Over the continued vociferous objections of Valentine and Pease, the marines worked through the day and much of the night, preparing the *Nanina* for departure. On June 14, they were ready to set sail. Pease, knowing that none of the British on board had any knowledge of the Falklands' treacherous waters, or how to navigate through them, offered to take the helm on one condition: They had to stop first at Beaver Island to pick up the hunting party. When the British agreed to this humanitarian detour, the *Nanina* left Hooker's Harbor.

But when the *Nanina* drew abreast of Beaver Island, the British reneged on their deal. Valentine told them that the hunting party was on the other side of the island, and if he was allowed to send only Pease and Tennant ashore, they could quickly hike there and retrieve the missing men. But the British refused to send the boat, or even briefly come to anchor. Their only concession was to fire a few gunshots and wait a short while to see whether anyone appeared. Valentine pleaded with the British to do more, making clear that to leave the crew on this island, "in the depth of a dreadfully severe winter, without food, raiment, or shelter," was the equivalent of a death sentence. Unmoved, the British sailed off.

As Beaver Island receded into the distance, there was nothing that Valentine or Pease could do but seethe.

Justification

==

At 9:13 a.m. on June 15, the *Nanina* was sighted heading toward Jack's Harbor on Eagle Island. Lieutenant D'Aranda's prize had finally arrived. He immediately ordered his men to prepare the *Young Nanina* and a boat to capture the brig. At around two in the afternoon, D'Aranda's mini-armada, with him in the shallop, closed in on their target. The boat was the first to arrive. Heavily armed marines scrambled over the *Nanina*'s side, as Pease observed, "with much hostility as though we were armed and manned for war." The boat's commanding officer demanded to know whether there were any British on board. Upon hearing that there were, he asked for their assistance, and then ordered the three Americans—Valentine, Pease, and Tennant—to be stripped of their arms.

The *Young Nanina* arrived soon thereafter. D'Aranda informed the Americans that the *Nanina* was a prize, and they were prisoners of war. The startled Americans then heard the backstory that led to this denouement, learning that the *Isabella*'s longboat had succeeded in its improbable quest, and the arrival of the *Nancy* was the result. Before they had much time to digest this disturbing turn of events, they were sent below. D'Aranda was eager to bring his prize in right away, but the tide was running against them, so the British were unable to tow the *Nanina* into the harbor. They anchored for the night, taking the brig in the following morning.

D'Aranda questioned Durie about all that had transpired after the *Nanina* left Barnard's Harbor. Durie defended the British takeover of the brig, saying that they did so because Charles had violated the agreement they had reached when he laid up the brig during the bad weather, instead of pushing on to get back to the wreck. Even though Durie had initially been supportive of that plan, he chose not to share that fact with D'Aranda.

D'Aranda seized on this supposed American violation as a basis for claiming even worse offenses. He desperately needed justification for taking the *Nanina* as a prize, especially in light of the agreement and the Americans' otherwise compassionate behavior toward the British. To that end, in the ship's log that the Royal Navy required him to keep, D'Aranda wrote his June 16 entry: "Brought the *Nanina* brig in, belonging to New York, having taken possession of her in consequence of maltreatment experienced by everyone on board [as a result] of the infamous conduct of her master."

William Shepherd, D'Aranda's second-in-command, was also required to keep a log. His description of the events on June 16 was much more matter of fact, reciting the details of the *Nanina*'s arrival but saying nothing about Charles's purported egregious behavior, or claiming the *Nanina* as a prize. A few days later, when D'Aranda read Shepherd's entry, he realized he had a bit of a problem. D'Aranda had wanted Shepherd to corroborate his claim and support the justification for taking the *Nanina* as a prize, so he ordered or persuaded Shepherd to add some language to his entry. But Shepherd couldn't make a simple addendum to the log, since he had already added a few more entries, so he had to wedge the following comment into margins, at a right angle: "Got intelligence from passengers that the Americans had behaved to them in a scandalous, oppressive and fraudulent manner, and that this was the means of us seizing the brig as prize."

There was, however, something terribly misleading about D'Aranda's justification. He claimed that he declared the *Nanina* a prize *after* he had been informed about the purported "maltreatment," but that is not what happened. Instead, he declared the *Nanina* as a prize immediately upon boarding the brig, before he had questioned the British passengers, and, therefore, he would have known nothing about any supposed bad behavior or maltreatment from the Americans. It seems clear, as Joseph Holt believed, that D'Aranda had made up his mind to claim the *Nanina* as a prize almost as soon as he first landed on Eagle Island and was informed of the brig's existence. Indeed, the fact that D'Aranda had declared the

Young Nanina a prize weeks before the *Nanina* arrived, confirms that suspicion.

The most plausible explanation for D'Aranda's decision to take the *Nanina* and the *Young Nanina* as prizes is that he was motivated purely by the glory of capturing a prize of war and collecting the profit that would ensue. If the two American vessels were determined to be legitimate prizes by the Prize Appeal Court in London, they and their contents would be sold, and the money received would be split among D'Aranda and his crew, with D'Aranda receiving the largest share. If that had not been D'Aranda's ultimate goal, then why else would he have almost immediately claimed the *Nanina* and the *Young Nanina* as prizes, even after he had been informed of the amicable and compassionate rescue deal reached between the British castaways and the Americans?

On the same day that the *Nanina* was brought in, Valentine and Pease had urged D'Aranda to send the shallop back immediately to retrieve the hunting party on Beaver Island, but he refused. D'Aranda defended his inaction in his log, stating his belief that the "late crew left behind [was] . . . expected to follow." Such a blithe assumption was outrageous, given the circumstances. To expect a small open boat manned by five men to be able to journey successfully about 80 miles around treacherous capes and through much open water at the beginning of winter was assuming great persistence and a considerable amount of luck. But, more to the point, a compassionate and responsible commander—which D'Aranda was not—would have dispatched the shallop as soon as possible to rescue the men, who were, after all, not only American but also British.

Later that afternoon, the Americans were escorted roughly 7 miles over marshy land to Newtown Providence, arriving at 8 p.m., weary from their hike. Holt took Valentine and Pease into his hut, where they had a bittersweet reunion with Fanning and Hunter. Despite Holt's welcoming embrace, neither Valentine nor Pease was allowed to eat anything for thirty-six hours after landing. The men were also deprived of beds for many days, and, like Fanning and Hunter, they had to stay within the bounds of the camp.

Looking upon the new arrivals, Holt experienced feelings similar to those he had when D'Aranda first arrived and made Fanning and Hunter prisoners. "I felt for [Valentine and Pease] . . . with all my heart, and tried to make them as comfortable as I could, in their misfortune. But the old gentleman's case was the worst," for he had been forced to witness his son being left behind after he had unselfishly offered to lead a hunting party to feed all of those under his charge. "So that old Captain Barnard's case was doubly distressing, being made a prisoner himself, and losing his son. . . . I pitied these poor gentlemen very much, and my sorrow for them was nothing more than a debt of gratitude."

Despite all of his apparently heartfelt concern for how unjustly the Americans had been treated, Holt did what he had done before. Instead of standing up for the Americans, he remained silent, noting that "a shut mouth denotes a steady head." According to Holt, the Duries, too, "felt very sorry for our American benefactors," despite the fact that Robert Durie had contributed to the Americans' predicament. Like Holt, the Duries kept their misgivings to themselves. Though, truth be told, it was extremely unlikely that even a vociferous defense of the Americans by Holt and the Duries would have swayed D'Aranda from his chosen course, unless all of the British protested, which clearly was not going to happen.

THE FOLLOWING WEEKS WERE trying for the Americans. They were poorly fed, and Pease claimed that, for one stretch of days, he was given only coffee and sugar, and, "had it not been for the corporal," who surreptitiously provided him with food, he would have starved.

Using threats as motivation, the British ordered the Americans to work. This infuriated Pease, who argued that such forced labor "was contrary to the usage of prisoners, unless in cases of greatest necessity." He also told his fellow Americans that if they lifted a finger to help the British, he "would throw them overboard." Despite Pease's argument and threat, the other Americans said they had no choice in the matter, given the situation, and they proceeded to load cargo onto the *Nancy* and the *Nanina*.

Hearing of Pease's defiance, D'Aranda exploded in rage and ordered the marines to bring Pease to his cabin on the *Nancy*. As soon as the American entered, D'Aranda began haranguing him with "abusive language" that Pease said he "had never before heard from any low-bred character." D'Aranda also threatened to have Pease flogged and put in irons if he caused any more trouble. From that point forward, Pease kept his rebellious thoughts to himself.

The Americans' trunks were opened, and almost all their personal effects were either destroyed or taken by the British. D'Aranda justified the theft by stating that the items were "public property," and that everything was "free plunder." The purloined property included quadrants, spyglasses, guns, clothing, and charts. The Americans' beds were ripped open, scattering all the feathers. The crew then used the beds' ticking to repair sails. The British even cut up many of the sealskins that the Americans had so painstakingly prepared. According to Valentine, Joanna-Ann Durie and Mary Ann Spencer took the lead in plundering Charles's cabin in order to gain favor with D'Aranda and demonstrate their loyalty to the Crown. The two women presented the best of Charles's belongings to D'Aranda, who gratefully accepted them.

Throughout all of this period, the prisoners were placed on half rations of salt beef and pork, and bread. They were not allowed to hunt, so the only fresh provisions they ate were those few birds they could catch in snares set outside of their huts. And their allowance of wine and rum was completely cut off.

While the Americans were being mistreated so unconscionably, the British sailors and marines were kept busy stowing cargo and passengers' luggage, overseeing the prisoners' work, and making repairs to the *Nancy* and the *Nanina*—all to prepare them for their upcoming departure from the Falklands. The weather remained cold and unsettled—with intermittent squalls, gales, rain, snow, and fog—casting a dreary pall on the proceedings.

D'Aranda continued to focus on the bane of so many naval commanders—inebriation. One *Nancy* crewman who imbibed too much was given twenty-four lashes. Passengers from the *Isabella* were also punished for the same offense, though not bodily. Mattinson, along with Ms. Connolly and Elizabeth Davis, had their allowance of spirits stopped, "in consequence of their repeated drunkenness."

Another all-too-common problem also plagued D'Aranda—Norway rats—which, oddly enough, had nothing to do with Norway.* Semantic slander notwithstanding, the rats, which could grow to 16 inches, including their tail, and could weigh more than a pound, were a nuisance aboard

---

* They were brown rats that had mistakenly been dubbed *Norway* rats in 1769, when British physician and naturalist John Berkenhout wrote a treatise in which he claimed erroneously that the rats had arrived in England on ships from Norway. See Dave Taft, "A Rat with a Bum Rap. And It Isn't Even Norwegian," *New York Times* (January 31, 2017).

ships, eating their way through the provisions and occasionally biting sailors. Although rats were introduced to the Falklands by mariners in the late 1700s, it is almost certain that the ones infesting the *Nancy* had been on board when the brig left Buenos Aires. Since then, they had been multiplying. To rid the vessel of this scourge, glowing coals were covered with rolled sulfur and placed in iron pots. After these were lowered into the hold, the hatches were battened down. Overnight, the smoke did its work, and when the hatches were opened, down the men went to clear out the dead rats and pitch them over the side. Although a few hardy survivors remained, the purging was considered a success.

ON JULY 10, WHETHER compelled by the continued pleas of the Americans or just wanting to appear that he had tried to find them, D'Aranda sent out the shallop to look for the missing hunting party. Pease volunteered to go along, since he had extensive experience navigating the Falklands and knew New and Beaver Islands quite well. D'Aranda at first welcomed Pease's assistance, but when the time came for the shallop to leave, he forbade him from going along. Instead, the shallop was placed under the command of John Marsh, a *Nancy* midshipman, who was joined by a couple of marines and one foremast crewman from the *Nanina*. Unlike Pease, neither Marsh nor any of the marines had experience sailing in the Falklands, except for what they had gained on the *Nancy*'s inbound voyage. And while the *Nanina*'s foremast hand clearly had some knowledge of the Falklands, his expertise was nothing compared to Pease's.

The men on the shallop might have succeeded if they had given the search a serious effort, but that is not what happened. They returned on July 13, just three days after they left. Instead of going to New Island or Beaver Island, where the hunting crew was last known to be, or even going around Cape Meredith or Cape Orford, the shallop sailed only as far as Fox Bay, directly across Falkland Sound from Eagle Island. It seems likely that D'Aranda specifically ordered a merely half-hearted attempt, but, even if he hadn't, there was no further talk of rescuing the hunting crew after the shallop returned.

Although D'Aranda never provided his reasons for abandoning the hunting party, there was nothing he could have offered to make his actions acceptable. No doubt he was eager to leave, and he was reluctant to risk his men on repeated forays to find the party, but the callousness he exhibited in this instance remains astonishing and indefensible. To the Americans on Eagle Island, D'Aranda's atrocious behavior "was as destitute of the common feelings of humanity as it was contrary to common sense." Holt felt the same way. "I think that leaving these men on the island, was a disgrace to the British flag, and much worse in every respect than the seizure of the *Nanina*, considering the humane service in which she was employed."

BY MID-JULY, THERE WAS an air of anticipation running through the ranks of the British residents of Eagle Island. The pace of preparations for departure picked up. Newtown Providence was abandoned, and everyone was sent to live aboard the vessel that would take them back to civilization—the *Nancy* heading back to Buenos Aires and the *Nanina* to England.

After the sorting of crew, passengers, and prisoners was complete, the *Nancy* had fifty-two people on board, including the Duries, Henry Hayes, George Higton, Mary Bindell, and Mrs. Hughes. The *Nanina*, under prize master John Marsh, took on forty-four, including the Holts, the marines from the *Isabella*, Richard Lundin, and all of the men from the *Nanina*. To sustain the people on the *Nanina*, D'Aranda ordered 540 pounds of bread and 840 pounds of beef transferred to the brig.

The Americans' accommodations on their own brig were miserable. Crammed into the cold and damp starboard side of steerage, right next to coiled cables and cargo, with little extra clothing and continued poor rations, they shivered through the nights and days and cursed their captors. Most galling to them was that the *Nanina*'s captain's cabin was reserved for Marsh, Mary Ann Spencer, and Lundin, the latter two of whom were referred to by Henry Defrees as "a common prostitute and her fellow."

Finally, on July 27, 1813—exactly 170 days after the *Isabella* slammed ashore and 44 days since the five-man hunting party had been left on Beaver Island—the *Nancy* and the *Nanina* were fully loaded and ready to set sail. The passengers and crew on the two vessels could only imagine what had happened to the hunting party, but what they imagined was almost certainly not as dramatic as what had actually occurred.

Desperate Journeys

═══

O N JUNE 15, AFTER THE HUNTING PARTY SEARCHED FOR THE *NANINA* ON New and Beaver Islands and came to the shocking realization that the brig had abandoned them, they latched onto one final hope. The *Nanina* must have gone to Eagle Island, if for no other reason than the British would want to pick up their compatriots and the rescued cargo from the *Isabella* before departing the Falklands. If the five men could just make it there in time, they could at least confront those who had so callously left them behind and, perhaps, repair the relationship—or at least appeal to their humanity so as not to be abandoned again. Even if they arrived at the island only to find the British had departed, there might be a note explaining what happened, and perhaps some supplies awaiting them. On such a slender reed, Charles and the others placed their faith.

With no navigational equipment, and such a small boat, this was a dangerous gambit. But they decided, despite the risks, that they had no choice but to try, so they steeled themselves for the long voyage. To lessen their load and make the boat more seaworthy, they pitched four of the hogs overboard, retaining the other four to sustain them, along with any provisions they could procure at stops on the way. At midnight on June 15, the men and Charles's faithful dog, Cent, climbed into the boat, and set off in search of salvation.

They rowed through much of the night, making it as far as Island Harbor on the east side of Swan Island. The upper reaches of the beach, now exposed by the receding tide, were glazed in a thick crust of ice. Exhausted, and drenched in cold sweat and sea spray, they pulled the boat onto the shore beyond the reach of the water, flipped it over to use as a shelter, and crawled beneath it. Their threadbare clothes offered little protection against the elements, so the men huddled together for warmth and then spread out their only blanket, trying to cover as much of their bodies as possible. Before falling off to sleep, a couple of them shared their deepest fear, moaning that they would soon die.

When they awoke a few hours later, the men used a knife and a flint to ignite a small fire. Then they greedily consumed the seared strips of pork, this being the only food they had eaten in an entire day. Over breakfast, Charles laid out the best course of action. Sailing around Cape Orford, the most direct route, was out of the question. He was especially fearful of the 23-mile stretch between the cape and the entrance to Port Stephens, calling it "an inaccessible iron-bound shore," ringed by towering perpendicular cliffs. Almost the entire distance was buffeted by fierce winds, heavy seas, and dangerous tide rips, and, worse, there was no place to land without the likelihood of having the boat dashed against rocks and broken into pieces. In Charles's estimation, it was "the most perilous cape in this part of the world."*

There was, however, a way to avoid the perils of Cape Orford and still make it to their destination. They could head to McCockling's Lagoon,† which was to the east of Cape Orford and sheltered from the open ocean. The farthest reaches of this lagoon were separated by only a few miles from another sheltered body of water to the south called Port Stephens Harbor. By going to the lagoon, then carrying their boat overland and relaunching in the harbor, they could avoid the "ironbound shore" and exit to the open ocean just a few miles above Cape Meredith. The latter was by no means easy to navigate around, but it was much easier than Cape Orford, since the distance between landings was relatively short,

---

* The dangers of the waters around the Falklands were illustrated by comments Barzillai Pease had made during his first voyage to the islands in 1790, aboard the brig *Nancy*. He complained that without the services of a shallop, he and the other sealers had to use a small boat—just like the boat the five abandoned men had to use—to go from island to island in search of seals. This put them, he said, "under a disadvantage," and "obliged them to go through rips and breakers" and run "many risks. One time we were crossing from Beaver Island to New Island and were swept by the strength of the tide into one of those rips and before we got out were filled up to the thwarts." See Barzillai Pease Journals, Special Collections Research Center, Syracuse University Libraries, Journal 1, 17–18.

† Modern-day Fegen Inlet.

and the rips and races were not as threatening. And if they reached the mouth of Port Stephens Harbor and waited for a day of fairer weather, surely they would be able to round Cape Meredith with even less risk.

Confident in the plan, they headed out. Unfortunately, the wind was dead ahead, forcing them to keep their sail furled and row again. As the bow cut through choppy waves, rivulets of cold saltwater surged into the boat. Once darkness settled in, they pulled into a small cove, hauled the boat onto a beach, and once again flipped it over. Throughout the night, a light snow fell, coating the boat's hull in a velvety embrace. At daybreak, they could clearly see that they were at the mouth of a valley, with low hills all around. Charles believed that they were only a mile or so to the east of the entrance of the lagoon they sought. To get a better sense of their location, Charles climbed to the ridgeline of one of the hills and spotted another body of water in the distance.

Convinced that it was Port Stephens Harbor, he rallied the other men, and they spent the daylight hours carrying the oars, masts, sail, two dead hogs, and other items from the boat up and then down the hill to the water beyond. As darkness fell, they returned to their "wooden tent" for the night. Early the next morning, they flipped the boat, hoping to carry it over the same path they had trod the day before. That was, however, too much for them to accomplish in their fatigued state. Instead, they dragged the boat gently over the rocky ground, having to stop many times along the way to rest.

Shortly before sunset, the boat was back in its element. Charles believed that they were now at the head of Port Stephens Harbor. Therefore, he saw no risk to sailing into the darkness, even with the falling snow reducing visibility. If he was correct, they would be at the mouth of the harbor in about 8 miles, ready to brave Cape Meredith. Off they went, their spirits rising.

It came as a shock when, after having proceeded about 3 or 4 miles, they found themselves battling mounting seas and a freshening wind. Still thinking he was in Port Stephens Harbor, despite increasing evidence to the contrary, Charles steered the boat in the direction he thought would take them to the harbor's edge. But after having sailed a distance that was easily twice the breadth of the harbor, he suddenly realized he had no idea where they were. He was lost—which was not all that surprising. They had no compass or chart, and the coast in this area was so dotted with islands, coves, bays, inlets, and harbors that even sailors with a host of navigational tools and rudimentary charts—as they all were at this time—would have found it extremely challenging to get from place to place.

Charles did not have the luxury of time for chastising himself; he needed to get to land. As his mind raced, trying desperately to get his bearings, he heard breakers to leeward. Through the gloom, they could see the shore, which was lined with large, flat slabs of rock exposed by the low tide. Having no alternative, the men ran the boat as gingerly as possible into the shallow water, where a couple of them hopped out of the boat to pull it higher onto the ledge. ·

They had to drag the boat up a steep slope of the clay, rock, and sand bank to get beyond the high-tide mark. Clearing 6 to 8 inches of snow from a small area, they then overturned the boat, leaning one side against a raised bank, and climbed in. Cent could sense the men's distress, and, as he nestled among them, he repeatedly licked their faces, seemingly wanting to comfort them.

Charles cut a small depression in the clay bank, lit a fire fueled by driftwood, and dropped strips of pork into a pot they had brought along. Then he tied the pot to a string, the other end of which was looped around the gunwale resting against the bank. Suspended above the flames, the pork began to sizzle, sending a pleasing aroma into the air.

The next morning, June 18, was cold, made colder still by gales coming from the south. After crawling out from beneath the boat, the men examined their surroundings to see whether anything looked familiar. As Charles later recounted, "[A]ll appeared strange, and our suspicions, that we had in our haste hauled the boat to the wrong place, were confirmed. . . . I was completely at a loss to tell where or on what island we landed."

Preparing breakfast, Charles realized they had a problem: This meal would use all that remained of their water and their wood. So he sent Green and Ansell off to search the shore for both. They returned empty-handed and almost frozen. After the men ate their parboiled pork, and melted snow in the pot to drink, Charles took Albrook and headed off in the opposite direction from that taken by Green and Ansell, carrying the boat keg and their sealing implements. A mile later, after going inland, they came upon a frozen pond. Breaking through the ice, they found fresh water and filled their keg.

They had no luck finding wood, but they came upon something

almost as beneficial—elephant seals. With a few vicious blows from their clubs and thrusts of a lance, they killed the smallest one. They cut off a few hunks of blubber and took them back to the boat. Although blubber was a dirty burn, they could use it to light their fires. But with the gales showing no sign of letting up, the men soon worried that their fuel might run out if they were forced to stay in this place for many days. Hence, they returned to the place they had seen the elephant seals and killed a few more, providing additional blubber as well as some meat.

For the next two days, the raging winds kept the men mostly under their overturned boat. Each time they lit a fire to cook food, it threw off billows of smoke that mixed with the grease particles coming from the sizzling meat. This filled the space with a pungent cloud that enveloped the already-filthy men, coating them in a layer of grime that gave their faces a blackened hue.

On June 20, the weather finally broke. In line with Charles's new plan, they packed up the boat and headed in what they believed was an easterly direction, hoping to reach the land they had glimpsed earlier, which was about 10 miles off. Despite his failure at this point to determine his location, Charles thought that if they could just reach other harbors, he would soon figure out where they were, since he had visited so many places in the Falklands during his many seal hunts.

They rowed for several hours, finally reaching a rocky shore late in the afternoon, when they pulled up the boat for the night. Charles looked around, recognizing nothing. But he was almost certain they were on English Maloon. His confidence in this conjecture was supported by the appearance of a warrah, which at the time were thought to inhabit only this island. The curious animal had no fear of humans, so Charles went in close and hit it on the head with the pole of his lance. One of the men skinned the animal, using its pelt for a hat.

With their pork supply nearly exhausted, the men divided into two groups, each searching for provisions. When they reunited early that evening, all they had to show for their efforts were three wildfowl, killed with rocks.

After another night on shore, they launched the boat once again on June 22. The same pattern repeated itself. About 8 miles later, they landed on an unfamiliar beach and again split up to search for provisions. Charles's group came back empty-handed, so they waited at the boat for the others to return. As the hours passed, Charles grew concerned. Perhaps the others got lost, or became so weary from the hunger and fatigue that they were unable to find their way back. Finally, at dusk they appeared, so exhausted that they had a difficult time standing. But they had good news in their hands—seven Johnny Rooks, or striated caracaras, also known as carrion hawks. They were slain while dining on a rotting elephant-seal carcass. The next day, search parties were sent out again to find food, and they returned with meat and blubber from an elephant seal, as well as a few more caracaras. The men christened this place Pinch-Gut Camp, even though they had managed to find a fair amount of food, albeit rather limited in its gustatory range. Nevertheless, given their exertions and the unrelenting cold, they were burning through calories fast and rapidly losing weight.

Still confused and unsure of where they were, the men vowed to attempt to retrace their steps, hopefully leading them back to Swan Island and familiar surroundings. But it wasn't only geographic familiarity they sought. Swan, Beaver, and New Islands were the only places in this part of the Falklands where hogs could be found. Having run out of their supply of this meat some days past, the men were looking forward to adding it back into their admittedly sparse menu.

They left Pinch-Gut Camp on June 24, and the next place they landed quickly earned the name Hook Camp, when a caracara made off with the crew's last sealing hook. Such thievery was the norm for the caracara. As Charles wrote, "The sailors who visit these islands, being often much vexed at their predatory tricks, have bestowed different names on them, characteristic of their nature, as flying monkeys, flying devils. I have known these birds to fly away with caps, mittens, stockings, powder horns, knives, steels, tin pots, in fact everything which their great strength is equal to."

The persistent caracaras at Hook Camp, more than a hundred of them swooping in to steal food, soon lived up to their reputation, leaving the men with nothing more than a few hunks of rancid elephant seal blubber with some meat attached—provisions deemed so foul that Charles said it could only have been eaten by a "Greenlander, Eskimo, savage, or piratical rook." Ironically, in their search for food, the caracaras became food themselves. The men pelted the flying horde, scaring them off but leaving eighteen dead birds on the field of battle.

For the next several days, another gale blew in, pinning them down at Hook Camp. Additional hunting forays yielded a single sea lion and

two rooks. By June 26, they once again ran out of food, and despera-
tion forced them to pull up tussac grass and eat the roots. This caused
some of the men to vomit and become dizzy. "In this forlorn situation,"
Charles later wrote, "exposed to every hardship that man could sustain
without sinking under the pressure, with scarcely provisions sufficient to
sustain our sinking frames, our bodily strength and mental energy daily
declined, and most of us despaired of ever being relieved except by a lingering death."

The torturous stay at Hook Camp continued until July 1, when the
emaciated men, realizing that staying in this location meant certain death,
rallied to get the boat back in the water. But in the process of launching
the vessel, they suffered two more misfortunes. While trying to get into
the boat, Green, unsteady on his feet, slipped on the rocks and had to be
plucked from the surf just as he was about to be washed away. And then,
as they were putting in, the hull hit hard upon a ledge, splitting a plank
and creating a slow but steady leak. Still, they managed to get off and
sailed along the rocky, cliff-bound shore. The combination of the leak
and the waves breaking over the bow into the boat kept the men busy
bailing to stay afloat.

Under these extreme circumstances, Ansell shared some information
with his fellow wayfarers. His real name was John Stone, and he had
spent time on a British man-of-war. Unable to swim and fearing imminent death, he asked the others to promise, if they made it to shore and
ultimately back to civilization, that they would relay the news of his death
to his mother, the Widow Stone, who lived in Luton, outside of London.[*]

The men promised, but neither Ansell nor any of the others died that
day, and when they reached the end of the chain of cliffs, they pulled up
on a sandy beach. A quick search for food before sunset procured some
seal flesh, two foxes, and three geese. The cooked seal and goose meat
was palatable, but the foxes proved a challenge. As Charles commented,
the flesh is "so very strong that nothing but the sauce of extreme hunger
could force it down."

---

[*] According to David Miller, in his book on the wreck of the *Isabella*, Ansell was
known as John Stone in the Royal Navy, but his real name was Samuel Stone. Miller sur-
mises that he was a deserter from the navy, hence the name change to avoid capture and
possible court-martial. Miller, *The Wreck*, note 150.

The following day, July 2, the search for food continued, and another confession was added to the mix. Greatly depressed by their situation, and obviously haunted by his secret, Ansell began bawling. In between almost uncontrollable bouts of sobbing, he blurted out that he had been a "great fool . . . to volunteer" to accompany Charles and the three others on the hunting foray, for he had been in on the plan, hatched by Mattinson and others, to take over the *Nanina* and sail it to Eagle Island. According to Ansell, the plan had been in the works for some time, and the British who were privy to it were only waiting for the right opportunity to put it into effect—which the departure of the hunting party provided. Ansell was, however, shocked and disappointed that his fellow conspirators chose that moment to execute the plan, leaving him exiled along with the rest of them.

Understandably, this news greatly angered Charles. Instead of lashing out physically, which he was tempted to do, he told Ansell, "[Y]ou are just where you ought to be; your guilty conscience troubles you, and you are tormented in mind, which renders your sufferings greater than ours, whose consciences are clear of having plotted against the property or happiness of our fellow-creatures."

Charles had other reasons for disliking Ansell intensely. Since almost the beginning of their ordeal, Ansell had often been abusive toward Jacob Green, as well as Louder and Albrook, whom Charles called "excellent young men." At one point, Ansell, swearing violently, threatened to beat Louder over the head with his club. Louder turned to Charles, asking for protection and beginning to retreat in his direction. Ansell followed, swearing that protection or no, he was going to knock him down. Charles intervened and took Louder's side, telling Ansell that he should back off and, under no circumstances, hit anyone with a club. Instead, Charles said that if Ansell was determined to fight, he should do so with his fists, not with "a weapon, like an assassin, to revenge themselves by committing murder." That stopped Ansell in his tracks, but, from Charles's perspective, it had an unintended consequence. Ansell's anger, which had formerly focused primarily on Louder, Albrook, and Green, was now transferred to his new nemesis, Charles.

At the same time, Ansell displayed another characteristic that Charles found reprehensible. Becoming somewhat philosophical, he commented, "[W]hat was very singular about him [Ansell], and what illustrates the excellence of real virtue and courage is, [is] that though this fellow was the greatest bully breathing, and had domineered over the men and made them all afraid of him; yet, when we were in real difficulties and dangers, he was the very first to shrink back and despair; while they would bravely face them without a murmur or a tear."

The men remained at this place three more days, waiting for the weather to turn favorable for a final push. On July 5, they finally set off. When they arrived back at the neck of land where they had, many days earlier, hauled the boat and everything in it over a hill to another body of water beyond, they repeated the task in reverse. It took nearly two days of hard labor, but they overcame this obstacle and then sailed for Swan Island, reaching it at three in the afternoon on July 7. Reflecting on the crazy circular voyage he had just completed, and the total lack of recognition along the way, Charles was astonished that he had become so disoriented, despite having visited the Falklands many times. Perhaps the stress of his predicament had dulled his memory and judgment.

The first order of business was sustenance. Cent performed brilliantly, quickly capturing a hog, which the men devoured almost raw, their hunger too great to wait for it to be cooked properly. In the next few hours, Cent caught six more hogs, which the men clubbed to death. That night, after eating their fill of meat, there arose a renewed optimism and sense of purpose among the party. They vowed to make another attempt to reach the *Isabella* wreck site.

AT TWO IN THE morning on July 8, 1813, the five men left Swan Island. Their plan was the original one: to find McCockling's Lagoon and travel overland to the head of Port Stephens Harbor. Battling a fierce wind and driving snow, they reached what they thought was the head of the lagoon just before dawn. They emptied the boat, hauled it up the beach, flipped it, and made a fire to cook their food and keep the penetrating cold at bay. So great was Green's and Ansell's desire to know whether they were in the right place that they immediately set off to find the harbor. After they walked for a few miles, a large body of water came into view. Having been there many times, Green was sure he was looking at Port Stephens Harbor.

Getting to the harbor had been difficult enough and slow going, wading through high tussac grass and snow, but the hike back was far worse, given how spent the men were. They arrived at the bottom of the lagoon just after dark. There were two paths they could take, each one leading up a different side of the lagoon. Confused and tired, they chose poorly, picking the side that was opposite to where their boat lay. They finally realized their mistake when they saw the light of the fire beneath the boat—on the opposite bank. Back they went, retracing their steps, and then up the other side of the lagoon. Around midnight, starving and shivering, they arrived at the boat. The three others were elated to see them return, having assumed that the explorers had succumbed to the elements and frozen to death.

The next morning, the men discussed what potentially lay ahead if they continued with their quest to reach the *Isabella* wreck. It was all too much for Green, Louder, and Albrook to bear. They didn't think they had the strength to drag the boat and its contents over to Port Stephens and then sail around Cape Meredith, on to Eagle Island. To decide what to do, Charles put it up for a vote. Ansell was in favor of proceeding. But Charles knew that Ansell "possessed neither [the] resources nor [the] firmness" necessary for such a risky and difficult endeavor, and that the plan had virtually no chance of succeeding unless they all worked together. So Charles voted with the others. For the moment, that ended their quest to reach the wreck, but they vowed to try again when more favorable conditions presented themselves.

During the next two days, they were pinned down by another storm. With the wood and blubber expended, their only fuel was some withered grass and vines they were able to gather near the boat. This made for a weak flame that produced only half-cooked pork and scant heat. "The piercing cold," Charles related, "penetrated our emaciated bodies with the keenness of a dagger."

On the third day after they had reached their momentous decision, and with the storm abating, the crew set sail for Swan Island, ultimately landing at the island's Quaker Harbor. In the coming days, they ventured to New Island to check yet again whether there was any evidence that the people on the *Nanina* had searched for them, or at least had left a note. Finding nothing, the weary wanderers had to wait out some nasty weather on New Island before heading back to Quaker Harbor on July 25. At that point, they decided to remain there for the rest of the Southern Hemisphere's winter because of the advantages it afforded. From this spot, they could see any ship that visited New Island's main harbor, the traditional stopping-off point for vessels to stock up on food and water. The location was also only a mile from a seal rookery, and there were plenty of hogs on the island.

On the very day that the five castaways settled in at Quaker Harbor, the *Nancy* and the *Nanina* were still in the final stages of preparing to depart. If only their decisive vote had been unanimous, and the men had pressed onward instead of turning back, they might have made it to Eagle Island in time.

The *Nancy* Returns

D'ARANDA'S PLAN WAS FOR THE *NANINA* TO LEAVE JACK'S HARBOR FIRST, and for the *Nancy* to follow soon thereafter. Once the *Nanina* got clear of the Falklands, it was supposed to heave-to, waiting for the *Nancy* to arrive, and then both ships would sail in tandem as far as the mouth of the Río de la Plata. There they would diverge, with the *Nanina* heading to England and the *Nancy* to Buenos Aires. If the rendezvous off the Falklands did not materialize within two days, the *Nanina* was to return to Jack's Harbor, the assumption being that the *Nancy* had gone back, and that a new plan would have to be devised.

The *Nanina*, towing the *Young Nanina*, departed Jack's Harbor at 11:45 in the morning on July 27, 1813. The *Nancy* left a little more than four hours later. Late that evening, while the *Nancy* was off the northwest corner of Spanish Maloon, D'Aranda ordered three of the cannons to be fired to alert the *Nanina* to the brig's location. There was no response. D'Aranda assumed that the *Nanina* had gone a little farther ahead, so the following day, while still within sight of the Falklands, he continued to look for his prize. The sea, however, was empty as far as the eye could see.

At this point, D'Aranda discarded the rest of the plan. He neither waited another day nor returned to Jack's Harbor. One possible explanation for this decision is that the day after leaving Jack's Harbor, very strong gales, accompanied by rain and snow, began lashing the *Nancy*, and those conditions continued without letup for another week. The heavy seas ripped out the ship's taffrail and washed away the stern boat and some of the rigging. Tons of water coming over the sides kept the pumps in near-continuous service, and the wind shredded a number of sails. Not thinking of continuing to look for the *Nanina*, or returning to the Falklands, D'Aranda was just focused on keeping the ship together and getting to Buenos Aires.

Fortunately for the *Nancy*, the worst part of the voyage was over. During the next few weeks, there were alternating periods of fair and squally weather, and only one day where they encountered a violent storm. The crew remained busy making numerous, often jury-rigged, repairs. Finally, at 5:30 p.m. on August 19, the *Nancy* arrived in Buenos Aires, leaking badly. Most on board were very sick, and one British seaman, Matthew Lennon, was near death. The thirty-six lashes he had received for drunkenness back on Eagle Island no doubt weakened his constitution, allowing scurvy to take a stronger hold on him than on others who were also suffering mightily from the malady. While the *Nancy* was anchored off Buenos Aires, Lennon "departed this life," as D'Aranda noted in his log, and his body was "committed . . . to the deep with the usual ceremonies."

Upon arriving in Buenos Aires, one of the officers on the *Nancy* wrote a letter that was later published in *The Times* of London, detailing the dramatic nature of the brig's voyage to and from the Falklands.

[I encountered] the most tempestuous weather I have yet experienced; we from unceasing perseverance have executed the important service sent upon. . . . [The islands] upon which we discovered the wrecked people, are dangerous in the extreme, and surrounded by numerous and extensive reefs; . . . [We] had constant gales during our stay in the islands. The weather was so piercing cold, with snow and hail, that the crew could not keep the deck or perform the least duty, and we were all but a complete wreck when we returned. It was with great difficulty we patched her up to bring us here. . . . We found on the islands the unhappy people we went in search of . . . except two American seamen; but from our long passage there, and the prospect of another one back, we should not have been able, for want of provisions, to bring them all away, had we not most fortunately captured an American [brig].

The fact that the abandonment of two Americans, to say nothing of the three British, merited only a passing comment speaks volumes. Similarly, the officer's mention that it was their good fortune to capture an American vessel completely avoids the extremely troubling and dishonorable circumstances surrounding the taking of such a prize. No doubt, the officer didn't want his tale of derring-do marred by inconvenient facts.

As soon as D'Aranda disembarked from the *Nancy* in Buenos Aires, he reported the results of his trip to local British officials. Perhaps already realizing that his behavior might not stand up under scrutiny, D'Aranda wrote a defense of sorts to Captain William Bowles, of the HMS *Aquilon*, on station in Buenos Aires: "We had suffered so much in our passage to the islands, crew sickly and the vessel a complete wreck . . . that but for the American vessel I could not have brought more of the wrecked people from the island in the *Nancy* than I at present have on board, but could merely have removed them to one of the islands upon which were cattle or pigs." This probably was true, but that doesn't absolve D'Aranda. As historian David Miller argued, "[T]here seems to be no reason why he [D'Aranda] could not have come to an arrangement with the Barnards to achieve this [the use of the brig], without actually having to take the *Nanina* from them by force."

After submitting his report, D'Aranda was told that the *Nancy* was in such bad condition that she had to be condemned and sold, which occurred a few months later. Thus, D'Aranda lost his command. This bad turn of events, at least from D'Aranda's perspective, was somewhat counterbalanced by his dreams of wealth that were sure to come from his prizes, the *Nanina* and the *Young Nanina*, which he assumed were heading to England at that moment. But he was sorely mistaken.

Necessity

=

THE *NANINA*'S VOYAGE WAS WORSE THAN THE *NANCY*'S. NOT LONG AFTER leaving Jack's Harbor, the towrope parted and the *Young Nanina* drifted away. From Richard Lundin's perspective, this was not a bad thing. The bulky shallop had been slowing them down and making it more difficult to sail the brig. The *Nanina* waited around for two days for the *Nancy* to appear, but clearly not in a spot where D'Aranda could find it. Still sticking to the plan, prize master John Marsh tried to head back to Jack's Harbor, but the same storm that rocked the *Nancy* hit the *Nanina*, and, along with strong adverse currents, this precluded any attempts to turn around. On they went, but not to England. They were heading for Rio de Janeiro.

This change of plan was born of necessity. Nobody on board had any confidence that the overloaded, overcrowded, and poorly provisioned brig could make it to England. According to Lundin, when the *Nanina* left the Falklands, it was in "a most miserable plight, with a leak in her bows, with neither sufficient sails, rigging, or spars, or even provisions to last us one-fourth of the intended voyage." In the same vein, Holt said that the brig didn't have "as much spare rope as would fetter a frog, nor a second sail to put up, if we lost one." Part of the reason for the *Nanina*'s paucity of provisions was that, in the days before sailing, the brig had no British officer on board to take charge and restrict access. As a result, many of the marines and crewmembers of the *Isabella* rifled through the *Nanina*, taking off what they wanted and needed. D'Aranda, too, plundered the *Nanina* of rigging and yards, plus a cable, boat, and anchor, all to benefit the *Nancy*. According to Defrees, this free-for-all left the *Nanina* "a complete shell."

The *Nanina*'s sailing abilities were further compromised by the amount of cargo she was carrying, a combination of the Americans' stores and what was taken off the *Isabella*—so much cargo that a considerable portion of it was stored on the main deck, the hold being full. As Pease commented, "[O]ur decks [were] lumbered up in a shocking manner for sea." In addition, the week-long storm at the outset sent the *Nanina* significantly off course, which would have made it very difficult and time consuming for the brig to get back on track.

There were also grave doubts about the abilities of the prize master and the crew to lead the *Nanina* on such a long voyage. It quickly became apparent that John Marsh was not up to the job. He was young and had had little experience sailing in these waters, and he certainly was not skilled in handling a dangerously overloaded vessel in bad weather. Making matters worse was that he was forced to contend with a crew that Pease had called "Botany Bay convicts," and "as poor a set of men as ever navigated a vessel." There were more than a few times when the entire crew left their stations and went below, shirking their responsibilities in favor of drinking, playing cards, and quarreling with one another. To top things off, the brig's charts, compass, and most of its quadrants had been transferred to the *Nancy*, a strange and dangerous move by D'Aranda, especially if he wanted to ensure that his prize made it to its destination.

Once again, the Americans came to the rescue. The *Nanina*'s captains had managed to save one of their quadrants and a few books on navigation, and they shared them with Marsh. Despite being prisoners, the Americans stepped up to help sail the vessel, offering Marsh navigational advice and working with the crew when necessary. Their help was critical, and, without it, Lundin believed that the ship would not have made it to port.

Joseph Holt described a particularly harrowing example that confirms Lundin's claim:

> On the fourteenth of August we got in sight of Grande Island [about 60 miles southwest of Rio de Janeiro], and only for old [Valentine] Barnard, who knew the coast, we should have been lost. The Americans, for self-preservation, often went up aloft to take in reefs and handle the sails. Old Barnard said to me that

we had gone within five feet of the rock, when we went through a passage only about one hundred feet wide, and with very dangerous rocks on both sides; but he got us out of danger, and told Mr. Marsh, the prize master, where we were. We then bore out to sea, and sailed more by guess than by knowledge, as we had no maps on board nor anything to direct us, except old Barnard's memory; and a very fine old fellow he was, as I ever saw.

CONDITIONS ON THE *NANINA* remained miserable. The long periods of bad weather made the sailors weary and depressed, as well as wet for much of the time, since they had no other clothes. The *Nanina* would have been overcrowded even if it had had no cargo, but with all the cargo, there was even less space for the passengers and crew. The food not only was limited but also was rather monotonous, and lacking in anything that could provide vitamin C, which contributed to the malaise that settled over some of the passengers and crew.

Finally, on the twenty-third of August, the *Nanina*'s lookout sighted Sugarloaf Mountain, the majestic peak rising 1,300 feet above Rio. Two days later, the brig dropped anchor in the harbor, and in short order a fascinating diplomatic dance ensued.

Entrance to the port of Rio de Janeiro, circa 1854,
showing Sugarloaf Mountain in the distance.

Protest

===

AVING REACHED RIO, AND STILL FEELING BADLY ABOUT HOW THE AMERI-cans were treated, Joseph Holt offered to help the captains in any way he could. As prisoners, the Americans were not allowed to leave the brig, so he volunteered to deliver their letters protesting the taking of the *Nanina*. Taking him up on this, the captains wrote a letter to General Thomas Sumpter, the US Minister Plenipotentiary (Ambassador) in Rio, telling him of their travails and asking for help in getting the *Nanina* back.

Holt went to Sumpter's office and told the minister the entire story, making clear that the Americans were wronged. Sumpter thanked him and later wrote to Portuguese authorities, requesting that they intervene. He wanted them to take the *Nanina* from the British, who he said were holding it illegally, and give it back to the Americans. Claiming a lack of jurisdiction, and not wanting to meddle in such international affairs, the Portuguese refused to get involved.

Five days after the *Nanina* arrived, the British commander-in-chief, Rear Admiral Sir Manley Dixon, stepped aboard. (Brazil was neutral at the time, hence having both an American and a British presence.) He was curious to meet the people who had been involved in such a dramatic tale of survival, which was already the talk of the town. Dixon walked up to Holt and asked him whether he was one of those who had been shipwrecked. After confirming that he was, Holt then proceeded to give the admiral a summary account of what had happened on the Falklands. Dixon then asked to meet the Americans, whereupon Holt called the captains up from below. After being introduced, they told the admiral the story once again, stressing the unfairness of it all. In concluding the tale, Valentine Barnard observed that the whole enterprise was a "bad job" for him. Dixon disagreed, saying that "it was the hand of God that guided you there to save so many lives."

To bolster the Americans' case for restitution of the *Nanina*, Holt decided to lobby on their behalf. "The Americans generously gave us plenty of food," he told Dixon. "It is my opinion, your worship, that a vessel taken up by British subjects, and for the purpose of saving their lives, ought to be considered as an exception to the general rule respecting prizes. Although there was a war between England and America at the time that the *Nanina* was seized, the conduct of the Americans towards us clearly showed that there was no enmity on their part." Dixon concurred, saying that the Americans were no longer prisoners and could freely go where they wanted. Overjoyed by this decision, Holt immediately hired a canoe, which carried his family and the American captains ashore, landing at Palace Square. From there, they repaired to a local pub and downed a few glasses of rum.

Next stop for the captains was the office of the US Consul, where they gave a sworn statement in the form of a protest to Acting Commercial Agent Philip Rutter. They laid out pretty much the entire story of what happened—from the time they left New York to their arrival in Rio de Janeiro. The protest had multiple targets, including the British who forcibly took possession of the *Nanina* at New Island; Lieutenant D'Aranda, for making the *Nanina* a prize, and for placing the Americans under military arrest; John Marsh for acting as prize master; and, in a catchall clause, everyone who played a part in the capture and detention of the brig. The captains also sought to avoid personal liability. All "damages, losses and detriments that have happened to" the *Nanina*, and all her cargo, "from wind, waves, or capture," should be borne by "the merchants and freighters interested," and not by the officers and crew of the brig, who did not cause those problems. Rutter placed the protest in the diplomatic pouch and sent it off to Washington on September 6.

ABOUT A MONTH LATER, Pease, Hunter, and Fanning joined the Philadelphia vessel *Bingham* as passengers. A few Americans in Rio lent money to the destitute captains so they could purchase supplies for the voyage. At the end of November, they arrived in Newport, Rhode Island, where

Fanning spoke to a local newspaper about their ordeal. The resulting story—only a few paragraphs long and reprinted widely—ended with the following indignant flourish provided by the editor:

> Such are the particulars, and allowing them to be correctly related, I cannot refuse to declare that a more infamous and detestable transaction, whether we consider its base rapacity, its ingratitude, or its downright injustice, has rarely been heard of since the days of civilization. In a light of such magnitude do I view it, that I hold the character of the English nation to be implicated in seeing prompt and effectual justice done to the injured, and if it is not, it will be a foul and indelible blot in their history.

UPON REACHING HIS HOMETOWN of Hudson, New York, Barzillai Pease shared with the *Hudson Bee* the sworn statement the captains had given to Rutter. Even though it was quite long, the paper published it in its entirety in January 1814 with the eye-catching title "British Inhumanity." The article, reprinted in many papers, was prefaced with the following searing commentary, which was fueled by the fierce animosity that so many Americans felt for the British at the time:

> We request the attention of the reader to the following account of the almost unparalleled ingratitude and treachery of the crew of a *British* ship to the crew of an *American* vessel—the latter having *saved the lives* of the former, whose vessel had been wrecked, and they in return for this humane act, seized and made prize of the vessel and property of their *preservers!* Were it not that such a nation as Britain existed, this act of treachery might be correctly styled *unparalleled*; but British history is full of incidents of such black ingratitude. Such conduct, even in our enemy, cannot fail to call forth the indignant feelings of every American who has a drop of patriotic blood flowing in his veins. [emphasis original]

MEANWHILE, BACK IN RIO, Rear Admiral Dixon had been thinking more about the *Nanina*. He was greatly troubled by the way the Americans were treated, and the disgraceful act of abandoning the hunting party.

He wanted to help set things right, but first he needed to know what kind of deal the Americans might accept. On October 14, he sent the British Consul to visit Valentine to find out, carrying with him a specific offer—would he accept the return of the *Nanina*, minus the cargo from the *Isabella*? Valentine replied that if Dixon would give him a passport to return to the Falklands to pick up the hunting party, and then go to the United States, he would give the admiral his "determination." The same day, Valentine sent the admiral a list of all the necessary repairs and provisions that would have to be supplied before the *Nanina* could make the voyage to the Falklands.

Two days later, Dixon agreed to Valentine's terms, sending him a letter in which he said that he would hand over the *Nanina* "as she now stands," and after the *Isabella*'s cargo was brought ashore. Valentine would also get the passport he requested. As a sweetener, Dixon noted that "the rigging and sails [of the *Nanina*] have now been completely put to rights for you." If Valentine did not agree to these terms, Dixon warned, the *Nanina* would remain the *Nancy*'s prize.

Valentine consented, and, to cement the deal, the consul sent Valentine a bond of acquittance on October 27. But, upon receiving it, Valentine changed the rules. He told Dixon that he wouldn't sign the bond unless language was added that reserved for him the opportunity to stake "a future claim for all losses and damages which might be sustained through the conduct of her captors." In his mind, Valentine was merely standing up for the rights of the owners, captains, and crew of the *Nanina* to be made whole. But Valentine had overplayed his hand. Dixon refused the new demand, and he ignored Valentine until December 6, when D'Aranda suddenly appeared in Rio.

Let the Court Decide

═══

Aᴏғᴛᴇʀ ʀᴇʟɪɴǫᴜɪsʜɪɴɢ ᴄᴏᴍᴍᴀɴᴅ ᴏғ ᴛʜᴇ *ɴᴀɴᴄʏ* ɪɴ ʙᴜᴇɴᴏs ᴀɪʀᴇs, D'Aranda wanted to return to England to recuperate from his recent adventure and keep tabs on the ultimate disposition of the *Nanina* and the *Young Nanina* by the Prize Appeal Court. He decided to go aboard the HMS *Hermes* as a passenger, which would be stopping in Rio before continuing on to Plymouth. When the *Hermes* entered Rio's harbor on December 6, 1813, D'Aranda was thunderstruck. There, riding at anchor, was the *Nanina*. What, he wondered, was going on?

He soon found out. Upon hearing that D'Aranda was in port, Rear Admiral Dixon summoned him. Despite his recent disagreement with Valentine over terms, Dixon still wanted to make a deal. He told D'Aranda this, and the two of them agreed to the following: Valentine would get back the *Nanina*, minus the *Isabella*'s cargo, as long as he paid the harbor fees the *Nanina* had accrued, which amounted to 400 Spanish silver dollars. Although this was a little worse than the original deal, as Valentine would have to come up with the money, Dixon thought that Valentine would relent, realizing that some deal was better than no deal. Armed with this offer, D'Aranda met with Valentine in the British consul's office on December 9.

How things had changed. No longer a prisoner, but a peer, Valentine no doubt had to control his anger, sitting across from the man who had caused him so much financial, emotional, and physical pain. D'Aranda, too, must have been angry to be on the verge of giving away his prize.

But, when presented with the deal, Valentine "promptly declined." The *Nanina*, he said, had been "completely pillaged," and he had no way of coming up with such an exorbitant sum. Without the right to make a claim at a later date, the deal was worth even less.

If Valentine expected Dixon and D'Aranda to come back with another proposal, he misread the situation. Dixon had finally had enough of the American's haggling, and he broke off communication with him and ordered the *Nanina* to sail to London, where the Prize Appeal Court could sort things out. Valentine and the six crewmen who were still in Rio were ordered to vacate the *Nanina* immediately. Of this dénouement, Valentine later complained that it was "contrary to the remonstrances of the . . . American ambassador, the dictates of common justice, and the universally expressed opinion of almost every individual, whether British subjects or other who were acquainted with the circumstances. I was thus stripped of everything."

D'Aranda, pleased that he didn't have to relinquish his prize, departed Rio aboard the *Hermes* on January 19, 1814. Although he was a passenger and thus was supposed to have no formal interaction with the officers and crewmen, he stepped over the line. After penning a few reports on the *Nancy*'s rescue mission, D'Aranda asked the ship's sailmaker to enclose the documents in a roll of sailcloth, stitched up at the ends. The sailmaker refused, pointing out that he was ordered not to use any sailcloth unless so instructed by the captain. Angered by the temerity of this lowly seaman to deny his simple request, D'Aranda verbally abused the man, hoping to change his mind. When that didn't work, D'Aranda called over the warrant officer, assuming he would take his side in the matter. Instead, he supported the sailmaker's refusal. Furious now, D'Aranda ordered the sailmaker to sign a document—which, incidentally he could not read because he was illiterate—stating that he had disobeyed the orders of a superior. Cowed into submission, the sailmaker placed an X next to his name.

After the warrant officer told Philip Browne, captain of the *Hermes*, what had transpired, the captain accused D'Aranda of meddling with the crew. D'Aranda protested, which only made Browne angrier. According to D'Aranda, the captain let loose with a barrage "of the most opprobrious language which was ever uttered in the hearing of a man." Browne then called all the parties involved, and, after hearing each person present his version, he exploded, being particularly outraged that the sailmaker had been coerced to sign a document he couldn't even read. Browne ordered D'Aranda confined to his cabin, effectively placing him under arrest.

Many other serious problems occurred on the *Hermes* voyage, including one altercation that ended up forcing Browne to endure a court-martial after the ship docked in Plymouth on March 31, 1814. D'Aranda, too, was brought up on charges for his behavior. The Royal Navy ultimately court-martialed Browne, but it was later overturned. As for D'Aranda, the charges against him were dropped. He was released from custody and allowed to go home to London.

THE *NANINA*, IN A convoy, departed Rio on February 6, 1814, with Marsh remaining in charge as prize master. Its voyage was as eventful and dramatic as that of the *Hermes*. At one point, Edward Grimmit, a seaman with a long history of making trouble, tangled with Marsh, striking him twice. The second blow sent Marsh running to his cabin to retrieve his dirk, a long-bladed dagger. Upon returning to the main deck, Marsh told Grimmit, "[I]f you hit me again, I'll run you through." Hit he did, and Marsh kept his word, thrusting the dirk into Grimmit twice—once in the groin and once in the back. Four days later, he succumbed to his wounds. Back in England come spring, Marsh was court-martialed, but the verdict was "not guilty," on account of Grimmit's mutinous conduct.

WITH THE *NANINA* GONE, and no viable means of saving his son, Valentine made his way back to the States "after much vexation and difficulty," catching rides on various American ships, his progress slowed by the ongoing war. He arrived in Thomaston, Maine, on November 23, made his way to New York a few days later, and immediately visited the offices of John B. Murray and Son, where he told them the entire story from start to finish. If the Murrays, Valentine, or any other of the captains who had been aboard the *Nanina* attempted to lobby for Charles and his companions, or to launch a rescue effort to retrieve them, there is no record of their having done so. Such an effort would have been quite expensive and difficult to mount, especially with the United States just coming to the end of the very costly and fatiguing War of 1812 and the Treaty of Ghent still months away from being signed. From a purely financial perspective, it would be hard to justify spending so much money to potentially save just five men, only two of whom were American. And even if the humanitarian impulse were added to the balance, it is not at all clear that any men living in the Age of Sail—when so many mariners lost their lives while doing their jobs—would argue that compassion or the welfare of a few men engaged in an inherently dangerous business should trump financial concerns. The prospect of success, no doubt, also argued against rescue. It had been seventeen months since the hunting party had been abandoned. Given that amount of time, it was not unreasonable to assume that they had perished. Even if they hadn't, it would not only take months to prepare a rescue mission but also take quite a few more to sail to the Falklands. By the time another vessel arrived, given the best scenario, two years might have elapsed, making survival an even less likely possibility.

Of course, neither Valentine and the other captains, nor the Murrays, had any idea what had actually happened to Charles and his companions. Had they known, they would have been amazed and impressed.

Routine, Then Deceit

===

SOON AFTER BARNARD, GREEN, LOUDER, ANSELL, AND ALBROOK SETTLED ON Swan Island at the end of July 1813, they established a schedule of duties necessary to sustain them. With their trousers, shirts, and jackets worn and ripped, and their shoes in an equally poor state, there was an immediate need to replace them. Two men, therefore, were assigned responsibility for procuring seals and transforming their skins into clothing. Because food was the most pressing and constant need, two other men, with Cent's assistance, were tasked with hunting. The last man was to stay near the boat and cook, and also keep an eye on the harbor across the way at New Island, in case any ships arrived. To ensure that all the duties were borne equally, the men switched positions every day. All of them would also periodically collect driftwood, vines,* and dried tussac grass to fuel their fires, as well as plants for nourishment.

In short order, about fifty seals were killed and skinned, and the clothes-making commenced. The beginning of the process was very similar to that used when they were procuring skins for sale. After stripping the pelt and cutting off the remaining flesh, they would dry the skin

---

* One of the vines that the men made use of, no doubt, was that of the red crowberry. Not only was its small red fruit edible, but it was great for building fires. According to British botanist Joseph Dalton Hooker, who visited the Falklands in 1842, "The stems and leafy branches are much used for fuel in the Falklands, where the plant is called 'Diddle-dee', they are especially employed in kindling fire, for even when sodden with rain, they speedily ignite, and burn with a bright and hot flame." Joseph Dalton Hooker, *The Botany of the Antarctic Voyage of H.M. Discovery Ships* Erebus and Terror *in the Years 1839–1843* (London: Reeve, Brothers, 1844), 345.

Charles H. Barnard, depicted in Charles Ellms, Robinson Crusoe's Own Book; or, The Voice of Adventure, *1843.*

by laying it out in the open when the weather was clear, and bringing it under the boat when it rained or snowed. The dry and stiffened skins would be massaged, rolled, and rubbed with stones to make them more pliable. Then they were cut to order, the size and shape of the resulting pieces dictated by the type of clothes they were producing—a pair of trousers, a coat, a vest, a shirt, a cap, or moccasins.* To bind the pieces together, the men used sail-needles and thread from a large ball of twine, both of which they had fortunately brought with them from the *Nanina.* When the twine ran out, which it did in the coming months, they began cutting small strips from the mainsail, which was made of light duck, a relatively thin cotton canvas. Those strips were then raveled into thread. The clothes they produced were much more comfortable and warmer

---

* An American sealer described the process of making these moccasins on the Falklands as follows: "Our shoes were not expensive here as we generally wore moccasins, taking green [untanned and dried] seal skin, put a foot on it and cut around it, sew up the heel and run a string around the toe, which draws it up, and tie it on the instep. By walking it becomes leathered and soft to the foot." Townsend, "The Diary of Mr. Ebenezer Townsend, Jr.," 36.

than what they replaced. Charles was so envious of the men in their new outfits that, even though he had brought along a change of clothes still in reasonably good shape, he chose to make a new suit for himself. In addition to clothes, the men also made blankets out of the sealskins. Finally, Charles took the thinner skins from young seals and transformed the inner sides into parchment pages that were sewed together to form a logbook in which he recorded daily events, using a combination of soot and plant juice as ink, and quills from birds, likely geese,* as his stylus. It wasn't only their skins that made the seals so valuable to the men. They were also prized for their blubber, which was used as fuel, and their meat was eaten as well.

Hogs were the main target for the hunting party. Killing them was an exciting and sometimes dangerous endeavor. Upon smelling, seeing, or hearing a hog, Cent raced off in hot pursuit. If it was a pig, or an immature hog, Cent pounced, jaws first, retaining his grip until the men arrived to deliver the coup de grâce—a thrust of a knife or a blow to the head. But if Cent found himself confronting a large sow or boar, he was much more cautious, all too aware that mature hogs had lower and upper teeth, or tusks, that were protruding and pointed, serving as excellent weapons that could severely wound any foe. When dealing with such a formidable opponent, rather than rush in and attack right away, Cent would lock eyes with the hog and stand his ground. Usually, when the men arrived and closed in with their clubs raised, the hog would forget about the dog and charge them. That was Cent's cue. The minute the hog turned its attention to the men, Cent clamped his teeth upon whatever part of the hog's body was closest, avoiding the mouth. The ensuing battle could last ten to fifteen minutes. Sometimes the hog's wild gyrations flung Cent into the air. But, back into the fray he would go, seizing the hog again. All the while, the men would be hitting the hog with their clubs, trying to land a blow on the small of the back, where it often had the most crippling effect. When the hog was beaten down enough, or thoroughly exhausted, one of the men would go in close and smash its skull or plunge in the knife, multiple times if necessary.

Hogs used to be evenly distributed throughout Swan Island. The men soon discovered, however, that the ones that remained had relo-

---

* According to Pease, there is "no better quill written with than the Falkland Island geese quills." See Barzillai Pease Journals, Journal 13, 21.

cated to the opposite side from where they made camp, perhaps because
the side closest to New Island was the one most frequented by sealers.
This forced the men to hike 8 or 9 miles in order to find their quarry, the
path taking them over hills, across valleys, and through streams in good
weather and bad, the latter of which kept their feet and lower legs perpetually wet. In order to make the hogs easier to transport back to camp,
they were dressed in the field. Their heads and their entrails, except for
the liver, were left behind. Considerably lighter now, the fore and hind
legs were tied together, and the carcass was flung over someone's shoul-
der for the return hike.

Whether a boar or a sow, the hogs were fast and relatively skinny, a
combination that made them lean, with only a thin layer of fat. Hence,
the meat tasted more like venison than beef. According to Charles, it provided a "very light diet, easy of digestion, which leaves a vacancy in the
stomach that gives rise to unpleasant feelings, which it requires another
meal to remove."

Besides killing hogs, the men sometimes downed birds, but they
didn't have the option of shooting them. While they had a gun and a
few charges of powder, their ammunition was gone, having been used up
during their first couple of days on Beaver Island. Instead, they obtained
birds either by flinging their clubs at them or grabbing them if they came
in close.

During one group foray for food, that day's designated hunters and
sealers came upon a large old sea lion, sleeping in among the tussac grass
a considerable distance from the water. The men wanted to kill it both for
its blubber and its thick skin, which made for very sturdy moccasins. But
there was a problem. They had inadvertently left their only lance back at
Hook Camp on July 1, when they were in the midst of their failed attempt
to reach Eagle Island. Without that lance—the usual means of attacking
a large sea lion—they were not sure they could dispatch it. All they had
were clubs and skinning knives. They knew that a club to the head of
a seal this large would infuriate it but not kill it. Furthermore, getting
close enough to inflict such a blow would be very dangerous, placing the
attacker in jeopardy of being crushed under the sea lion's great bulk or
bitten by its massive jaw, which is studded with large and pointed canine
teeth. Alternatively, using a skinning knife in close quarters would subject the assailant to the same risks.

To prepare himself for battle, Charles lashed his knife to the end of

Charles and his companions' perilous encounter with a sea lion, depicted in Charles Ellms, Robinson Crusoe's Own Book; or, The Voice of Adventure, *1843.*

a club, making an ersatz lance that, while hardly ideal, put a little more distance between man and beast than would have been the case if only the club or knife were used. The other men loaded up on rocks. The plan was for Charles to sneak up on the sleeping beast and thrust his club-lance under one of its flippers, hoping to reach the heart and inflict a mortal wound. Simultaneous to the thrust, the other men would hurl their stones at the sea lion's eyes, attempting to blind it. This would keep the creature from seeing the water and making its escape, which would, in turn, give Charles more time to stab the seal multiple times, until the life was drained from its body.

Things didn't work out exactly as planned. The makeshift lance barely injured the seal since its skin and blubber were too thick. It did, however, enrage the animal. The bloodied seal reared up and thrashed about, ripping up nearby clumps of tussac grass in its fury. Then it made for the water. But the rock throwers' aim was true, and the animal was blinded before it got too far, giving Charles the opportunity to drive home the knife numerous times. Eventually, the loss of blood became so great that the seal died, and the men then stripped it of its skin and blubber.

Obtaining food was one thing, but safeguarding it was another. Almost as soon as they arrived, the men's camp—really just their boat at

John James Audubon's drawing
of the brown or Norway rat, circa 1845–48.

the moment—was overrun by rats, which were such a nuisance that the
men called their temporary abode "Rat Camp." To protect their stores,
the men tried a number of stratagems, but, as Charles observed, the rats'
"sagacity in committing their felonies was greater than ours in prevent-
ing them." Finally, they got the better of their rodent foes by making
their food inaccessible to the four-legged poachers. They lashed three
oars together, creating a tripod, with a high point in the center. Then
they used the boat's painter* to haul the meat off the ground. The final
touch was to grease the lower reaches of the oars with seal blubber so that
the rats would fail to gain purchase. This solution came none too soon,
because before instituting the new plan, there were times when almost
an entire hog carcass was stripped bare by the swarming rats in a single
night of ravenous feasting.

---

*   This is the rope that is typically attached to the bow of a small boat and used to tie up
or tow the boat.

Southern elephant seal pup,
New Island

Adult male sea lion,
New Island

Adult male Southern
elephant seal with
newborn pup,
New Island

*Adult male sea
lion roaring,
New Island*

*Adult pair of striated
caracaras, New Island*

Black-browed albatross pair, New Island

Southern fur seal mother and pup, New Island

Landsend Bluff with nesting black-browed albatrosses, New Island

Settlement rookery cliffs in stormy weather, New Island

*Settlement rookery with tussac grass in the foreground and
black-browed albatrosses beyond, New Island*

*A view of Grand Cliff on New Island, with Beaver Island in
the distance, all under a canopy of asperitas clouds*

A view of New Island, showing Grand Cliff, South Hill, and Tigre Harbor

Cliff Peak on New Island (also called Queen Victoria Peak)

Cathedral Cliffs on New Island, looking to the northeast

Wild celery on New Island, with a view of Saddle Island in the distance

Stormy seas near Stanley, the capital city on East Falkland Island

A patch of sea cabbage on the beach along South Harbor, with the West Cliffs in the distance, New Island

COME LATE SEPTEMBER, the men headed to New Island. Whaling and sealing ships used the island for replenishing water supplies, so being on the island would give them a better chance of contacting visitors, as opposed to remaining on Swan Island and then rowing or sailing over to New Island whenever they saw a ship. New Island also had a healthy seal rookery, along with an albatross colony, and the birds were about to start laying eggs, giving the men a chance to expand their diet.

By early October, they had set up their new camp on the edge of Hooker's Harbor. Their first venture was to visit the albatrosses, each man carrying a sealskin bag to collect the eggs. The species they were planning to pillage was the black-browed albatross (or mollymawk). They are strikingly beautiful birds, the female of which lays only a single white egg each year, about as large as a goose's. Their nests are around 15 to 20 inches high and composed primarily of mud and guano interspersed with tussac grass and seaweed. Although not the largest albatross species, they are a very sizable bird, weighing up to 10 pounds or more, with a wingspan than can reach nearly 8 feet. The Falkland Islands currently have the largest concentration of black-browed albatrosses, comprising about 70 percent of the global population, or around a half-million pairs.

Rookery cliffs on the west side of New Island.

Black-browed albatross with chick on nest.

Black-browed albatross rookery on West Falkland Island.

When visiting the Falklands in 1800, the American mariner Amasa Delano found himself fascinated by these birds:

> To stand at a little distance and observe all their movements, was worthy the contemplation of a great mind. The observer would see them going round the outside walk, in pairs, fours, sixes, and

different numbers in a company, appearing like officers or soldiers walking on a parade, whilst the camp or rookery seemed to be in continual motion, some going through the alleys to their mates, while others were coming out. To view all that was doing, and the regularity in which it was performed, appeared incredible, when we consider that it was effected by no higher a rank of animals than birds.

On their first trip, the castaways collected six eggs. A few days later, they returned with many more, and had a "noble feast." Collecting the eggs was tricky. The males and females take turns incubating the egg, with one of them always on duty. They are very protective and wield their sharp beaks very effectively, biting when threatened. On more than one occasion in the ensuing months, the men sustained wounds to their hands while in the process of pilfering.

ON OCTOBER 10, 1813—exactly 119 days after the hunting party was abandoned—Charles decided to visit Sea Lion Point at the south end of the island to kill some sea lions. It seemed like a good idea. When Charles asked for volunteers to join him, Green and Louder bowed out, saying that it was their turn to gather vines to feed the fire. Albrook said it was his "cook day," and Ansell said he wanted to mend his trousers. With no takers, Charles decided to go himself, but before doing so, he crawled under the overturned boat and spent a few minutes sharpening his knife. When he emerged, he grabbed a club and called for Cent, who didn't show up. This puzzled Charles, so he asked Albrook whether he knew where the dog was. Albrook suggested that he probably went with Green and Louder, who had just left on their search for vines. Since the two had gone in the opposite direction from that which Charles wanted to head, he said he would wait for their return because he needed Cent to flush out the seals from among the clumps of tussac grass. Hearing this, Ansell jumped up, saying he would go. Charles repeated that Cent was needed, whereupon Ansell replied, "Oh, if there is any there, I will hunt them up."

Charles relented, and off the two went. They skirted a hill and entered a valley that was like a tussac obstacle course, with clumps growing in a jumbled pattern, forcing the men to weave through and around them.

The two talked while they walked, often not seeing each other, since the tall grass blocked their views. Barnard was speaking as he exited the valley onto an open plain, and he waited for Ansell to appear. He didn't. Charles called out. No answer.

A combination of panic and anger swept over him. Fearing some treachery, Charles quickly retraced his steps. When he rounded the hill, he could see the boat pushing off from the beach, with all the men on board. He placed his hat on the top of his club, waving it about and screaming, but the men took no notice. When he arrived at the camp, he found no note explaining this precipitous flight. Worse still, they had taken everything of value, including a blanket, sewing needles, tinder, flints, fouling gun, his clothes, a powder horn, and four charges of powder, the last of which he had been carefully saving for lighting a fire if all other methods failed. Also gone was an array of dried fur-seal skins that he was planning to use to make more clothes. But what crushed his spirits more than anything else was that they had taken Cent.

Charles's greatest immediate concern was keeping the fire going, because if that was lost, he wasn't sure he would be able to generate another one. There were still a few embers glowing, so he fed the fire with dried tussac grass and vines, plus one of his shirtsleeves. With the fire saved, he considered the cruelness of this turn of events: being abandoned for a second time, and by people with whom he thought he shared a bond of friendship, or, at least, reliance. "By thus depriving me of every necessary article," Charles later reflected, "it appeared evident that they expected I could not survive long, if destitute of everything, and that they wished my existence at an end."

Alone

═══

AFTER TENDING TO THE FIRE AND GETTING OVER THE SHOCK OF BEING abandoned in such a heartless manner, Charles turned to the task of providing for himself and making the best of a very bad situation. In the coming days, he built himself a small shelter out of rocks, turf, and tussac grass. He also gathered a large stockpile of dried grass and vines, which he used to keep the fire alive. And even though he had been kicked out of the Hudson Quaker Meeting, he was still a religious man, and on more than one occasion he prayed to God for strength and fortitude to survive this ordeal.

A few days after being abandoned, Charles remembered that while walking along the beach a week or two earlier, he had seen at low tide an old tin pot with a hole in its bottom. It had been used by the men as a bailer in the boat, but it was discarded when it could no longer serve that purpose. Charles returned to the spot and retrieved the pot. Turning up its edges and pushing in its sides, he created a serviceable pan, which he thereafter used to cook albatross eggs, his only sustenance for many days.

Charles knew that his reliance on eggs would not last long. The egg-laying season is roughly from late September through October, and, once laid, the eggs are incubated for about seventy days. At some point during the egg's development, it is no longer good to eat. So, in his race against time, Charles made as many as four trips a day to the colony, bringing back many eggs. During each excursion, he was under surveillance. Dozens of Johnny Rooks would fly overhead, looking for a chance to steal an egg, while others were on the ground, with the same intention.

*Charles annoyed by rooks (striated caracaras),
as depicted in Charles Ellms,* Robinson Crusoe's Own
Book; or, The Voice of Adventure, *1843.*

The persistent hawks followed him back to his hut, so Charles employed defensive measures to protect his egg hoard. He arranged a few eggs at a time, on their ends, and then covered them with dried grass and soil taken from the bases of tussac clumps. He repeated this process as many times as necessary to secure all of the eggs he collected. But, despite this, the wily birds would take every opportunity to swoop down and start digging with their beaks and talons to uncover the eggs, puncture them, and slurp out the contents. Fortunately for Charles, they were not entirely successful in their raids, leaving a good number of eggs behind, unmolested. Still, Charles grew to hate the rooks, viewing them as annoying competitors, and he sometimes spent almost the entire day throwing rocks at them to keep them away.

Even while Charles was terrorizing the rooks, he continued to focus on his need for rescue. So, just as the survivors of the *Isabella* had done, he erected a signal pole designed to capture the attention of any passing ships. He didn't have the benefit of spars and masts, but he did have a very small tree, about 12 feet tall and as thick as a man's arm. During their stay on Swan Island, the men had found it washed up on the shore. They had brought it with them, intending to carve it into new clubs to replace those that had broken or split after being brought down on the hard skulls of so many seals and hogs. Charles carved his name and the date into the pole, and he took strips of skin from a seal he had recently clubbed to death and tied them to the top of the pole, creating a furry flag of sorts. He planted the pole on a small rise not far from the hut. Every morning, he visited the pole and carved a notch into it, each one indicating the passage of another day. To keep better track of the weeks, the notches for Sunday were longer than all the rest, and thus more readily seen and counted.

ONE DAY, WHILE GATHERING vines on a hillside, Charles found a place where they grew in profusion. Casting down his club, he began pulling them up and throwing them into a pile. He had planned to use the seal-skin string attached to the club to tie the vines together, making it easier to carry them back to camp. But when he went to retrieve his club, it was gone. A search of the area turned up nothing. This was indeed alarming. The only thing that made it slightly less so was that he had recently discovered another club, which had been left behind by one of the *Nanina*'s crew many months earlier, before the Americans knew anything about the *Isabella*.

Charles returned to his shelter, the bundle of vines in his arms, and cooked yet another egg dinner. While eating, he heard a piercing noise very close by, like the screeching of a cat. Investigating, he spotted a large owl, probably a barn owl, that was perched upon the edge of the shelter, on top of the tussac grass that formed the roof. Charles grabbed his club and approached the bird, which, instead of flying off, just continued screeching at regular intervals. Standing right next to the bird, Charles took a swing. But instead of losing its life, the agile owl latched onto the club with its talons. Grabbing a nearby rock, Charles hit the owl in the head with a powerful blow. Victorious, he reveled in the silence and then went to bed.

A few days later, club in hand, Charles returned to the place he dubbed Fairy Hill,* where some unknown creature had absconded with his origi-

---

* Modern-day Barnard's Hill.

nal club. Despite what had happened before, he put down the club and proceeded to collect vines, frequently looking around to see whether there was any animal that might snatch this one too. He extended his search radius to about 30 feet, and when he returned to where he had left his club, it too had disappeared. Charles frantically searched the area, to no avail. He then "began to believe [that this place] was the residence of some evil genius, who thus punished me for invading his retreat." But there was no supernatural being or enchantress at work. The reason for the loss was more prosaic. While descending the hill, carrying the vines, Charles looked up at the Johnny Rooks flying overhead. There it was. Holding onto the club was one of the birds, its talons hooked onto the iron ring that sealers placed around the larger end to keep the wood from splitting. After pelting the thief with stones, and watching it drop the club, Charles rescued it and continued on his way. From then on, he kept his club close by.

EVERY MIDDAY, AFTER COLLECTING vines, tussac grass, various plants, and driftwood, Charles climbed to the highest point on the island and gazed in every direction, in hopes of spotting a sail in the distance. On October 24, while thus engaged, his mind wandered to thoughts of the real-life Robinson Crusoe, Alexander Selkirk. In the early 1700s, this

Barn owl, New Island.

Map labels: Landsend Bluff, Cathedral Cliffs, Settlement Rookery, Ship Harbor (Coffin), Barnard's Hill, South Cliff, Hookers Harbor (Settlement), Cliff Peak, Grand Cliff, South Hill, Sea Lion Point, NEW ISLAND, 0 1 2 Miles

British sailor spent four years and four months alone on the island of Más a Tierra,* located in the Pacific about 400 miles from the Chilean coast. Charles recalled a poem written by British poet William Cowper, which the latter imagined Selkirk himself might have written had he had a lyrical bent. The opening stanza reads:

> I am monarch of all I survey,
> My right there is none to dispute;
> From the center all round to the sea,
> I am lord of the fowl and the brute.
> O Solitude! where are the charms,
> That sages have seen in thy face?

---

* Modern-day Robinson Crusoe Island.

Robinson Crusoe,
from the 1720 French
version of Daniel
Defoe's book by
the same name.

> *Better dwell in the midst of alarms,*
> *Than reign in this horrible place.*

Charles then mused on his predicament as compared to Selkirk's:

> My similarity of situation to that of the celebrated Selkirk extended
> only to a few particulars; the difference was all in his favor. He
> voluntarily landed on the beautiful island of Juan Fernandez,*
> situated in a delightful climate, . . . [His life was] uninterrupted
> by the roaring of the wintry winds, the nipping frosts, snow and
> hail falling on a body weakened by the want of sufficient food,
> and only protected by tattered garments; [and I had] a shelter, or

---

* Juan Fernández is the South Pacific archipelago that includes three islands, the second largest of which is Robinson Crusoe Island, formerly known as Más a Tierra, which
is where Selkirk spent more than four years in isolation.

rather an imitation of one, that could neither exclude nor with-stand the fury of the storms of these tempestuous latitudes. . . . . He was landed with all his clothes, and fully supplied from the ship with every article that could contribute to his comfort and secu-rity. I at first was most scantily furnished, and of that scanty sup-ply I was deprived, by treachery and ingratitude, to the last flint, and compelled, sorely against my will, to remain on a rocky island.

Charles's claim that Selkirk had an easy time of it is way off the mark—for example, Selkirk was not particularly well supplied when dropped off on the island. Also, after first asking to remain on the island rather than continue on board the ship *Cinque Ports* because he feared it was in danger of sinking due to wood rot, Selkirk changed his mind and asked to rejoin the crew, only to be rebuffed by the captain, who viewed him as a mutineer.* Nevertheless, it is not surprising that Charles compared his situation to the man who inspired Daniel Defoe to write *Robinson Crusoe*, a fictional tale about a man who spends twenty-eight years as a castaway. Both Charles and Selkirk faced exceedingly trying circumstances.

Charles also took some measure of comfort from Selkirk's story: "And as his misfortunes and exile were terminated by a happy deliverance from this island, hope cheered me by intimating, that as my fate in some mea-sure resembled his, it might please the Almighty, in his own good time, to convert my sorrows into joys."

The following day, Charles's thirty-second birthday, was a milestone that "gave rise to many melancholy reflections," as he contrasted his cur-rent miserable situation with the times he had spent at home, surrounded by his family and friends, sharing hearty meals and good cheer. He did, however, receive a valuable birthday present, so to speak, which consid-erably brightened his day and improved his prospects for survival.

To take his mind off his misfortune, Charles decided to do some test-ing. Walking along the beach, he picked up various rocks and struck them with the spine of his knife, trying to generate a spark that might be sufficient to light tinder on fire. One rock delivered just what he was look-ing for, and that removed the dread of losing his tenderly tended fire. To

---

* After abandoning Selkirk, the *Cinque Ports* continued on its mission of plundering Spanish ships, but it soon succumbed to the very threat Selkirk had feared. Leaky and unseaworthy, it sank off the coast of Peru, and everyone who survived was promptly thrown into a Spanish prison.

better ensure that the fires he lit were well protected from the wind, he built a low rock wall to surround his cooking area.

A few days later, Charles made another discovery that was even more propitious. While exploring a hillside covered in burned-over clumps of tussac grass, he could see that the fire had eaten into the boggy surface of the ground, creating deep holes, or burn pits. The walls of the holes had partially collapsed, exposing something that looked familiar. In Wales, Barnard had seen peat, which he knew burned brightly and gave off considerable heat, almost as much as coal. Looking at the material before him at that moment, he surmised that it was peat. He took some to his fire and learned to his delight that his notion was correct. Quickly returning to the hillside, he collected more fuel. Now he had an abundant and, from his perspective, inexhaustible source of fuel that eliminated his fears of being able to survive the cold winter months.

His heating and cooking problems solved, Barnard started building himself a sturdier and larger hut, this one made out of stone, with a shielded fire pit inside. It was laborious work, as many of the rocks had to be brought from quite a distance. The project also necessitated the killing of more seals, whose skins would be used to make the dwelling's roof. The hut measured roughly 9 by 7 feet; its walls were about 5 feet high and from 3 to 4 feet thick.

In mid-November, Charles visited the potato patch, the same one from which he had taken fifteen "fine ones" the previous June and gifted them to Joanna-Ann Durie and Mary Ann Spencer. The mere thought of that magnanimous gesture to people who ultimately abandoned him upset Charles. But he hadn't come to revisit old wounds. Instead, he wanted food. Unfortunately, all he found this day were three small potatoes, each the size of a pigeon's egg. He even viewed that pitiful bounty in a favorable light, for he could use them as seed potatoes, which he hoped would yield a bigger crop in the future—should it be his misfortune to remain on the island for many more months or even years.

Charles continued to fill the long days by working on his hut, gathering fuel, scanning the horizon, killing the occasional seal, and spending a lot of time letting his mind wander. He often thought about what might have become of his erstwhile companions who deserted him. Given the dangerous rip tides that were particularly bad around the time of year they had departed, it was certainly possible that their boat had overturned, and they had perished. However, Jacob Green was a talented sailor who had spent a considerable amount of time in the Falklands, so, perhaps his skills and judgment would have spared them that fate. Charles's anger at being abandoned yet again was tinged with great sadness:

> I began to feel so very solitary, and time moved so slowly on leaden wings, that bad as they were, I wished for the return of the men. Company, even were it that of a savage, like Crusoe's Friday, or that of my poor faithful dog, would have been a great comfort to me; as it would sometimes amuse my attention, and prevent my thoughts from dwelling so continually on my forlorn situation and distant home. In this solitary state, agitated by hopes and fears, wishes and anticipations, I continued performing my customary daily labor.

ALSO IN NOVEMBER, CHARLES'S diet improved somewhat when the rock-hopper penguins began laying eggs, each pair producing two that are about the size of a chicken's egg. He collected the penguin eggs and took them back to his hut, where he arranged them on their ends and covered them. Every six days, Charles uncovered them and flipped them over, in

Rockhopper penguins, adult pair, New Island.

order to keep the yolk from settling through the white and spoiling the egg. Unlike albatross eggs, which went bad within weeks no matter what Charles did, the penguin eggs, if properly rotated, could last for months, providing Barnard with a calorie-cushion of sorts.

Having many hours during the day, and not that many tasks to perform, Charles took to observing the natural world around him. He found penguins particularly fascinating. Watching them race through the surf and run the gauntlet of sea lions was to witness a great life-or-death struggle. Charles often saw "the lions swimming with their heads above water, and with their rapacious jaws distended, among those poor, defenseless little birds, dealing destruction, and enclosing within a living tomb all that were within the deadly circle." Even after the penguins made it back to shore, their trials were not over, for caracaras would lie in wait, ready to swoop in and pick off wounded birds and make a meal of them.

On the fourteenth of December, while on his daily perambulation and appointment at the top of the highest hill, Charles saw large plumes of smoke rising from Beaver Island. Given the size of the plumes, he knew that this was not coming from a solitary fire. Some person or persons had to have set the tussac grass ablaze. He thought it was probably the men who had deserted him, or perhaps, hope against hope, it was men from the *Young Nanina*—maybe they had not left after all. Charles realized how unlikely this last possibility was, but he held onto it nonetheless.

That evening, even though the wind was wild enough that a boat would have a difficult time getting to New Island from Beaver Island, Charles made a large peat fire on the beach as a signal. Unable to sleep, worried about who or what could possibly come, he wandered back and forth much of the night. The following morning, the wind had become much more favorable, raising Charles's expectation that he might soon have visitors. He increased the size of the fire on the beach and spent hours on the nearby hill looking toward Beaver Island, where smoke was still rising. Finally, exhausted from his vigil the previous night, Charles fell asleep, only to be awakened by a rook attempting to steal his moccasins right off his feet. Alert again, he continued his vigil until nightfall.

As another day passed, still with no arrival, Charles became wary. Perhaps his former companions had sailed over during the night, landing in another harbor or cove beyond Charles's range of vision. If so, maybe they were there not to reunite, but to attack him. While these thoughts were racing through his head, and he was cooking eggs for dinner, he heard a noise, "like the snapping of a gun." Startled, he jumped up and looked around. Nothing. A few minutes later, he heard it again. Thinking that the men could be concealed behind nearby clumps of grass, Charles did a search. Still nothing. Turning back to his meal, the sound came a third time. Looking around the inside of his hut, suddenly he figured it out. A pair of spoons he had made out of twigs and shells and hung on a pin sticking out of the wall, were clanking against one another with every gust of wind.

Despite finding the cause of the noise, Charles remained worried that his former companions, or possibly even the people on the *Young Nanina*, were stalking him. To "banish or confirm . . . [his] suspicions" on the morning of December 17, Charles walked to the south end of the island to look around. That afternoon, after finding no sign of any human being and once again feeling despondent, he returned to his hut. Then, while cooking eggs, he looked up and saw a boat coming around a point of rocks, about a mile away.

Reconciliation

===

THE BOAT LANDED NEAR THE MOUTH OF THE HARBOR, ABOUT A HALF-MILE from Charles's hut. At that distance, he couldn't identify who had arrived, but there were four of them. The passengers got out of the boat for a few minutes, then got back in and shoved off, rowing to the middle of the harbor, where they laid on their oars, apparently to consider their next move. Then they began rowing again, toward Charles, who finally recognized his former companions. When they were about 20 yards off the beach, they stopped and remained silent, just staring at him. Cent, upon seeing his master, became agitated and tried to jump off the boat to get to shore, but Ansell held him tight.

Charles asked them why they didn't come ashore. "We wish to land," James Louder replied, "but are fearful that we have so offended you, that you do not want us to rejoin you. We have put a hog ashore for you on the point, with some old newspapers that I picked up at the wreck, as I had often heard you wish that you had some books or papers to read." Charles answered, "Let my dog come ashore, and you may go where you please with the boat; but, if you do not land him and my gun, you may depend upon it that, if ever a ship arrives, you will be made to repent of your late infamous conduct." Louder and Joseph Albrook chimed in that they wanted to land and live with him once again, and they hoped he would forgive them for what they had done. Replying that he would forgive them, Charles bade them to come ashore.

As the men began pulling for the beach, Samuel Ansell—who, Charles later learned, had the most reasons to repent—said, "I hope you will for-

Return of the deserters, engraved by T. R. Whitney,
in Charles H. Barnard's narrative of his experiences in the Falklands, 1829.

give me, captain, as well as the others?" Charles replied, "You are four, and, if it is not your choice to land, let my dog come, and you may go to any other place; I can get my living alone as well as with company; and last winter I instructed you how to get yours, and prevented you all from perishing. If you desire to remain here, I am agreed, but do not wish to control you, neither shall I refer to what is past, unless you commence the subject." Amenable to those conditions, the four men hopped out of the boat, and each "cheerfully" shook Charles's hands. With that, his sixty-nine days of isolation came to an end.

It surprised Charles to learn that they had visited the *Isabella* wreck, and now he learned more details. Nobody was there, the men said. The *Nancy*, the *Nanina*, and the *Young Nanina* were gone. A letter that the four "had found in a bottle, was left," Charles noted, "to induce a belief that every possible search had been made for us, and that it was therefore concluded that we were lost." They reported that a number of items were strewn around the old camp, from which they had brought some newspapers, plain paper, canvas that was later converted into thread for sewing sealskin clothes, and some rags that were used for tinder. At least they all were now certain that the vessels had left the Falklands.

The men were quite impressed with Charles's hut and surprised to see such a roaring fire, inquiring whether he had found coal. Charles told them about the peat and also showed them the potato vines that were beginning to sprout from the seed potatoes he had planted just weeks earlier. The men also congratulated Charles on the great supply of vines and eggs he had collected.

Since it was the season when fur seals were giving birth to their pups, the men decided to go on a hunting trip to North Island, about 8 miles away. Pup skins, very soft and pliable, were excellent for making blankets, that being their plan. North Island is small and almost entirely encircled with towering cliffs that would not allow them to land or even jump ashore. There was one area, however, that Charles knew quite well, where part of the cliffs had tumbled down, creating a jumbled expanse of large rocks frequented by seals. They reared their young in the hollows between the rocks, which offered considerable protection.

Louder and Ansell had volunteered to be left in this relatively exposed place for two days to hunt seals, while the other two men went back to New Island to do the same. Maneuvering the boat close enough to the

Cliffs on the north side of New Island.

rocks so the two men could jump off was incredibly risky, and it took all of the men's skills to keep the boat from smashing against the rocks. In addition to clubs, Louder and Ansell carried a keg of water and some cooked meat.

Not long after Charles and Jacob Green left their companions behind, the aspect of the water and sky began to change. Large swells were building, and dark clouds were scudding in. Leaving Louder and Ansell in their exposed position, with a storm approaching, would be the equivalent of letting them die. They couldn't climb up the steep cliffs to escape, so they would most certainly be crushed to death or drowned by the pounding waves. Hence, even before they had made it back to New Island, Charles and Green turned around to retrieve the others. Although they had been hunting only a few hours, Louder and Ansell had already killed five seals. Charles and Green, in yet another display of great seamanship, pulled the boat in close, managing to retrieve not only the men but also the dead seals. Then they beat a fast retreat to their camp on New Island.

IN NEED OF SKINS to make clothes and to shore up the hut's roof, Ansell, Albrook, and Green set out on December 23 to search for seals at the north end of the island. Louder remained behind, as it was his day to cook. Charles stayed busy dressing skins and sewing new clothes. While the hunting party was away, he learned some disturbing information.

Explanation

==

CHARLES HAD LONG WONDERED WHY THE OTHER MEN HAD DESERTED HIM. Now he pressed Louder for an answer. Becoming visibly uncomfortable, Louder told Charles that he couldn't share the information, because just a day earlier, while he, Albrook, and Ansell were skinning seals, Ansell had said that if either Louder or Albrook ever breathed a word about the trip to the wreck, or about why the men left Charles behind, he would kill them. Louder told Charles that he had better be careful, because Ansell was a dangerous man, and he had "formed some bad design against" him.

Charles persisted. He told Louder that, having shared this much, he should tell the rest of the story. Only with that information, Charles said, could he know how best to fight back against anything Ansell might attempt to do to him or any of the others. To allay Louder's concerns further, Charles promised that what Louder told him in confidence would never become known by Ansell, "unless he attempts to carry his threats into execution," and then Charles would protect Louder. Reassured, Louder then related the saga.

It was, Louder said, all Ansell's idea. He believed that the *Nanina* had left the Falklands without first returning to the wreck site. As a result, if they went to Eagle Island, they could get more supplies and also pick up prostitute and ex-convict Elizabeth Davis, whom Ansell fancied. Once they had done that, they would rejoin Charles on New Island, where they could all wait in relative comfort for the arrival of a ship. Despite the fact that Ansell's assumption that the *Nanina* would just take off like that seems more than a little implausible—given that the British on board had demanded that the Americans fulfill the agreement by going directly back to the wreck—Louder, Albrook, and Green didn't question it. According to Louder, "Without reflection, we thought that all he proposed was practicable and so very easy, that we almost considered it accomplished." And off they went. As to why they didn't share this plan with Charles, tell him where they were going, or leave him with anything that he could use to survive, Louder provided no answers.

After abandoning Charles, the four men went to Beaver Island. They remained on the island for three days, killing hogs to build up their food supply. Since Green was the most familiar with the Falklands and sailing its treacherous waters, he was chosen to lead the rest of the expedition.

It took them three weeks to make it to the wreck, and, when they did, their hearts sank. Although they were able to gather some useful items, there was no reunion with Elizabeth or anyone else. A pall descended, and they all became quite depressed—especially Ansell, since it was his idea that had failed so miserably. He "fretted and cried like a vexed child," said Louder. Soon, however, Ansell's depression turned to anger. He needed a target for his rage, and Louder unintentionally provided one.

On their way back to New Island, the men stopped off at Bird Island, about 4 miles off the coast of English Maloon, abreast of the mouth of Port Stephens Harbor. It was an excellent place to collect penguin eggs, and the men went ashore. After gathering enough eggs to sustain them until they reached Beaver Island, Ansell, unprovoked, went into "one of his mad freaks," cursing and raging at the other three. To release or satisfy his anger, Ansell began wildly clubbing penguins to death, leaving corpses in his wake. The three others were disgusted by Ansell's behavior, but they were too afraid to intervene. Louder, however, did say to Albrook that he thought Ansell's actions were exceptionally cruel; the birds had given no offense, and had, instead, provided them with much-needed food.

Overhearing this criticism, Ansell turned his fury toward Louder, rushed at him, and hit him on the head. As Louder crumpled to the ground, Ansell continued the attack, pummeling him. Albrook, no hero, stood mute and didn't intervene, fearing that Ansell's rage would be turned upon him. Green, however, had more courage. To keep Ansell from committing murder, he pulled him away, calmed him down, and urged him to be more forgiving, especially given their perilous situation.

The following day, the men landed on Beaver Island and set fire to the tussac grass. It was smoke from that fire that Charles had seen. On a few occasions, they had tried to make it over to New Island, but each time Ansell stood in the way. He feared that Charles would blame him for the desertion, and he was scared of what Charles might do. One time, when they were about halfway to New Island, Ansell grabbed the helm of the boat. Threatening to put his foot through its bottom, he forced them to go back. During this dramatic turnaround, Ansell exclaimed that he hoped Charles was dead. When the other men asked him why he would wish for such a thing, Ansell replied that if Charles was alive, he would want his greatcoat that he had lent to Ansell, and Ansell didn't want to give it back. Finally, Ansell relented, and the men completed the final leg of their five-week trip back to New Island.

After finishing his tale, Louder reiterated his fear that should it get out that he had told Charles what happened, Ansell would kill him. Charles tried to allay his concern, telling him that if Ansell abused him again, Charles not only would stand up for him but also would maroon Ansell on another island. However, Charles was not only interested in reassuring Louder, he also wanted to create a confrontation to flush Ansell out and bring the situation to a climactic head. To that end, Charles told Louder to stand his ground and refuse to obey Ansell if he tried to treat him like a servant. If Ansell lashed out at Louder's resistance, Charles would intervene. Then, Charles believed, "the affair will soon be decided."

Reprieve, Relapse, and
Return to Eagle Island

===

THAT NIGHT, GREEN, ALBROOK, AND ANSELL RETURNED FROM THEIR HUNT-ing trip with a paltry five sealskins. At dinner, Charles acted as if nothing was wrong, even though he was silently seething. That Ansell had wished him dead just to keep the greatcoat infuriated Charles, especially since Charles had lent it to Ansell in the first place. Nevertheless, Charles kept his anger in check. Rather than ask that his coat be returned, and risk having Ansell shift all of his bile to him, Charles let Ansell have it for the night, as a kind of peace offering. Charles was confident that if Louder stuck to their plan, a quarrel between Ansell and Louder would soon happen. When it did, Charles would try to engineer the situation in a manner that would array everyone against Ansell and end up with his banishment.

After breakfast the next morning, Ansell ordered Louder to wash the sealskins brought in the previous night. "You lazy devil," Ansell added, "you don't do anything unless I tell you." Screwing up his courage, Louder responded, his voice quavering a bit, "I do not expect or want any of your skins; of course I shall not wash them, peg them out to dry, or have anything to do with them: when I want skins, I shall go and get them myself." This refusal, especially from a man who had typically been timid, enraged Ansell. Seizing his club, he rushed toward Louder.

But Charles was ready. He sprang in front of Louder and used his own club to knock Ansell's out of his hands. Charles demanded to know what Ansell was planning to do. "It is my intention," Ansell angrily replied, "to kill that damned rascal who is skulking behind you." To defend himself—and Charles, if need be—Louder picked up his own club. Looking unflinchingly into Ansell's eyes, Charles said in a cool, measured voice that if it really was his intention to murder someone, he should start with him.

This unexpected turn of events stunned Ansell. He assumed that Louder must have told Charles their secret. Turning to Green, Ansell said, "The villainous rascal has sold us." Before letting the accusations go any further, Charles demanded a vote of sorts. He was not sure how Green and Albrook would respond, but he forged ahead, asking all of those who stood with Ansell to go stand by his side, while those who didn't should come to him. Green and Albrook quickly joined Charles and Louder, leaving Ansell alone.

Pleasantly surprised by Albrook's allegiance, Charles said to him, "[H]ow is this? I thought you would choose Ansell for your leader." Albrook replied, "[N]o, captain; I do not like him, but I never dared to mention my dislike of him to you, for fear that he would do me some great injury; for he frequently threatened us all to our faces, that if ever we told you anything, or did not as he ordered us, we should suffer for it; and when you were not present, he would abuse and threaten you." This admission opened a floodgate of complaints by Albrook, Green, and Louder, all directed at Ansell, highlighting his "depravity and savage temper." Rather than continue to put up with this, the three urged Charles to banish Ansell.

Seeing all aligned against him, Ansell began bawling and begged for forgiveness, promising to behave better if the others would just give him a second chance. Charles, moved by the apparent depth of Ansell's contrition, was inclined to accede to this request, but first he had to sound out the others. Charles instructed Ansell to take a walk and return in a little while.

Charles proposed to Louder, Albrook, and Green that they take Ansell at his word and let him stay, but that if he violated his pledge, they would take him to one of the neighboring islands and leave him there. They agreed, and when Ansell returned, he was told of his conditional reprieve. Greatly relieved, he thanked them all profusely, to which Charles responded, "We don't need your thanks, but rather your good behavior from here on out."

———

A FEW DAYS AFTER the confrontation, the entire party hiked about a mile to a favorite sealing place between Cliff Peak and South Cliff, on the western side of the island, where a steep gully cut into the cliffs and ran down to the sea. After clambering down the side of the ravine, over and around rocks and boulders, they found themselves separated from the seals by a fissure carved out by the ocean's ceaseless pounding. To get across this relatively narrow expanse of extremely cold water that violently sloshed back and forth with each rolling wave, Louder took one end of the rope and dove in, soon reaching the other side. Green then jumped in and swam over. Ansell was up next, but he couldn't swim, so Charles fastened him to the middle of the rope. With Louder and Green on one side, and Charles and Albrook on the other, all holding fast to the rope, they slowly pulled Ansell over, holding him so high that he didn't touch the water. Charles then swam over. After that, Albrook tied all of the sealing instruments and some extra clothes to the end of the rope, which was drawn to the opposite side. Finally, Albrook jumped in to join the others.

The sealing was exceptionally good that day. The men killed and skinned 125 pups and adults. They piled the skins at the edge of the chasm and then crossed it in the same manner as before, the only difference being that now they also had to convey all of the skins. By the time they reached the bottom of the gully, it was getting dark, so they left the

Cliffs on the western side of New Island, engraved by T. R. Whitney, in Charles H. Barnard's narrative of his experiences in the Falklands, 1829.

skins behind, climbed to the top of the cliff, repaired to their makeshift camp, ate dinner, and went to sleep.

The next morning, back at the head of the cliff, they tied one end of the rope to a stake pounded into the ground. Taking the other end, each man descended into the gully. Grabbing as many of the rolled-up skins as they could hold, they climbed to the top of the cliff multiple times, using the rope for an assist. Once all of the skins were collected at the top, the men began their even more laborious task: carrying the skins back to the camp. This done, all the skins were placed in a pile. Charles then began the selection round-robin, with each man taking a single skin, and repeating the process until all were claimed. That way, Charles hoped, no disputes would arise over who was responsible for cleaning and drying the skins, as each man would have his own stash to attend to.

A DAY LATER, LOUDER, Albrook, and Green spoke to Charles privately, reporting that Ansell had gone back to his old ways. Specifically, he was being verbally abusive while Charles was out of earshot. Admitting that Ansell had seemed to be in a sulky mood of late, Charles said that he did not doubt what they were telling him. Rather than allow the situation to escalate, Charles wanted to get rid of Ansell once and for all. To that end, the four of them agreed that Charles would propose a trip to Swan Island to capture hogs. Everyone would go except Charles, who would say he was staying behind to be on the lookout for any vessel that might come by. Then, at the island, the coconspirators would contrive a means of leaving Ansell behind.

At eight the next morning, the boat left with the four men on board. Charles busied himself with various chores, all the while hoping that the plan would succeed and worrying that it might not. His biggest fear was that Ansell would realize what was going on, and, in his rage to keep the other three from abandoning him, he might damage the boat.

The following evening, Charles was roused from sleep by somebody or something pulling dried tussac grass from his bedding. He woke with a start, but he relaxed once he saw Louder looking at him. At the same moment, Charles heard Green say, "Jim, come away, you will alarm the captain." It was too late. Charles was up, and Louder couldn't wait to tell him what had happened, so excited was he about their elegant solution to the problem.

The boat had sailed to Quaker Harbor, at the north end of Swan Island, under the guise of picking up some driftwood they had seen on an earlier trip. Ansell was convinced to go gather the wood, while the other three hauled up the boat. As soon as Ansell had gone partway down the beach, the other three put Ansell's things on the shore and shoved off.

Ansell saw the boat in the surf and immediately ran back, frantically screaming for them to stop. He even pulled out his knife and threatened to kill himself. Calling across the water, Louder told Ansell that he shouldn't kill himself, but rather accept that he had brought this punishment upon himself. They promised to return and pick him up when a ship arrived at New Island. Ansell continued to plead, at one point claiming that the island was haunted and that he couldn't survive there for long. The men in the boat told him they felt bad for him, and with that, they sailed away. Before heading back to New Island, though, the men stopped at Beaver Island to kill some hogs.

Charles commended the men on their actions, and while he also felt sorry for Ansell, he was glad they no longer had to fear for their safety. Charles then proposed that, from this point forward, the men would set aside a day during the week when they could cease their labors and spend the time like "Christians and immortal beings," conversing with one another and pursuing spiritual reflection and rest. This new tradition was launched the following Sunday, when Charles read aloud part of a prayer he had found printed in one of the newspapers brought back from Eagle Island.

> O, God, who commands us when we are in trouble to open our hearts and let out our sorrows unto thee in prayer, and does promise to listen with compassion to our humble supplications, give us grace to approach thee; that we offend not in word or deed, take away from us every impatient feeling, silence every unworthy expression; let not our prayer assume the language of complaint, nor our sorrows the character of despair.

According to Charles, the prayer had a most profound effect upon the men. "That a little piece of paper, with only a scrap of a prayer upon it, should produce an impression upon the crew, . . . so as to change the whole tenor of their profanity and thoughtfulness, to a course of devotion and proper sense of their situation, is really a remarkable circumstance at first sight; but it is no less strange than true." In the weeks to come, the men memorized the prayer and repeated it often, providing them some comfort that God was listening and they would soon be delivered from their trials.

WITH ANSELL OUT OF the immediate picture, the rest of the men got along quite well and worked in a coordinated fashion to make their time on the island as pleasant as possible. In early January 1814, Louder, Green, and Albrook approached Charles with a proposal. They wanted to go back to Eagle Island to do a thorough search of the *Isabella* wreck site to gather anything of value they could find. Charles consented, but he insisted that Cent stay with him. Agreed, the three men loaded the boat with the few remaining hogs, got in, and with Charles wishing them well, sailed off, a fine breeze at their back. As they disappeared from sight, Charles mused that he had become "Robinson Crusoe again," but this time it was voluntary isolation.

His provisions nearly gone, Charles went on a hunt the morning after the boat departed. Cent was soon straining on his leash. Before long, Charles realized what had him excited. About 50 yards off, in an open area, he saw a fine sow and eight pigs grazing on the low, white grass (a different species from tussac grass). Charles released Cent, and he made for the sow, but it was too fast, escaping into nearby tussac that was so high and thick that the dog did not follow. Charles, fleet of foot for a large man, chased down one of the pigs, snatching it before it could follow its mother.

The moment Charles plunged his knife into the pig, a large boar bolted from the tussac. It charged so quickly that Charles had no chance to prepare for the assault and only was able to deliver a glancing blow to the snout with his club. Slowed hardly at all, the boar rammed into Charles's side. Then it pulled back and lunged at Charles's legs. Charles saw this coming, so he was able to avoid a second blow while grabbing onto one of the boar's ears. Holding the creature as best he could, Charles rained down blows on the boar's head, while yelling for Cent. In a flash, the dog was there, and he latched onto the boar's other ear.

Ignoring Cent, the boar continued attacking Charles. With an errant swing of his club, Charles accidentally hit Cent on the head, nearly knocking him unconscious and causing him to release the boar's ear and stagger back, out of the fight. Charles alone now faced the boar, which, despite the punishment it had received, showed no sign of giving up or even slowing its assault. Fearing that if the fight continued much longer, he would succumb, Charles sprang onto a mound of tussac to gain the higher ground. Gripping his club with two hands, Charles hit the charging boar a few more times. Finally, it was over. Injured and perhaps cowed by its foe standing higher, the boar slowly retreated into the grass, "frequently stopping and looking back, his eye-balls glaring with fury, and his teeth gnashing and foaming with rage."

Charles rushed to Cent, still dazed and lying about 30 yards off. Relieved to find that the dog appeared to be more stunned than injured, Charles comforted him with a warm embrace and soothing words. Cent then followed Charles to pick up the dead pig, and both went back to camp.

It would have been a disaster had Cent been permanently disabled or, worse, killed—not only because it would devastate Charles, but also because of the dog's crucial importance. Ever since their arrival on the Falklands, Cent had taken the lead in virtually every hog hunt, service that had left him with numerous gashes and cuts. Once, he received a blow to the genitals that nearly neutered him. On another occasion, a boar's tusk gouged out one of Cent's eyes, causing him to collapse. Fortunately, instead of going in for the kill, the boar took off. For a week after that horrific injury, while Cent recuperated, the men's meat diet was reduced to a few birds they were able to club to death. As Charles wrote, "[N]o one can judge how serviceable he was to us."

ON JANUARY 26, 1814, gazing out at the harbor at midday, Charles saw a small boat heading in his direction. Since his three companions had left a mere three weeks earlier, Charles assumed something must be wrong, since he didn't think they could have made it to Eagle Island and back in that time. But when the boat came closer, his concerns evaporated. His companions had returned, and their reunion on the beach was joyous, with warm embraces. As it turned out, they had completed the round trip to the *Isabella* wreck site, and, even though they had failed to bring back much of value, at least they had returned safely.

Forgiveness

═══

ALITTLE MORE THAN TWO WEEKS LATER, IN EARLY FEBRUARY, THE MEN decided to hunt seals at Sea Dog Island, located about 30 miles from New Island and about a mile from Cape Orford. They gathered Ansell's share of the sealskins, as well as anything else that was his, and placed it all in the boat, their plan being to deliver the items to his place of exile, Swan Island, on the way to their destination. Before leaving, Barnard wrote a note and placed it in the powder horn, which he hung on the door to the hut:

TO THE CAPTAIN OF ANY SHIP THAT MAY PROVIDENTIALLY STOP AT this island. We beg leave to state to you, that there are five men of us, two citizens of the United States, and three subjects of Great Britain, who were left hereon, since which time we have been in a most deplorable and suffering condition, destitute of every necessary of life except what these barren islands afford. We are now gone to Sea Dog Island to procure skins for clothing, to prevent, as far as possible, a renewal of our dreadful sufferings last winter, from the excessive cold and frequent tremendous storms. If this falls into the hands of any one disposed to assist suffering humanity, we implore him to remain with his ship a few days, till our return, if possible, and take us from these desolate regions; but if circumstances positively forbid his awaiting our return, we solicit, as the next greatest favor, to leave us some supplies of food and clothing; for we have long been strangers to these necessary articles, commonly used by man in a civilized state. We also request that information may be given to the American or British Consul at the first port where the ship may arrive, or if an opportunity offer to write, to inform them of our dreadful situation, from which we entertain but faint hopes of being relieved, unless they should send a vessel for us.

(SIGNED.).

CHARLES H. BARNARD.

JAMES LOUDER.

JOSEPH ALBROOK.

His

JACOB X GREEN.

Mark

As the four men neared Quaker Harbor, they saw Ansell standing on the shore, next to a small hut he had built out of dried tussac leaves and clumps of soil. Their boat pulled up to the beach about a half mile away. They dropped off all of Ansell's belongings and then rowed back out through the surf, quickly enough so that he couldn't reach them, which he attempted to do. When Ansell was abreast of the boat, he fell to his knees crying, and he implored Charles to let him return to live with them. Ansell was "almost reduced to a skeleton," and clearly was having a difficult time feeding himself. Charles told him that while he was sorry to see him in that state, they would not take him off the island. Charles added that Ansell should be able to obtain food, since he had been provided with the means for doing so, and he certainly was in a much better position than Charles had been when he was marooned.

Ansell's continued begging led Charles to apologize again. He added that, even if he wanted to rescue him, he could not do so without the approval of the others. Ansell then pleaded with them, but they, too, were unmoved, with Albrook threatening to leave the boat if Ansell got in. There was nothing else to be done, Charles said. To give Ansell some shred of comfort and hope, Charles pointed out that since it was still summer, there was no chance of his freezing to death for many months, and a ship was sure to arrive before winter set in.

Realizing that his pleas were having no effect, Ansell changed his tack. He said that he wanted to move his camp to the other side of the harbor, where he could more easily keep an eye on New Island and, thus, see whether a ship was approaching. Where he was now, his view was blocked by one of the islands at the harbor's mouth, and the only way he could get a line of sight to New Island was to climb up one of the hills behind his camp.

The spot to which Ansell wanted to go was about 4 miles by sail, and considerably more by foot. As a result, he begged the others to use their boat to transport all of his belongings to the new location. They agreed, telling Ansell that if he walked around, he would find his belongings waiting for him. Ansell looked to the sun, which was already starting to set, and asked Charles whether he would be able to make it to the new location before nightfall. Charles said no. Worrying that, in the dark, Ansell would not be able to find his new camp, Charles conferred with the other men to see whether they would be willing to transport Ansell as well. Although they were still very leery of Ansell's intentions, they reluctantly consented.

Ansell and his belongings were taken into the boat and rowed to the other side of the harbor. Instead of just dropping him off, though, the men went a step beyond. Feeling more sympathy for their erstwhile companion, and in consideration of his miserable state, they decided to provide him with meat. Green took Cent into the grass and soon came back with a hog. Charles had thought about having dinner with Ansell, but then he had decided against that, fearing that the longer they stayed, the more likely it was that Ansell would become despondent and do something rash. So Charles cut off enough meat to make dinner for himself and his three companions and left the rest of the animal for Ansell. Still concerned that Ansell was not capable of providing for himself, Charles told him that he and the others would visit the island periodically to deliver a hog. They then said their good-byes and the four of them rowed the boat to a small island at the mouth of the harbor, where they built a fire and ate dinner.

The next day, the men went to Beaver Island, where they caught five hogs, enough to support the cruise to Sea Dog Island. While they were hunting, the recent interaction with Ansell weighed on Charles's mind. Perhaps banishment had made Ansell truly repentant for his horrid behavior in the past. Maybe he was a changed man. Charles broached this possibility with the others and proposed to give Ansell one more chance. If they took him along to Sea Dog Island, and he behaved well, he could rejoin them on New Island. If he reverted to his old ways, they would drop him back at Swan Island, but then leave him utterly alone, with no support at all. The others consented.

On February 16, the men sailed back to Swan Island. They could see the smoke rising from Ansell's fire, and soon they saw Ansell rushing to the water's edge. Once again, Ansell pleaded to be taken off, and when he understood the plan, he was overcome with joy.

To Sea Dog Island
and Back

==

THERE BEING NO GOOD PLACE TO SET UP CAMP ON SEA DOG ISLAND'S ROCKY and wave-swept shore, the men established a temporary base on Cape Orford. Green and Ansell were then rowed to the island and dropped off, along with their sealing equipment and enough meat to last a couple of days. While they were away, the rest of the party searched the coastline of Cape Orford and found treasure in the form of driftwood. The best and longest pieces were collected to be used as rafters in the hut on New Island that Charles had started building months earlier. They were all anxious to complete it before the arrival of winter.

A few days later, fire and smoke spotted atop a hill on Sea Dog Island signaled that the hunting party was ready to be picked up, whereupon the men rowed over to collect Green and Ansell and the eighty sealskins they had procured. From there, they all set out for New Island.

The winds from the west blew so hard that they sent them in the opposite direction from their destination, all the way to Fox Island.* Bad weather kept them pinned there until March 1, when they set sail again. This time, they only made it as far as the northeastern shore of Swan Island before the wind forced them to go ashore. They remained a few days, killing another thirty seals and using the opportunity to peg out the skins to dry.

---

* Modern-day Tussac Island.

One night while they were there, everyone in the makeshift camp was awakened by barking, but it wasn't coming from Cent. Charles crept out from under the overturned boat and peered into the darkness, looking for the mysterious visitor. Barely discernible in the shadowy landscape stood a dog staring right at him. When or why it had been left on the island, Charles had no idea, but he quickly formulated a plan. He unleashed Cent, hoping that he would grab hold of the dog until the other men awoke, at which point they could catch it, and, perhaps, eventually tame it. Having another dog for companionship and hunting would be a very welcome addition.

Cent ran to the other dog, but instead of grabbing it, he began sniffing. The two of them appeared, Charles said, to "be on very friendly terms." When Charles got closer, he urged Cent to clamp on, but Cent ignored the command. Instead, both dogs ran away and were soon out of sight. About an hour later, Cent finally returned, alone, and the other dog was never seen again.

WHEN THE WEATHER MODERATED, the men sailed around Loop Head to Ansell's old camp, where they hauled the boat. Over dinner, Charles told Ansell that because his behavior had been exemplary on the foray to Sea Dog Island, his probation was over and he was welcome to join the others on New Island. Thrilled, Ansell gladly accepted the invitation and offered his profound thanks.

That night on the edge of Quaker Harbor, Charles grew reflective. He thought about all the men who had visited the islands over the years, and those who hadn't survived. Charles remembered that just about a mile up the bay were two graves. How old they were was unknown—the letters on the headstones had eroded to the point of illegibility. Still, they stood as silent sentinels—yet another reminder of the fragility of life, and the toll that the Falklands could take on men.

Everyone was eager to get back to New Island, and even though the weather was still questionable for such a heavily loaded boat to navigate roughly 12 miles of open water, they headed out the next day. It was just as difficult as they had anticipated, the boat riding low in the water and often in danger of being swamped. But by evening they arrived back at Hooker's Harbor.

They rushed to the hut to see whether their note had been read or responded to, or whether there was any other evidence that a ship had landed in their absence. Nothing. Everything remained as it had been left. With the summer season soon coming to a close, Charles informed the group that he was growing more pessimistic that a ship would arrive before the bad weather descended. He recommended that they settle in and prepare for the harder times they knew would come.

Building, Hunting, and Skinning

Back on New Island, the most immediate task was transforming Charles's rudimentary hut into a more substantial structure that could house the five men through the long, cold winter. After about four days of cheerful and concerted work, it was completed. The dimensions of this expanded abode are not known, but it was certainly considerably larger than the original hut Charles had built by himself, which was only 9 by 7 feet. The most difficult part of the construction process was the roof. Using the ribs of whales found washed up on the beach, and the driftwood gathered at Cape Orford, the men built a rough frame. Onto that they layered tussac grass tied into bundles with rope yarns retrieved from the *Isabella* wreck site. With its thatched roof, sturdy stone walls, and stone chimney, the finished hut might not have seemed out of place on a farm in the English countryside.

At the end of March, a hunting party left for Beaver Island. Ansell stayed behind. He used his time productively, piling dirt around each side of the hut. This insulating barrier reached to the top of the walls and then sloped away at an angle. At the bottom edge, it was roughly 8 feet thick. To keep all the dirt from washing away during rainstorms, Ansell covered it with clumps of sod.

Meanwhile, on Beaver Island, the hunting got off to a horrific start. After leaping out of the boat, Cent raced after a very large boar feeding in a stand of tussac grass. The boar charged, and Cent did not back

*A view of the hut built by Charles and the other castaways on
New Island, as depicted in Charles Ellms,* Robinson Crusoe's
Own Book; or, The Voice of Adventure, *1843.*

down. A ferocious fight ensued, and before the men could enter the battle, the two gladiators fell into a large burn pit. As the men approached
the pit, the boar leapt out, rushed at them, and then darted off into the
maze of grass.

Lying at the bottom of the pit, Cent was whimpering, clearly in great
pain. The men got him out and examined his wounds. He had two
large gashes in his hind quarters, about 6 inches long and nearly to the
bone. They carried Cent back to the boat and dressed his wound as
best they could.

Rather than go back to New Island empty-handed, the men decided to stay until Cent had healed and recovered his strength. Over the next four days, while the four-legged patient remained near the boat, the men improvised. They flung their clubs at birds, killing a few, and turned over rocks in the shallows, catching small fish and collecting mussels.

On the fifth day, the men decided they could wait no longer, their meager diet beginning to take its toll. With the leash to restrain him, Cent was taken into the high tussac grass. As soon as he caught the scent of a hog, he was off, pulling as hard as he ever did, forcing the man holding onto the leash to run to keep up. Any lingering doubts about Cent's thirst for the hunt quickly evaporated. When five hogs were spotted in the grass, and Cent was let loose, he savagely attacked them, gravely injuring two, which were quickly dispatched by well-placed blows. Dinner that night was a feast, greedily consumed.

AFTER A BRIEF RETURN to New Island, where the men spent a few days making clothes and blankets, everyone except Louder went on another foray. Their first stop was Beaver Island, where they spent two days killing hogs. After that, it was on to Tea Island, which was located between Beaver and Swan Islands and known to be a good place for sealing. It did not disappoint. There were upwards of three hundred seals, young and old, at the rookery.

As the four men walked from the water's edge, the seals became agitated and began undulating their blubbery bodies in a hasty retreat down the beach for the safety of the ocean. This is what the men expected, so, using their clubs, they felled the first seal that approached. But then, moving almost as a single mass, the seals quickly engulfed the men, who were swinging wildly and struggling to keep from being bitten, knocked over, or, possibly, crushed by the panicking animals. In the end, they killed twenty-three seals. The men managed to escape largely unscathed, with Charles sustaining the only injury when a large male seal bit one of his knees. Fortunately, it was only a flesh wound.

Back on Beaver Island, the party killed more seals. They also captured a pregnant sow and two boars. Rather than kill them, though, they managed to tie their feet together and load them into the boat.

Their last stop was New Island, where they landed at its south end to release the hogs. Since there already was a thriving hog population on the north end of the island, the hope was that, by seeding the south end in this manner, a healthy population would also thrive there. If the men had to remain on the island for years more, both hog populations could prove critical to their survival.

When the hunting party finally returned to the hut, they were warmly greeted by Louder, who had found his solitary time quite tedious and unpleasant. Never again, he proclaimed, did he want to be left alone.

Return to Hook Camp

======

SINCE YOUNG FUR SEALS PROVIDED THE SOFTEST PELTS, THE MEN WANTED to obtain more of them before winter set in. Those pelts were good not only for making clothes but also for bedding. Now that the geese had arrived and were molting, the men could also use their shed feathers to stuff the bed sacks made from the pelts. Sleeping on those sacks was far more comfortable than sleeping on either the ground or a layer of dried tussac grass.

Charles knew a place where fur seals gathered in great numbers to birth their pups. It was at the southwestern end of New Island, where the seals congregated at the foot of nearly perpendicular cliffs more than 200 feet high.* Over eons, large rock slabs and boulders had broken off the sides of the cliffs, tumbling down and shattering into smaller pieces. This created a rocky field that provided a perfect spot for hauling out and rearing young seals.

But there were two problems with this location. First, it was impossible to land a boat there. Large waves almost continuously hammered the rocky shore, and the men could not risk damaging their boat, no matter how great the prize. They could, however, land a hunting party if they could get close enough to the rocks so that the men could jump onto the shore. It was risky, but possible if done with great care and

---

* The exact location and identity of these cliffs—and the name they were given, either at the time or now—is not clear from the information Charles provided in his memoir.

skill. Still, even if this worked, there was the second problem—getting the men and the skins they had collected safely off that rocky outcropping. Jumping back into the boat was not feasible, given the weight and mass of a large number of skins. The only way out was up, but the men could not climb out unassisted because the cliff face was too steep. They could use a rope to help them, but, unfortunately, the rope the men had earlier used to scale other cliffs on New Island was not long enough to conquer these.

Charles came up with a potential solution to their dilemma. They could, he said, venture back to Hook Camp, where they had left their only lance. If they went back for it, Charles said, they would then have the means to kill very large, old, male sea lions. Their thick skin could be cut from their bodies, in the same manner that one peels an orange in one continuous ribbon. Long strips of skin could then be dried, bundled, and tied together to make a strong rope, capable of reaching all the way to the bottom of the cliffs and strong enough to take a man's weight.

The other men, with bad memories still fresh in their minds, did not relish the idea of going back to Hook Camp. They had had a miserable sojourn there while sailing and rowing about, desperate to find their way to Eagle Island. Not only were they forced to stay at Hook Camp for days, pinned down by a storm, but also the camp was quite a distance from Swan, Beaver, and New Islands, and therefore far away from their only source of hogs.

Charles parried their concerns, pointing out that the current weather was much better than what they had experienced before, it being the middle of fall and not the depths of winter. And with plenty of geese along the way, they should be able to find an acceptable substitute for hog meat. Furthermore, he said, since there was no guarantee that their boat would remain in good shape, they ought to take their chances now, rather than risk waiting until a time when the boat could no longer go to sea. Finally, the prospect of reclaiming the lance was a strong inducement, because with it they would be that much more capable of killing sea lions, as well as elephant seals, in the future. Persuaded by Charles's arguments, everyone agreed to the expedition.

With fair winds under sunny skies, the men set off. The trip back to Hook Camp turned out to be far easier this time, and far more familiar. On his earlier visit, Charles had had no idea where they were. His great distress at their being abandoned, their near-starving condition, and the layer of snow covering the ground, had all confused him. Now, things were different. Hook Camp, he could clearly see, was on Doane's Head.*

After they retrieved the lance from the camp, the men headed south-west to Barnard's Harbor to see whether the wheat they had sown while the *Nanina* was there had sprouted and was ready for harvest. They were too late; the wheat had rotted. They did, however, discover that another effort had succeeded. While the brig was in the harbor, Charles had brought a few live hogs back from Swan Island, in the hope of establish-ing a population on English Maloon. The patches of ground that were dug up all around were clear evidence that hogs had been there, but the men saw none during their brief stay.

Back at New Island, the men set off to Sea Lion Point. Wielding the recovered lance, they were able to kill a number of huge male sea lions. After the creatures were skinned, the strips, cleaned of meat and blub-ber, were tied into a long rope that was stretched out to dry. Three days later, the sea-lion-leather rope was ready for use, and, to make it even longer, the men added the boat's painter. Off they sailed to the perilous cliffs on the twelfth of May.

THE ROCKS AT THE base of the cliffs were covered with seals, and the large waves crashing onto the shore made it extremely difficult to land the hunting party. The men on the boat waited for a break in the waves and then darted in. Louder and Ansell jumped onto a rock, and Charles threw them a large hunk of cooked pork. No sooner had this transfer been accomplished than the other three men began pulling furiously to get back out to open water. Just then another wave rolled in, flinging the boat against the rocks. Only through their superior boat-handling skills did the crew manage to get off without damage to the hull. Had the boat been dashed to pieces, all of the men would have soon perished, being marooned, as it were, at the base of those forbidding cliffs.

After arriving back at the hut, the three men gathered up the rope, all 330 feet of it, and hiked to the top of the cliff. They drove their strongest club deep into the ground about 90 feet back from the edge and looped one end of the rope around it. For added stability, Green and Albrook

---

* The promontory where modern-day Dunnose Head on West Falkland Island is located (see Barnard's map).

*Sealing adventure
along the cliffs
of New Island,
depicted in Charles
Ellms*, Robinson
Crusoe's Own Book;
or, The Voice of
Adventure, *1843*.

sat down on the rope near the club and held on. Ready, Charles walked
to the edge of the precipice with the other end of the rope. When he
looked down, he could see Louder and Ansell almost directly beneath
him. After Charles threw down a few small stones to get their attention,
they looked up. Charles tried to yell out instructions, but the crashing of
the surf and the bellowing of the seals drowned him out. So he threw the
rope over the edge. When it reached its end, it was still about 30 feet from
the bottom. Fortunately, there was enough of an angle to the cliff's base,
along with conveniently placed footholds and handholds, that Louder
was able to scramble up and grab the dangling rope.

Next began the hard part, which took great courage. Louder proceeded to climb, hand over hand, with his feet walking up the slightly

angled rock face, each step bringing him higher, and at greater peril of falling farther. At ledges along the way, he stopped and rested, and then continued upward. Reaching the top, Louder was in good spirits, and he told Charles that the climb, though hard, was not as difficult as he had expected. He said that he and Ansell had skinned a great quantity of seals, and he was willing to go back down to collect them, as long as someone accompanied him. Green and Albrook, gripped with fear, absolutely refused. They would not even go up to the edge, much less climb down the cliff. Given their intransigence, Charles came up with another plan.

About halfway down the cliff, there was a large ledge that could be used as a staging area. Charles suggested that Louder climb down to that ledge and then call down or gesture to Ansell, telling him to tie four or five skins to the end of the rope. Louder would then haul the skins up to his resting place, after which Charles would pull them up the rest of the way. They repeated this procedure until all of the skins were at the top. Then Louder climbed back up and helped Charles move the skins to just beyond the club. From there, Green and Albrook transported them back to the hut, where they were washed and pegged out.

In the meantime, Charles and Louder climbed down the rope to help Ansell skin more seals. That night, all three of them slept huddled together right up against the cliff's base. That was yet another gamble. If a gale kicked up the seas, waves could wash them away.

The next day, at about noon, Charles, Louder, and Ansell were busy skinning seals when rocks began raining down on them. Charles knew that neither Green nor Albrook would peer over the edge, and even though he couldn't see them, he assumed they were signaling their return. Louder climbed up to see. With Charles's assumption confirmed, Green and Albrook used the same process they had the day before to get the skins up to the top of the cliff, after which Charles, Louder, and Ansell followed. By nightfall, the skins had all been taken back to the hut and the exhausted men sat down for a pork dinner, after which they got some well-deserved sleep.

Near Disaster

Over the next few weeks, and into the middle of June, daily life for the five men continued in a predictable pattern, with a few twists. There were repeated trips to the north end of New Island and over to Beaver Island in pursuit of hogs. Some hunts were successful, others not. The worst one was on Beaver Island, where Cent had another mishap. While chasing a hog late in the day, he fell into a pit. Green located Cent by his whining, and when he peered into the deep hole, he could see Cent with his forelegs on the pit's side wall and the rest of his body enveloped in a slurry of mud. The only way to get Cent out would be for someone to climb down and get him, but the rope was back at the boat, as were Albrook and Ansell. Charles and Louder were back on New Island. Green was too far away to call for Albrook and Ansell, and he feared that if he left the pit to get them, he might not find his way back, there being such a wide expanse of grass and no real landmarks for guidance. All he could do was wait with Cent, hoping that the others came soon.

Green stayed with Cent through the night, trying to comfort him. The next morning, Ansell and Albrook found them, and, after the rope was retrieved, Albrook went into the pit and rescued Cent. They brought the miserable and shivering dog back to the boat and warmed him up by a fire. The next day, he refused to hunt. In fact, he wouldn't go beyond the edge of the tussac grass. Instead, when they reached the edge, he would lie down, looking up at them with a fearful gaze, as if to say, "That's it, I'm done." For six days, the men tried to coax Cent into hunting, with no success. Finally, they returned to New Island, famished. Charles told them not to be discouraged. He was sure that Cent would hunt again, given some encouragement from his master. In the meantime, however, Charles and Louder had found a new way to get meat.

While the boat was away on Beaver Island, the two of them had begun using snares to catch geese. They twisted rope yarn into a thin but sturdy line with a slip knot at one end. Placing the knot on the beach, they took the other end up to the hut's door. When the geese landed on the beach, which they did quite often to sip from a small freshwater stream not far from the hut, Charles and Louder waited for one of the geese to step within the knot's open loop. Then they would yank the line, ensnaring the bird. Sometimes Charles even sent Louder out to drive the birds toward the knot. Although this hunting method was hit or miss, they got better at it over time, and soon they had a fairly continuous supply of geese to eat.

Since snaring the geese worked brilliantly, and the men had become more confident that they could feed themselves on trips farther away from New Island, Louder, Albrook, and Green proposed yet another trip to the *Isabella* wreck, despite the fact that winter was just about to begin. There were, they said, even more things they could collect that might be of use, and the last time they were there, they had seen a patch of potato sprouts, which might have produced some potatoes they could harvest. With rising hopes, off they went.

A few days later, a severe storm blew in. Charles and Ansell were sitting by the fire in the hut when they heard voices in the distance. Stepping outside, they saw the boat in the surf, where its occupants were calling for help to haul it up on the beach. Once back at the hut, Louder, Albrook, and Green relayed what had happened.

They had gotten as far as Cape Orford when the wind blew them onto the rocky shore so violently that one of the boat's garboard planks had separated from the keel and been split in several places. Although leaking, the boat was still sailable, but not nearly in good enough shape to continue on to Eagle Island. The crew even feared that the boat might not make it back to New Island. Then, while sailing from Beaver to New Island, a gust split the boat's mast near its base, knocking it over. This put the men completely at the sea's mercy. Fortunately, they had brought along the adze that Charles had found on the beach, and they used it to cut away the jagged stump. They then stepped the shortened mast and thereby were able to raise part of the sail. This jury-rigged fix enabled them to make it the rest of the way back to New Island.

For the next few days, the men worked on repairing the boat, fixing the hull with nails they had earlier procured from the wreck. They also refashioned the mast and its rigging. To test the boat's seaworthiness, Charles, Louder, and Ansell sailed over to Swan Island to replenish the supply of hogs. The boat performed admirably, as did Cent, and they returned four days later with eight hogs.

Confident that the boat could make the trip, Louder, Albrook, and Green set out again for Eagle Island on July 20.

A Long Wait

＝

WEEKS TURNED INTO MONTHS, AND THE BOAT DID NOT RETURN. THIS anguished Charles and Ansell, but there was nothing to do but wait. In the meantime, they spent long hours in the hut. It was surprisingly cozy and warm, given that the winter temperatures stayed roughly between freezing and 40°F, and with the nearly constant winds, the air felt much colder still. The only time they left the hut was to snare birds, gather water, and collect peat in hogskin bags to fuel their fire.

While sitting around the fire in the evenings, Charles and Ansell carved plates out of wooden planks and fashioned crude knives, spoons, and forks from iron hoops. Cups made from tin scraps, riveted together with copper nails and fitted with wooden bases, added to the domesticity of the place.

Charles also taught Ansell to read. The numerous scraps of newspaper brought from the *Isabella* wreck provided the teaching materials, and through repetition Ansell learned to make out all of the words. He was quite proud of this, and Charles once overheard him carrying on an imaginary conversation with his mother, telling her of his achievement. "Fancying himself at home, he would begin with 'Mother, have you got a newspaper?' 'No; what do you want with a newspaper?' 'I want to read it.' 'Poh! you can't read.' 'Can't I? send to the Bell* and borrow one; I would read it.'" Charles broke into Ansell's reverie, asking, "'Well, Sam, what

---

* He was most likely referring to *Bell's Weekly Messenger*, a popular London newspaper, printed on Sundays.

did the old woman say?' He would laugh, and reply that she would be frightened, and say, 'Sam, who learned you to read?' I would say, 'that American captain I was so long with.'"

In September, with the arrival of spring, the men's prospects brightened. Temperatures rose, and the sun was not as much of a stranger. It was time to begin gardening. In addition to beans and turnips, the descendants of plants brought years earlier by other mariners, Charles and Ansell sowed seed potatoes. One other encouraging development was the return of the albatrosses to mate. Before long, there would be plenty of eggs to eat.

ON THE MORNING OF October 5, Charles and Ansell saw smoke rising on Beaver Island. It had to come from the missing men, they surmised, and that buoyed their hopes that their companions were alive, and they would soon be reunited. The following day, Charles and Ansell scanned the horizon for signs of the boat. At 10 a.m., it came into view. Fighting the wind and straining at the oars to enter the harbor, the three men finally reached the beach at noon.

It was another joyous reunion, followed by the story of their travels. This trip, which had lasted nearly three months, had cured the men of any desire to return to Eagle Island. The first five weeks after leaving New Island, they reported, they "suffered everything but death." But upon reaching Eagle Island, their situation improved. They set up the only tent that the wreck survivors had left on the island and kept a good fire burning within it. Daily searches of the area, in an ever-widening arc, uncovered many useful items, and, after about four weeks, the heavily loaded boat began sailing back toward New Island. The return trip was not as arduous or death-defying as the earlier leg of their expedition, but it took many weeks nevertheless, with frequent stops along the way to ensnare birds for food. Among the presents they brought back were pieces of old boards and canvas, rope, nails, a pair of spectacles, and thirteen small potatoes, which they planted immediately.

37

"Two Ships, Two Ships!"

==

DURING THE NEXT MONTH, THE MEN FILLED THEIR TIME WITH NUMEROUS activities, all involving food, clothing, or housing. Albatross egg collecting netted enough to fill a hundred barrels, if only they had them. It was a greedy haul, since that number was far more than they could possibly eat in a few weeks' time, at which point the eggs would go bad. Mending clothes and making new garments was another focus. With a single needle, however, only one man could serve as tailor, but Charles doubled the workforce in an ingenious manner. He dismantled his pocketknife and scraped the blade against a rock until the steel was pointed and thin. The rivet hole at one end, which had served to connect the blade to the handle, became the eye of the makeshift needle, and it worked quite well. Charles also found a clever use for the spectacles retrieved from the wreck. Holding them in the proper orientation, he could concentrate the sun's rays and set dry tussac grass alight, providing another means, besides flints, for starting a fire.

To make their abode more commodious, the men tore down one of the end walls and extended the hut by about 18 feet. Using mud and clay they found under the beach sand as mortar, they built the new walls even better and tighter than the old ones. Before they could finish their addition, however, they ran out of wood to complete the framing for the roof. This was rather annoying, but with the summer fast approaching, the men were not that concerned about leaving the hut in this state. Confident that they would soon find more wood to complete their project,

Mounds of balsam bog on New Island.

Charles, Louder, and Albrook went to Swan Island in mid-November to gather driftwood and also kill hogs.

The trip to Swan was nearly a disaster. The men encountered "a very cross sea" that constantly threatened to swamp the boat. When they finally landed, rotten weather kept them pinned down for days at a time and foreclosed any attempt to reach Loop Head. Their only excursions were short trips rowing around States Bay,* pulling onto the beach whenever they saw hogs. The hunting was poor, so they caught only a few scrawny ones. One bright spot was the killing of a couple of elephant seal pups, whose skin would be used to make more parchment for Charles's logbook.

On November 25, with the squally weather continuing, and the seas between Swan and New Islands very rough, the men put off their plan to return that day. After breakfast, Charles asked Albrook to accompany him to the top of a nearby hill to collect balsam bog, a creeping evergreen ground cover that grows in rolling, dense, cushiony mounds that carpet the landscape. According to Charles, the plant's sticky and fragrant resin

---

* Modern-day Chatham Harbor.

The arrival of the Asp *and the* Indispensable, *engraved by*
T. R. Whitney, in Charles H. Barnard's narrative of
his experiences in the Falklands, 1829.

was an excellent balm for cuts and bites. Louder joined them, carrying
the boat's keg to collect water.

As they ascended the hill, Louder headed off to a nearby pond, while
the other two continued higher. Soon after parting, though, Charles
and Albrook heard Louder scream. Rushing down the hill to see what
was wrong, they found Louder rolling on the ground and crying—not
from pain, but from joy. Agitated by this display, Cent began jumping
around and over Louder, seemingly intent on learning whether he was
hurt. Before Louder could explain what was going on, Albrook grabbed
Charles's hand and he, too, began to cry. "Two ships, two ships!"
Albrook exclaimed, and when Charles looked toward New Island, he
saw them too.

Deliverance

=

For a few minutes, Charles, Albrook, and Louder alternated between looking at the ships and crying, then jumping up and down and embracing each other. Suddenly, though, Charles froze. At that moment, the ships were near the northern end of New Island, and the men had no way of knowing where they were heading. What if they didn't stop at New Island and, instead, just sailed away? All the men could do now was wait and see. A few hours later, they had their answer. The two ships tacked and stood in for Hooker's Harbor, soon disappearing from view.

The three men ran down the hill and back to their boat. Louder and Albrook wanted to take off immediately, their excitement to get back to New Island overflowing. Charles, however, counseled patience. The tide was high, the surf heavy, and the wind in their faces. To try to launch now would risk disaster, and they had come too far to hazard that at this penultimate moment.

By midafternoon, the tide was low and the waves were not breaking as wildly upon the shore. Also, the wind, though still quite strong, had shifted a bit. Taking their chances, they shoved off and hopped in their boat with Cent in tow. Employing both the sail and the oars, they headed out into the open water separating Swan and New Islands. Charles, wanting to appear more presentable, pulled from his bag the last scrap of a shirt he had, the arms and tail of which had been ripped off to use as tinder. He slipped the rag over his head, where it rested rather awkwardly on his bulky sealskin jacket.

They reached the ships in the late afternoon. By 6 p.m., all three men were aboard the British whaling ship *Indispensable*, master William Buckle. The other ship was the *Asp*, master John Kenny. William Dunkin, the *Indispensable*'s mate, asked Charles to go down to the captain's cabin, where Buckle and Kenny were waiting. But Charles, standing on ceremony, said that he would not go until he received an invitation directly from the captain. Dunkin sent a man below to inform the captains, meanwhile informing Charles that Britain's war with America was still ongoing.

Soon Captains Buckle and Kenny arrived on the main deck and got their first look at the new arrivals. As Charles later wrote, "The whole of my dress, with the exception of the piece of old checked shirt, was composed of skins, and my face was almost entirely covered with a beard eight inches in length. I was reviewed with more attention and astonishment than any of my fellow-sufferers, whose beards, being very light and thin, their faces were not so fully and richly ornamented as mine." Buckle invited Charles to his cabin for some food, but again he declined, this time saying that the excitement of this turn of events was so great, and a bit unnerving, that he had completely lost his appetite.

Buckle and Kenny then broached a subject of considerable import, especially to them. Any master was considered the absolute ruler of the ship. Therefore, when a ship encountered another vessel in distress, or found men marooned or castaway, the ship's captain would usually ask to speak to the corresponding captain to determine whether his men had behaved properly toward him, and, if they had not, punishment would most likely ensue. If there was no captain to speak to, then suspicions were raised, and the inquiring captain would demand to know what had happened to the missing captain to determine whether there had been any foul play.

The British captains told Charles that their suspicions had indeed been raised earlier. The *Asp* had arrived in Hooker's Harbor before the *Indispensable*, and Kenny had planned to wait until the other ship was there to attempt to find an anchorage closer to shore. While waiting, he saw two men standing on a rock waving their caps, so he sent one of his boats in to find out who they were, telling his men not to bring them off the island. But when the boat's officer saw the miserable state of the two men, he decided that basic humanity demanded that he take them back to the ship. Once on board, Ansell and Green told Kenny a bit of their story, and Green offered his services to pilot the ship in, which Kenny accepted.

When the *Indispensable* anchored nearby, Kenny took Ansell and Green to meet Captain Buckle, who asked them to identify themselves and explain how they came to be on this island. Both men said they were Americans who had formerly been with the brig *Nanina* out of New York, captained by Charles H. Barnard. The reasons why Ansell claimed to be an American are not clear, but likely he didn't want to be revealed as a Royal Navy deserter. The two were going to continue, but Buckle interrupted them, demanding to know where their captain was. They told Buckle that Charles Barnard and two other men had left for Swan Island a few weeks earlier, and since the weather had been dreadful when they left, Ansell and Green feared that they might have been blown way off course and could be lost.

Buckle told Charles that, upon hearing this, he began to think that something was not right, and that perhaps these men had done something wrong. Swan and New Islands were so close to one another that being gone for a couple of weeks, bad weather notwithstanding, sounded dubious at best. Buckle kept his suspicions to himself and simply told Ansell and Green that they "must go ashore, and remain there until Captain Barnard returns." This caused Ansell to drop to his knees and beg not to be returned to the island to perish. Buckle replied coolly, "If Captain Barnard does not return, and inform me that you have conducted yourselves correctly towards him during the time you have been here, I shall certainly put you on shore and leave you."

Now, with Charles standing before him, Buckle asked directly whether his men had behaved properly. Charles vouched for all of them, including Ansell, the last for both practical and merciful reasons. Charles realized that if he had mentioned Ansell's earlier "villainy," Buckle would have left him on New Island. But Charles had no interest in exacting such a heavy penalty on a man who had since repented, and even had acted quite responsibly. Satisfied that there was no bad behavior on the part of Charles's men, Buckle let the issue drop, and everyone relaxed.

Buckle informed Charles that he and his companions had not been entirely forgotten. When the *Indispensable* was in Peru earlier in the year, Buckle received a letter from the British admiral in Rio de Janeiro that requested he look for Charles and the others if the *Indispensable* stopped by the Falklands on the way back to England. Other ships had been given the same instructions. Buckle hadn't been able to visit the Falklands on that voyage. On this current voyage, of course, he did come by the islands, but not with the intent of picking up the castaways. In fact, Buckle had forgotten all about the admiral's request until Ansell and Green boarded his ship.

The conversation next turned to the war. Buckle mentioned that an American frigate in the Pacific had captured every British whaleship in that ocean except for his ship and one other. When Charles asked the name of that frigate, he was told it was the USS *Essex*. Charles had only a few moments to bask in this American naval success before Buckle added, "but one of our frigates went round and captured her." This was the first Charles had heard about the war's progress, and it considerably dampened his mood. If Charles had known the full story, he could have parried Buckle's blow, or at least placed it in a more favorable light.

In fact, Captain David Porter of the United States Navy had led the *Essex* on a dramatic and bold cruise that damaged the British whale fishery and gave Americans something to cheer about. After becoming the first American naval ship in the War of 1812 to capture a British warship—the sixteen-gun *Alert*—Porter sailed the *Essex* into the Pacific, racking up another distinction as the first American warship to enter that ocean. While there, he learned that heavily armed British whaleships were soon going to be ordered by their government to attack American whaleships in the region and take them as prizes. That would spell disaster for the many American whaleships operating near the Galapagos Islands that had no idea that war had broken out between America and Britain. Therefore, they would "fall an easy and unsuspecting prey to the British ships."

Porter decided to strike first, and he did an admirable job protecting the largely defenseless American whaling fleet and damaging the British whale fishery. In the end, he burned three British whaleships and captured another nine, although five were later retaken by the British. Of Porter's exploits, Theodore Roosevelt wrote, in his sweeping history *The Naval War of 1812*, that "it was an unprecedented thing for a small frigate to cruise a year and a half in enemy's waters, and to supply herself during that time, purely from captured vessels. . . . Porter's cruise was the very model of what such an expedition should be, harassing the enemy most effectually at no cost whatsoever." And a Member of Parliament complained that because of Porter's captures of British whaleships,

Commodore David Porter of the US Navy, the protector of America's whaling fleet in the Pacific Ocean during the War of 1812. Mid-eighteenth-century engraving based on a painting by Alonzo Chappell.

London "had burnt dark for a year." While it is true that Porter lost the greatest prize of all, his ship, in a battle against two British warships in the harbor at Valparaiso, Chile, he was greatly outmatched, and his men fought valiantly.

Right after painting the *Essex* as a failure, Buckle delivered another blow, talking about how HMS *Shannon* had defeated the USS *Chesapeake* in a battle not far from the mouth of Boston Harbor. Having been informed of two major American losses, Charles remained silent for a while and began to wonder whether "the same disastrous fate had attended the whole of our little navy." Captain Kenny, perceiving Charles's distress, observed that the *Essex* had been at a great disadvantage in its final battle, and that Captain Porter "behaved remarkably well, and defended his ship bravely." Then he added, "[S]ome of your frigates have taken some of ours in a crack, before they had time to look around them." This intelligence greatly improved Charles's disposition, and with that, all discussion of the war ceased.

Over the next few days, the British went ashore a number of times to get water, shoot geese, kill hogs, gather eggs, and collect peat, which

Engraving by Robert Dodd, circa 1813, titled, "To Captain P.B.V. Broke commanding his majesty's ship Shannon, *his officers, seamen, & marines, this representation of their gallantly boarding the American frigate* Chesapeake *being 110 men superior in force and hauling down the enemy's colors in fifteen minutes from the commencement of the action."*

Buckle preferred to use in his cabin, claiming that it burned hotter and cleaner than coal. James Choyce, second mate of the *Asp*, recorded his observations after meeting the Americans and inspecting their encampment. "They had built a house, but it being too small for comfort they had commenced a larger one which was nearly completed when we arrived." The potatoes, turnips, and beans in the garden, the hundreds of stiff sealskins waiting to be transformed into clothes, and the vast collection of albatross eggs, which had to be turned on a regular basis, fascinated and impressed Choyce. The men, putting on brave faces, "said they were comfortable enough, and wanted nothing but wives to make them happy; still, they wished to revisit their native countries."

THE INDISPENSABLE AND THE ASP rode out a powerful gale on November 29, 1814, both dragging their anchors, and the *Asp* losing one of theirs. That night, as the winds calmed, the two ships finally departed, with

Green and Ansell on the *Asp*, and Charles, Louder, Albrook, and Cent on the *Indispensable*. Also on the *Indispensable* was the *Nanina*'s trusty boat, brought on board by Buckle in the event that Charles might want to use it again, or sell it to raise funds for his ultimate return home. To help in that regard, the *Indispensable*'s carpenter was tasked with repairing and painting the boat.

Rescuing the five men had no impact on the British captains' plans. They headed their ships south, intent on rounding Cape Horn and sailing into the Pacific to continue their whaling voyages. Their new passengers were along for the ride and they would have to take advantage of any opportunities to return home, if and when they arose.

All told, the five castaways had survived on the Falklands, both together and apart, for 534 days.[*] In an unusual coincidence, on the very day that Charles and the others left the islands for good, the Prize Appeal Court in London was ruling on the disposition of the *Nanina*.

---

[*]   This does not include the few days the men spent in the company of the two British whaling ships before sailing from the Falklands.

Prize

===

LIEUTENANT WILLIAM D'ARANDA ARRIVED BACK IN PLYMOUTH, ENGLAND, on March 31, 1814. About two months later, the *Nanina* showed up in Portsmouth. D'Aranda went to inspect the brig and realized he had an immediate problem. The cargo, primarily the oil and sealskins, had already begun to rot during the voyage over, and it was in danger of being damaged further if forced to remain on the brig. To keep his expected prize from losing any more value, D'Aranda petitioned the High Court of the Admiralty to allow the brig's cargo to be taken off and stored in a proper warehouse while the legal proceedings moved ahead. His motion was granted, and the brig was offloaded.

The prize case appeared to be quite simple. D'Aranda submitted his side of the story, and no one was there to dispute it. The firm of John B. Murray and Son had learned of the infamous proceedings in the Falklands, based on the article that Pease had published in the *Hudson Bee*, which described everything that happened up until the arrival of the *Nanina* in Rio de Janeiro at the end of August 1813. However, the merchants knew nothing about the prize proceedings in the High Court of the Admiralty, and even if they had, the War of 1812 would have precluded them from traveling to London to state their case. Given all of this, it is no surprise that the court's judgment on November 29, 1814, favored D'Aranda. The prize was his, they ruled, as long as no one came along in the following year to submit an appeal.

Just a few days before that ruling was handed down, Valentine Barnard had walked into the New York offices of John Murray and Son. He told them what had transpired among himself, Dixon, and D'Aranda in Rio, and that the *Nanina* had indeed been sent to London as a potential prize. The Murrays decided to bide their time, since peace negotiations had begun in Belgium a few months earlier, and it appeared that the war would soon be over.

The Treaty of Ghent was signed on December 24, 1814, and the US Senate ratified it on February 16, 1815. Peace made it possible for the Murrays to plead their case in person, and John Murray arrived in London in June to do just that. In the meantime, the *Nanina* and all of its cargo was put up for auction, the proceeds of which were invested in the Bank of England until such time as the possibility of appeal had expired.

With the help of a local barrister, Murray launched a legal attack, supported by new statements from Valentine Barnard and Barzillai Pease that bolstered the argument that a travesty of justice had occurred, and letters from Rear Admiral Sir Manley Dixon, which cast doubt on the legality, or appropriateness, of the *Nanina*'s capture. This, along with additional testimony from D'Aranda, induced the Advocate-General of the Doctors' Commons* to hand down an opinion on September 15, 1815, that favored the Americans. It was a devastating blow to D'Aranda, who, no doubt, had already begun to figure out how to spend the prize money. The Advocate-General urged Murray to "appeal instantly" the condemnation of the *Nanina*. "There is reason to think," the opinion continued, "from the acts done by Admiral Dixon and the propositions for restitution and other circumstances, that perhaps the capture ought not to have been made." Appeal Murray did, his barrister submitting the paperwork on November 28, 1815, a day before the one-year grace period would have run out.

Unfortunately, some of the records associated with the subsequent prize case have been lost or misplaced, but the outlines of what occurred are clear. It was painfully obvious that the wheels of the British judicial system, at least in this case, moved very slowly. At the Murrays' urging, the US State Department sent protests of its own in 1816 and 1817, addressed to the British Ambassador to the United States. One of the latter, penned by Acting Secretary of State Richard Rush, argued: "It

---

* A society of lawyers in London that would consider civil cases.

Doctors' Commons in London, circa 1815.

would appear that the crew of the *Nanina* had the strongest titles to the treatment due to generous friends, instead of being handed over to hostile captivity. On behalf of the owners, the peculiar and affecting circumstances attending this loss of their property makes a powerful appeal to the fairest principles of comity between nations." Rush urged the ambassador to ably present the Murrays' case so that the outcome would result in their being indemnified in a manner that "a spirit of kind and liberal justice may be found to dictate."

At the same time, D'Aranda continued to defend his actions. In 1817, he wrote to the Secretary of the Admiralty, rehashing his false and reprehensible argument that it was the Americans who were to blame, and that it was why he had no other alternative but to take the *Nanina* as a prize. "The infamous proceedings of the Americans and the inhuman treatment the Wrecked People received from them prior to my arrival rendered *Nanina*'s detention indispensable. . . . I am satisfied that it was never the intention of the Americans to remove the Wrecked People from Eagle Island. . . . The treatment several individuals received when first on board the *Nanina* was unpardonable."

Finally, on February 5, 1818, the Prize Appeal Court of the High Court of the Admiralty ruled in favor of the Murrays. They would be compensated for the cost of both the *Nanina* and its cargo, but, in turn, they had to pay the captor's expenses, which included legal fees and the cost of storing the cargo and selling the ship.

Justice was served, and D'Aranda was left with nothing.

Long, Strange Trip Home

CHARLES'S JOURNEY BACK HOME WAS LONG AND FASCINATING. IT INCLUDED stops in Lima, the Sandwich Islands (Hawaii), and Canton, as well as time on another whaling ship and a sealing vessel, plus various other adventures. His experiences also offer insights into the lives of peripatetic mariners of the day and show how difficult it could be in the Age of Sail to get back home from faraway lands. Rather than fully document his travels, the following presents a few of his most interesting and dramatic interludes.

After rounding Cape Horn on the *Indispensable*, Charles witnessed the ship's whaling operations as its crew captured three sperm whales. In the middle of January 1815, off the coast of the Viceroyalty of Peru, Charles faced a hard decision. He wanted to get to Peru's capital, Lima, where he hoped to obtain a passport from the viceroy to transit the Isthmus of Darien,* and then on the other side find a ship going to the States. But Captain Buckle planned to whale another four months before stopping in the capital city. Charles didn't want to wait that long. Even though the *Indispensable* was about 45 miles from the continent and roughly 150 miles south of Lima, Charles said he was prepared to take his boat and head for the coast, alone if need be. Buckle pleaded with him to remain on the *Indispensable* until it arrived at Lima. He urged Charles to consider the great distance he would have to sail in a small boat on the open

---

* Modern-day Isthmus of Panama.

ocean, and the dangers he might face from Spanish rebels or thieves who would take advantage of his defenseless position when he landed.

Charles would not be dissuaded, so Buckle ordered the boat to be put in order and provisioned for the trip. The provisions, however, were for three people. When Louder and Albrook heard Charles's plan, they asked to go along, notwithstanding their great fears of being captured and imprisoned by Spaniards. To better prepare them, Buckle gave Charles money, two watches he could trade, extra clothes, a chart of the coast, and letters of introduction to an American merchant in Lima and to the British captain of the port of Callao, just outside of Lima.

Before they could leave, however, a major problem arose. The boat had been baking in the sun on the ship's deck for so long that its planks had dried and shrunk, pulling away from each other and leaving gaps in between. Therefore, when the boat was launched in the morning, it began leaking at an alarming rate. In that state, it was not seaworthy. Confident that contact with the water would cause the wood to swell, thereby closing up the seams, Charles decided to let the boat remain tied off next to the ship, and to postpone leaving until later in the day. By the early afternoon, the leak had slowed to the point that one man bailing could keep the boat from filling up. The three men then climbed into the boat and pushed off.

Within a day, they were just offshore, preparing to land when they saw a group of heavily armed men on horseback galloping along the valley floor in their direction. The men dismounted at the water's edge and yelled and waved, encouraging the boat to come in. To avoid what was almost certainly a trap, Charles and his companions headed back out to sea and continued sailing north. That night, the men feared for their lives, as there were many whales swimming and spouting around the boat, any one of which could have easily launched the men into the water, intentionally or not.

They sailed for many miles before landing on the small, uninhabited Sangayán Island, about 3 miles from the Peruvian coast. They killed a few seals, saving the skins and roasting the meat. Next stop was Pisco, 15 miles farther up the coast. Even though they were wary about stopping there, for fear of being detained or attacked, and would have preferred to press on to Lima, they were down to less than half a gallon of water and desperately needed more. Arriving ashore, they were surrounded by soldiers who took them to a nearby fort and locked them in a prison cell.

Sealing adventure on Sangayán Island, off Peru, engraved by T. R. Whitney, in Charles H. Barnard's narrative of his experiences in the Falklands, 1829.

Fortunately, the local governor was welcoming. Using broken Spanish and English to communicate, he told his visitors that it would be too dangerous for them to continue on to Lima in their boat, given the rough seas along the way. Instead, the governor proposed a different plan. His brig was returning from Lima in a month or so, whereupon it would take one to two weeks to prepare the cargo for its return to the capital. In the interval, the governor offered the brig and ten men to Charles, if he would go sealing at Sangayán Island. Charles could keep any skins he procured, while the governor wanted only the oil that could be made from the seal's blubber, which was needed as a lubricant in local textile mills. After Charles returned from the island, the brig would be loaded, and it would take him and his companions on to Callao, from which he could easily get to nearby Lima. The deal struck, the three men had a very pleasant stay in Pisco as the governor's guests, and they sailed to Sangayán after the brig arrived on March 17.

The ten-day trip was a success. The men returned with nearly 900 skins and plenty of blubber. Most of the killing, however, was done by Charles, Louder, and Albrook. None of the Spaniards had ever gone sealing before, and many were so frightened of the bulky animals that they either froze when confronting them or used their clubs without conviction. Yet, when the Spaniards returned to Pisco, they were full

of bravado. According to Charles, they "gave a minute and most roman-
tic account of their perilous adventures and daring achievements, to the
wondering and credulous inhabitants of Pisco." Louder and Albrook,
"remembering how boastful the Spaniards were on deck, and how pusil-
lanimous they had been on shore, when among the seals," were indignant
upon hearing "the lies those cowardly rascals . . . [were] telling."

CHARLES, LOUDER, AND ALBROOK arrived in Callao in early April, whereupon the latter two signed on as crew aboard the British merchant ship
Wildman, seeing it as their best and quickest chance of getting back to
England. After Charles wished his long-suffering companions good-bye,
he bought a horse and traveled about 9 miles to Lima. His plan to cross
the Isthmus of Darien was thwarted by the Spanish viceroy, who refused
to issue him a passport to travel overland because of the war raging in the
country's interior. That avenue cut off, Charles headed back to Callao to
see whether he could find a ship to get him closer to home. Since there
was no American ship in port, Charles took passage on a British whaling ship, *Eliza*, for an extended cruise through the Pacific. The *Eliza*'s
captain, John Walker, told Charles that if they ran across another vessel
heading directly to Europe, Charles could transfer to it. Otherwise, he
could remain on the *Eliza* until it returned to England, where Walker
would help him avoid prison and get back home.

Just before leaving Callao, Charles learned that Jacob Green wanted
to see him. After leaving the Falklands aboard the *Asp*, Green had signed
on to the British whaling ship *Cyrus*, which was now in port. Captain
Davie of the *Cyrus* told Charles that Green was refusing to get back on
board until he had spoken to his former captain. When they reunited,
Green said that although the men on the *Cyrus* had treated him well, he
didn't like sailing under the British flag, since Britain was at war with
the United States (they had yet to hear of the peace treaty). Charles com-
plimented Green on his patriotism and allegiance, but he told him that
neither of them would be able to leave Callao if not on a British ship, as
no American ships were likely to come into port any time soon. Their
best bet for ultimately returning to the United States, Charles counseled,
was to take passage on a British ship and hope that it would get them one
step closer to home.

Convinced that this was the wisest course, Green returned to the

Cyrus. Another former member of the *Nanina* also boarded the *Cyrus* that day. While spending time with Charles, Davie had gotten to know Cent, and had heard about his sterling qualities. Davie was so enamored with the dog that he asked Charles if he could have him. Charles, who anticipated a long journey ahead of him, with many unknown twists and turns, consented, confident that he had "secured the dog the protection of a good master." How the rest of Cent's life played out is unknown, but, given his critical role in keeping the five men alive, one earnestly hopes that he was treated with great love.*

BY AUGUST 20, 1815, Charles had wearied of being on board the *Eliza.* He was not involved with the whaling, so he was merely a passenger. Wanting to feel useful and pursue his livelihood, Charles asked Captain Walker to be let off at the island of Más Afuera, part of the Juan Fernández Archipelago. Charles proposed sealing for a month or so, and then, when the *Eliza* returned to obtain more wood and water, as it often did, Charles would get back on board. Walker thought it a bad idea, but Charles persisted and was dropped off with a great array of provisions, as well as clubs, lances, fishing lines, and hooks. Accompanying Charles was a seventeen-year-old American boy who was eager to join the escapade. "Now my character was complete," recalled Charles years later. "I had obtained a Friday [Robinson Crusoe's sidekick] without encountering the least danger," and was ready to resume "a Crusonian life, but under much more favorable circumstances than those in which I commenced and terminated my former one."

The sealing didn't work out as Charles had hoped, and since the *Eliza* had not yet returned, he took advantage of another opportunity that literally appeared out of the blue about six weeks after he was left on the island. One morning in early October, Charles saw a ship offshore. Thinking it might be Spanish, he and "Friday" hid in the bushes near the shore as the ship's boat approached. When the boat came close, one of the men on board commented, in English, on the smoke rising from Charles's just-abandoned fire. Hearing this, Charles and "Friday" jumped out of the bushes and shouted greetings, whereupon the startled

---

* The whereabouts of Samuel Ansell after he sailed from the Falklands on the *Asp* are not known.

*View of Más Afuera Island (now Alejandro Selkirk Island, Chile),
engraving, 1760.*

Arrival of the Millwood, *engraved by T. R. Whitney,
in Charles H. Barnard's narrative of his experiences in the Falklands, 1829.*

man asked where he could land. Charles directed him to a nearby beach,
and he and "Friday" helped haul the boat onto the sand.

The men were from the American ship *Millwood*, out of New York,
captained by Samuel G. Bailey, heading to the Sandwich Islands (now
Hawaii) and then on to Canton before returning to the States. Charles
was invited to have dinner on board. When Bailey heard Charles's sur-

name, he immediately asked Charles, "Whom did you marry?" "Mary
Ann Paxton" came the reply. As Charles later recalled, "[A]t this he
appeared to be astonished. 'Is it then possible,' said he, 'that you are
here? that you are yet in existence? for I have, in common with all your
friends and acquaintance[s], concluded that you were long since num-
bered with the dead,' and hastily added, 'just previous to my sailing, I
saw your wife and children, and I am happy to say they were enjoying
good health.'"

An enormous load was thus lifted off Charles's shoulders, and delightful images of home flooded his thoughts, made more delightful still by
the news that the war was over. Bailey urged Charles to leave with him
and not wait for the *Eliza*, because some unforeseen mishap might occur
that would preclude Captain Walker from returning, and then Charles
would truly be abandoned. Readily agreeing, Charles left a note on the
island explaining what had happened, and why neither he nor "Friday"
was there. Years later, Charles ran into a mate from the *Eliza* who told
him that they did find the note, and that it was a good thing that he left
with the *Millwood*, since the peace treaty had resulted in orders for the
Eliza to return to England.

IN EARLY DECEMBER, THE *Millwood* pulled into Kealakekua Bay on
Hawaii's Kona coast. Charles was taken by the beauty of the place and
the "ingenuity" of its people, especially their great skill in building excellent single and double canoes, which they deftly handled. Captain Bailey was there to obtain sandalwood to sell in Canton. The heartwood
and roots of these relatively small trees contain a fragrant oil that made
the fine-grained, yellowish-brown wood highly prized in China, where
it was carved into exquisite, aromatic furniture and used to make sweet-
smelling incense that was burned in houses of worship. Bailey negotiated
with King Kamehameha I, and, after they settled on a price, a load of sandalwood was soon delivered to the ship.

The *Millwood* set sail for Canton in the middle of December, and on
April 4, 1816, it came to anchor off Whampoa (Huangpu), a long, narrow
island located in the middle of the Pearl River, roughly 12 miles below
Canton. Charles accompanied Bailey to Canton, where he met the Amer-
ican Consul and the captains of other ships, both American and British.
Recognizing that Charles had little money of his own, one of the captains

graciously offered Charles free lodging, and another gave him some gifts
to take back to his wife.

When the *Millwood* contracted to take a load of cargo to Holland,
instead of heading directly to the United States, the American Consul recommended that Charles transfer to the *Trumbull*, out of Rhode
Island, since it would get him back to his loved ones much faster. The
Trumbull's captain welcomed Charles on board, and the ship left Canton
on April 7.

The voyage home by way of the Cape of Good Hope was largely routine, with the exception of a hurricane that greatly damaged the ship.
At one point, the storm nearly knocked the *Trumbull* on its beam ends,
and it only righted itself after the mizzenmast was cut away. On October 23, 1816, at three in the afternoon, the men on the *Trumbull* spied
Martha's Vineyard through the haze. Four hours later, as darkness fell,
they saw the welcoming beam from Gay Head Light. The following
afternoon, after battling a heavy squall throughout the night, the *Trum-*

Trumbull *in a
hurricane, as
depicted in Charles
Ellms,* Robinson
Crusoe's Own Book;
or, The Voice of
Adventure, *1843.*

bull came to within 3 miles of the island, and a pilot boat sailed out to meet it.

Disagreement over the piloting fees led the captain to decide to continue on to the mainland, but Charles could not wait to get ashore, so he took his leave with the pilot boat. Finally, at seven in the evening on October 24, 1816, Charles had "the unspeakable happiness" of setting foot on his native land. "Weary of wandering round the world, and encountering the hardships incident to the ocean, I thought that if I should be so fortunate as to experience again the joys of domestic felicity, nothing would ever tempt me to risk again their possession." Shortly thereafter, he made his way to New York to reunite with his family and report to the *Nanina*'s owners, all of whom were astonished and delighted to see him alive.

Epilogue

=

Of all the passengers and crew on the *Nanina* and the *Isabella*, none left much of a mark on the world in the years after their ordeal. In fact, most of them largely disappeared from the historical record. However, for some of the main characters, a bit more can be said. As for the British, Joseph Holt returned to his beloved Ireland as a fairly wealthy man, settling first in Dublin and then in Dún Laoghaire, where he lived a relatively quiet existence as a pub owner and a real estate builder/investor until his death at age seventy in 1826. An obituary noted: "The insurrectionary chieftain has at length gone to the house appointed for all living." Richard Brooks made it back to Australia with his family and became a prominent landowner who ran a general store and supported many religious charities. After being gored by a bull, he died in his sixty-eighth year. Robert Durie and his family moved to Edinburgh, where he inherited the family estate and earned the honorary title of Robert Durie of Craigluscar.* He died at the age of forty-eight in 1825 and was survived by his wife, Joanna-Ann, who died in 1835. Nearly a year after returning from the Falklands, Durie revisited his ordeal when he wrote a letter to the British Admiralty, in which he, not surprisingly, supported D'Aranda's actions and behavior, calling the lieutenant a "meritorious officer to whose determined perseverance in surmounting every obstacle towards effecting our relief we are so much indebted."

Sir Henry Browne Hayes returned to Cork, Ireland. Upon entering

---

* Craigluscar is an area in Dunfermline, Scotland.

the city, he was described as "[a] portly person, wearing striped trousers, and a blue coat with brass buttons, having a rubicund face, charged with effrontery, and shaded by the broad leaf of a straw sombrero." He appears to have lived out the rest of his years as a gentleman-about-town with no clear profession. He died in 1832 at the age of seventy, after a long illness. Coincidentally, that same year, Mary Pike, the woman Hayes had abducted decades earlier, also died, leaving a fortune estimated in excess of £55,000.

William D'Aranda returned to London to rest and recover his health, which was compromised by his journey to and from the Falklands. Still a relatively young man of twenty-six, he served additional stints in the Royal Navy and spent a few years in the merchant marine, but in neither service did he do much to distinguish himself. His capture of the *Nanina*, far from burnishing his career and fortunes, as he had hoped, haunted him. His reputation, despite Durie's glowing praise, was damaged when word of his less-than-honorable behavior in the Falklands spread through London's maritime community. He remained quite bitter about the Prize Appeal Court's ultimate decision, which stripped him of his best chance for a financial windfall. The owners of the *Isabella* ignored his heroics in saving the passengers and gave him nothing for his efforts. Over the years, D'Aranda repeatedly complained about how shabbily he had been treated. For example, in response to an Admiralty questionnaire in 1848, he grumbled that he had "rescued 46 British subjects from wreck and starvation . . . [for which] I never received reward or compensation." He died in 1872, at the age of eighty-four.

Richard Lundin was promoted after returning to London. This elevation was no doubt due in part to the glowing letter Admiral Dixon wrote to the Lords Commissioners of the Admiralty, in which he lauded Lundin for "his active and persevering spirit" during his perilous journey in the longboat, and the rescue mission on the *Nancy*. Lundin served briefly in the Napoleonic War. When it ended, he was placed on half pay, and soon left the military. He retired to the family estate in Scotland, never married, and died in 1832 at the age of forty-one.

A FEW OF THE Americans, as well, left a trail. Captain Edmund Fanning went to sea in subsequent years, going on a number of sealing voyages. In 1822, in Coquimbo, Chile, he committed suicide, shooting himself for reasons unknown. Perhaps it was due to his financial woes. Apparently his success at sea, and in life, was limited; the estate he left behind was worth only $111.17, not nearly enough to pay off all of the debts he had accrued.

Henry Ingman Defrees relocated to Nantucket from Boston sometime after his trip on the *Nanina*. Like Fanning, he also returned to the sea, going on multiple voyages (at least one as a master) to Guadeloupe, Gibraltar, and Brazil, among other places. Upon retiring from shipboard life, it appears that he worked at various times as a lawyer, landlord, and proprietor of a general store. He also served as a director of the Pacific Bank. Over the years, he took out numerous ads in the *Nantucket Inquirer*, offering for sale an array of items, but most prominently and persistently brown sherry, coffee, and canvas, which he either had in profusion or just had a difficult time selling. Defrees died in 1871, at the age of eighty.

When Barzillai Pease returned home to Hudson, New York, he was met with the tragic news that his six-year-old son, Leonard, had drowned while swimming in the river just a few months earlier. In subsequent years, Pease held various maritime positions. For a while, he captained a scow transiting up and down the Hudson River, delivering cotton bales and machinery to textile factories. Near the end of the War of 1812, he commanded troop transports on Lake Ontario. A few years after the war, he fell on tough times and was briefly imprisoned in Boston as a result of a dispute over the ownership of a piece of property. Later, he was declared an "insolvent debtor."

In 1826, Pease went on a somewhat confusing and mysterious cruise, when he shipped as mate on the schooner *Margaret* out of New York. He said he offered the captain $5,000 to take him to Anguilla and wait while he "performed a certain voyage." The money, however, would only be forthcoming if Pease found some sort of treasure there, the nature of which he did not specify.

In all his years going to sea, Pease had never seen "so shabby a crew," which didn't bode well for the trip. Nevertheless, the *Margaret* arrived safely at its first stop, Bermuda, on June 23. After unloading its cargo, and just before it was to sail for Anguilla, the *Margaret* caught fire at two in the morning of July 1, while anchored in Mangrove Bay, just 6 miles from Hamilton, Bermuda's capital. Although much of the gear was taken off, the vessel itself was a total loss. Pease bemoaned his situation, writing, "[M]y voyage at an end, my prospects of getting my money blasted."

Over the next few weeks, Pease met with various captains of American vessels who were in port and finally convinced one to take him to Anguilla on terms similar to those that had enticed the captain of the *Margaret*. Pease's revived dream of riches, however, was destroyed on August 12, when the ship pulled into Anguilla's Rendezvous Bay. Pease took a boat to shore and searched frantically up and down the coastline, but, as he later wrote, he "could not find" the tree under which the "treasure" was supposedly buried. This failure infuriated the captain of the vessel, and he upbraided Pease and told him he wanted him off the ship as soon as possible. When they docked at Dominica a few days later, Pease booked passage on the Rhode Island schooner *Ann Rosina*. On September 9, Pease disembarked in Providence and made his way home. The course of his later life and the date of his death remain unknown.

VALENTINE BARNARD NEVER WENT to sea again. He retired in New York City, where he died in 1823 at the age of seventy-four. When Charles returned to the city in 1816, Valentine told him everything that had happened after he was left behind in the Falklands. Learning the details of his abandonment enraged Charles, and he let loose with his condemnation of the main authors of his suffering, among them Mattinson, D'Aranda, and Durie, the last of whom received most of Charles's ire. "Fourteen armed royal marines had been placed under his command during the passage home, and were ready to act at his nod. With these he was sufficiently powerful, even though all the rest combined to violate their agreement. By declaring his consent, he need not have ordered a trigger to be drawn or a bayonet presented, to have deserved a just claim to his pretended title of being an officer of honor or humanity." Instead of standing tall, Charles believed that Durie—whom he called "chicken-hearted"—was ruled by Joanna-Ann, who was the true architect of the treachery. "But this contemptible Sir Jerry had surrendered all his manliness and honor to his lady wife, for safe keeping, for the sake of being occasionally warm at a dinner party or review. He had emasculated himself in feeling, and was a mere puppet that moved as she pulled the strings, so that it was she who actually held the balance; . . . Madam Durie governed the automaton Durie, he the marines, and they the sailors and passengers." As support for his jaundiced view of Joanna-Ann, Charles pointed to a conversation he had had with Holt, in which the latter observed that, as compared with Mr. Durie, his wife "was the better soldier; as she was accustomed to all the pomp and circumstances of war, (having been the wife of a late colonel, and had accompanied him in all his campaigns;) and from her callosity of nerves, she could view all the events of a battle without any emotions of pity or fear."

Despite the anger Charles felt when recalling his travails, he was very happy to be home. "After an absence of four years and seven months, I had returned without a shilling in my pocket; but, notwithstanding my penury, my joy was far beyond the power of words." A month after his return, his financial distress was advertised to the world when Richard Riker, the Recorder of New York City, placed ads in local newspapers identifying Charles as "an insolvent debtor," and inviting all his creditors to come to the Recorder's office to present their claims as to why Charles should not be allowed to declare bankruptcy and, thereby, have all of his debts forgiven.

Strangely, given the dramatic nature of the story of the *Isabella* and the *Nanina*, there was virtually no coverage of the events in the American or British press, beyond a flurry of articles that appeared after Edmund Fanning's brief account appeared in a Newport paper, and Barzillai Pease published the protest that he and the other captains had lodged in Rio. Nor did any of the participants publicly write about their experiences in the years immediately after coming home.* Everyone involved, it seems, had moved on with their lives, and were not particularly interested in dredging up the past.

ALTHOUGH CHARLES HAD SAID he would rather stay home than go to sea again, he soon changed his mind and went on to captain a number of sealing voyages. The draw of the ocean and the very real need for him to replenish his fortunes were too strong for him to resist. On one of those expeditions, Charles met a man who caused him to revisit his earlier involuntary stay on the Falklands.

---

* Joseph Holt's *Memoirs*, published in 1838, included a considerable section on the *Isabella* and its trials.

The brig Jane *and the cutter* Beaufoy, *February 1823, off Antarctica,*
"passing through a chain of ice islands." Drawn by A. Mason, circa 1825.

British ship captain James Weddell was on a sealing expedition to
the South Shetland Islands, aboard the brig *Jane*, when he stopped off
at New Island in the Falklands in 1821.* He was there to stock up on
supplies, including water, bird eggs, and peat. During his stay, Weddell encountered Charles, who was on a similar voyage on the New
York brig *Charity*. After the two exchanged pleasantries, the conversation turned to the time that Charles and his four companions had
spent on the island almost ten years earlier. As Weddell later recalled,
he "greedily devoured" Charles's tale, and he observed that "a particular account of this residence on an uninhabited island would not fail of
being considered almost as wonderful as the celebrated fiction of Robinson Crusoe."

In 1825, Weddell published *A Voyage Towards the South Pole*—in
which he devoted nearly five vibrantly written pages to Charles's story.
Even before the publication of this book, some of Charles's friends had
encouraged him to write his own book, telling the world what had hap-

---

* A few years later, Weddell would gain fame for sailing 532 miles beyond the Antarctic Circle, going farther south than anyone ever had and discovering the eponymously
named Weddell Sea. Also, Swan Island in the Falklands, where Charles and the others
had spent a considerable amount of time, was later renamed Weddell Island.

pened in the Falklands. Now that the popularity of Weddell's book cast a warm light on Charles and his ordeal, his friends redoubled their efforts to get Charles to put pen to paper. He ultimately did, publishing a tome in 1829 with a ponderous title: *A Narrative of the Sufferings and Adventures of Capt. Charles H. Barnard, in a Voyage Round the World, During the Years 1812, 1813, 1814, 1815, & 1816: Embracing an Account of the Seizure of His Vessel at the Falkland Islands, by an English Crew Whom He Had Rescued from the Horrors of a Shipwreck; and of Their Abandoning Him on an Uninhabited Island, Where He Resided Nearly Two Years.* In the book, Charles offered some context:

> I now submit my journal to the inspection of my fellow-citizens, by whom I hope it will be received with indulgence, as it respects the literary part, as it proceeds from one who has passed the greater part of his life in traversing the boisterous ocean, encountering difficulties and dangers, and who never thought of appearing before the public as an author. The conduct of those British subjects, sons of the self-styled mistress of the ocean, their violation of every agreement, to the faithful observance of which they affixed their signatures, and pledged their honor; and rending thus asunder, and trampling under foot, every tie of gratitude which is always held sacred by civilized man, and which the wild, untutored son of the forest, who looks to nature and nature's God, holds inviolate, with my sufferings subsequent thereto, I present as a plain, unvarnished tale of truth. The publication has been delayed in consequence of the reluctance I felt to appear as an author, or inform the world of the actions of those monsters in human shape, whose bones might now, had it not been for my interference, possibly be blanching in the storms, on a barren and inhospitable island.

Reflecting on his own experience, Charles warned people not to make the same mistake he had made. If there were ever another war with Great Britain, and American sailors came across a shipwrecked crew of a British ship in desperate need of saving, the Americans should first find out how many people had been castaway, Charles argued. If the British outnumbered the Americans, the latter should sail off and leave the castaways behind, even if doing so goes against every humanitar-

A

NARRATIVE

OF THE

SUFFERINGS AND ADVENTURES

OF

CAPT. CHARLES H. BARNARD,

IN

A VOYAGE ROUND THE WORLD,

DURING THE YEARS

1812, 1813, 1814, 1815, & 1816;

EMBRACING AN ACCOUNT OF THE SEIZURE OF HIS VESSEL AT THE

FALKLAND ISLANDS,

BY AN ENGLISH CREW WHOM HE HAD RESCUED FROM THE HORRORS OF A
SHIPWRECK; AND OF THEIR ABANDONING HIM ON AN UNINHABITED
ISLAND, WHERE HE RESIDED NEARLY TWO YEARS.

———————

EMBELLISHED

WITH SIX COPPERPLATE ENGRAVINGS;

ALSO

A CHART, DRAWN BY HIMSELF.

———————

New=York:

PRINTED FOR THE AUTHOR BY J. LINDON, 165 CHATHAM-STREET.—
SOLD BY E. BLISS; G. AND C. AND H. CARVILL; AND D. FELT.—BOSTON,
D. FELT AND CO.

....

1829.

*Title page of Charles H. Barnard's narrative
of his experiences in the Falklands.*

ian impulse, because if the Americans attempted a rescue, the rescuers might be overwhelmed by those they sought to save, and thus their fate would be similar to Charles's. But, Charles added, if he were ever on another trip, and he came across shipwrecked British in numbers less than his own, he would extend the hand of friendship and rescue them. Indeed, on the way back from one of his later expeditions to the South Shetland Islands, Charles did run across a British sailor on the Falklands who had been marooned there by his "iron-hearted captain, and left there to perish." Rather than leave him to that fate, Charles took the sailor on board and delivered him to the British Consulate in New York. Charles ended his book with a hope and some suggestions: "May the sufferings of all others similarly close! I conclude by recommending reparation to all who are injured; patience and perseverance to all in adversity; and gratitude to every American for all the inestimable privileges he enjoys."

Charles's book received only cursory coverage in a few publications. The reviewer for *The New-York Mirror and Ladies' Literary Gazette* said, "[T]he book is not badly written . . . this narrative is well worthy of a perusal . . . we have read it with pleasure, and can honestly recommend it to such of our readers as have a taste for wild adventure; it is as interesting as Riley's farfamed narrative,* and, to say the least, quite as veracious." *The Georgian* newspaper, out of Savannah, gave the book a paragraph, stating that the author "is said to be a person of unquestionable veracity; and the book one of much interest, containing singular adventures and perilous escapes." The book nevertheless did well enough to merit another edition, which was published in 1836.

BEYOND CAPTAINING A FEW sealing voyages in the late 1810s and early 1820s, and writing his book, not much is known about Charles's later life. He spent some time as the commander of a lightship stationed off

---

* In 1817, the American sea captain James Riley published *An Authentic Narrative of the Loss of the American Brig* Commerce, *Wrecked on the Western Coast of Africa, in the Month of August, 1815, with an Account of the Sufferings of Her Surviving Officers and Crew, Who Were Enslaved by the Wandering Arabs on the Great African Desart* [sic], *or Zahahrah; and Observations Historical, Geographical, &c. Made During the Travels of the Author, While a Slave to the Arabs, and in the Empire of Morocco.*

The Captain Charles H. Barnard Museum on New Island.

Located on the edge of Settlement Harbor on the spot where Barnard built his hut, this museum contains exhibits that explain the island's whaling, sealing, and farming history. The research and restoration of the building was carried out by Ian J. Strange MBE, and many other volunteers, from 1973 to 2011. Strange was a British naturalist, conservationist, wildlife artist, and photographer who devoted much of his life to the protection of New Island. He wrote a number of books on the history and wildlife of the Falklands and founded the New Island Conservation Trust in 1995. The trust merged with Falklands Conservation in 2020, and the latter organization currently owns and manages New Island and the museum.

Sandy Hook, New Jersey, and was also the Warden of the Port of New York for a number of years. He clearly was respected within the maritime community, being elected to both The Marine Society of the City of New York and the New York Nautical Institution and Ship Masters' Society. Charles died on November 13, 1863, at the age of eighty-three. Few newspapers covered his passing. One that did, the *New York Herald*, published an announcement that was a mere one sentence long; it said nothing at all about his ordeal on the Falklands so many years earlier. His life ended as it had begun, in relative obscurity.

*Photo showing the settlement on New Island, along the edge of
Settlement Harbor. You can just make out the Barnard Museum at
the head of the harbor. The larger body of water beyond the settlement
is South Harbor. In the distance, Beaver Island is visible.*

*The back of the Barnard Museum on New Island. The wooden ship
beached in the shallows is Protector III, an old sealing/
fishing/trading vessel. It was beached in 1969.*

ACKNOWLEDGMENTS

—

Fɪʀsᴛ ᴀɴᴅ ꜰᴏʀᴇᴍᴏsᴛ, ɪ ᴡᴏᴜʟᴅ ʟɪᴋᴇ ᴛᴏ ᴛʜᴀɴᴋ ᴛʜᴇ ɪɴᴅɪᴠɪᴅᴜᴀʟs ᴀᴛ Lɪᴠᴇ-right who supported, edited, produced, and promoted this book: Zeba Arora, Steve Attardo, Nick Curley, Fanta Diallo, Dan Gerstle, Clio Hamilton, Rebecca Homiski, Kadiatou Keita, Anna Oler, Don Rifkin, and Pete Simon. Copyeditor Kathleen Brandes did a wonderful job, adding many improvements to the text. And my longtime agent, Russ Galen, was, as always, an invaluable source of advice and encouragement. My relationship with him is the most important in my writing life. I couldn't have asked for a better literary partner.

Early readers of my manuscript provided constructive comments that improved the book, and I thank Jennifer Dolin, Bethany Groff Dorau, Ruth Rooks, and Jean Uhlig. Other people who helped me out along the way include: Beth Alcock, David Bailey, Andrea Barlow, Alison Barton, Jessica Brady, David Cain, Rachael Crowie, Ross Chaloner, Julia Dudley, Andrew Maule Dewar Durie, Bruce Durie, Christian Frances Dewar Durie, Michael Dyer, Gail Grandinetti, Michael Harrison, Jeane LaPorta, Virginia Martin, Chris May, Lindsey May, David Miller, Nick Morton, Susan Mulvey, Alan Neumann, Jonathan Palmer, Mark D. Procknik, Renae Rapp, Jennie Rayner, Phyl Rendell, Amy Reytar, Sorrel Pompert Robertson, David Rumsey, Jaylyn Barnard Schultz, Mary Sears, Brenda Shufelt, Jennifer Sol, David Stanley, Georgina Strange, Tom Tryniski, Betsy Tyler, Robert Young.

Libraries and other organizations that assisted me include the Abbot Public Library; Caroline Simpson Library–Museums of History New South Wales; David Rumsey Map Collection; John Carter Brown

Library; Dixson Library–State Library of New South Wales; Falklands Conservation; Falkland Islands Tourist Board; Library of Congress; Mitchell Library–State Library of New South Wales; National Archives (United Kingdom); Nantucket Historical Association; National Maritime Museum (United Kingdom); Naval History and Heritage Command; New York Public Library; Phillips Library (Rowley, MA); State Archives and Records Authority of New South Wales; Vaucluse House Collection, Sydney Living Museums; and the Widener Library at Harvard University.

Members of my family, as always, have been my biggest source of strength. They have seen me weather the dramatic ups and downs of being an author and have never wavered in their support, although sometimes they have questioned my sanity. To my daughter Lily, son Harry, mother Ruth, sister Penny, and in-laws Ruth and George Rooks, I say thank you for always being there and not making fun of me too often. Above all, there is Jennifer, my wife. Without her backing, wisdom, and love, I would never have become a writer, nor would life have been as sweet.

Finally, I want to thank all of my readers, to whom I have dedicated this book. You have not only given me a career but also have given me the greatest compliment imaginable, your time and appreciation. If you keep reading, I will keep writing.

NOTES

=

ABBREVIATIONS USED IN THE NOTES

CHB   Charles H. Barnard, *A Narrative of the Sufferings and Adventures of Capt. Charles H. Barnard, in a Voyage Round the World, During the Years 1812, 1813, 1814, 1815, & 1816; Embracing an Account of the Seizure of His Vessel at the Falkland Islands, by an English Crew Whom He Had Rescued from the Horrors of Shipwreck; and of Their Abandoning Him on an Uninhabited Island, Where He Resided Nearly Two Years* (New York: J. Lindon, 1829)

BPJ   Barzillai Pease Journals, Special Collections Research Center, Syracuse University Libraries

HID   Journal kept by Henry Ingman Defrees, 1811–1817. KWM 978, New Bedford Whaling Museum Library

JH   *The Memoirs of Joseph Holt, General of the Irish Rebels, in 1798*, vol. II, ed. T. Crofton Croker (London: Henry Colburn, 1838). Vols. I and II will be indicated in endnotes.

NA   The National Archives, Kew, Richmond, Greater London

RL   Richard Lundin, "Narrative of a Voyage from New South Wales in 1812–1813," *Lowe's Edinburgh Magazine* (1846)

INTRODUCTION

1   **Charles H. Barnard, captain:** *CHB*, 33–35; and *BPJ*, Journal 13, pages 35–36. Please note that the dates recollected by Barnard are off by one or two days from the dates recollected by Pease. Since Pease was keeping his journal in real time, and Barnard's dates come from a book written many years later, I have, for the most part, used Pease's dates.

1   **"awaited the approach . . . that she had been [there]":** *CHB*, 33–35.

CHAPTER 1: A-SEALING WE SHALL GO

3   **Early in 1812:** *CHB.*, v–vii.

3   **prosperous New York:** *The Wealth and Biography of the Wealthy Citizens of The City*

of New York (New York: Published at the Sun Office, 1846), 22; and Walter Barrett, *The Old Merchants of New York City*, vol. 1 (New York: Thomas R. Knox & Co., 1885), 294.

5   **Ultimately, the Americans**: Eric Jay Dolin, *When America First Met China: An Exotic History of Tea, Drugs, and Money in the Age of Sail* (New York: W. W. Norton, 2012), 104–64.

5   **The king of furs**: James L. Bodkin, "Sea Otter (*Enhydra lutris*)," *Wild Mammals of North America: Biology, Management, and Conservation*, edited by George A. Feldhamer, Bruce Carlyle Thompson, Joseph A. Chapman (Baltimore: Johns Hopkins University Press, 2003), 736.

5   **The first American . . . three years earlier**: Eric Jay Dolin, *Fur, Fortune, and Empire: The Epic History of the Fur Trade in America* (New York: W. W. Norton, 2010), 146–51.

7   **One lucky seaman**: James Cook and James King, *The Voyages of Captain James Cook*, vol. II (London: William Smith, 1842), 529–32.

7   **The description . . . times that amount**: Stackpole, *The Sea-Hunters*, 183–86; and Kenneth J. Bertrand, *Americans in Antarctica, 1775–1948* (New York: American Geographical Society, 1971), 20–24; John M. Bullard, *The Rotches* (New Bedford, MA: Privately printed, 1947), 51–53, 60, 70; and Ebenezer Townsend, Jr., "The Diary of Mr. Ebenezer Townsend, Jr., The Supercargo of the Sealing Ship *Neptune*, On Her Voyage to the South Pacific and Canton," *Papers of the New Haven Colony Historical Society*, vol. IV (New Haven: Printed for the Society, 1888), 1–3, 28.

9   **The scope of . . . cleared $53,118**: James Kirker, *Adventures to China: Americans in the Southern Oceans, 1792–1812* (New York: Oxford University Press, 1970), 8–9, 71–72, 167. See also Amasa Delano, *A Narrative of Voyages and Travels, in the Northern and Southern Hemispheres: Comprising Three Voyages Round the World* (Boston: E. G. House, 1817), 306–7; Edmund Fanning, *Voyages to the South Seas, Indian and Pacific Oceans, China Sea, North-West Coast, Feejee Islands* [Fiji], *South Shetlands, &c.* (New York: William H. Vermilye, 1838), 341; and Briton Cooper Busch, *The War Against the Seals: A History of the North American Seal Fishery* (Kingston, Ontario: McGill-Queen's University Press, 1985), 8, 20–36.

9   **It wasn't only . . . as an illuminant**: Busch, *The War Against the Seals*, 3–22; and Kirker, *Adventures in China*, 10–17.

9   **This high-quality**: Busch, *The War Against the Seals*, 164; and George Brown Goode, *The Fisheries and Fishery Industries of the United States, section V, vol. II Senate, 47th Congress, 1st session, miscellaneous document 124, part 6* (Washington, DC: Government Printing Office, 1887), 403.

10   **Charles's father . . . learn his craft**: New England Historic Genealogical Society, *Vital Records of Nantucket, Massachusetts, To The Year 1850*, vol. III (Boston: New England Historic Genealogical Society, 1927), 8, 76; Bertha S. Dodge, *Marooned: Being a Narrative of the Sufferings and Adventures of Captain Charles H. Barnard, Embracing an Account of the Seizure of his Vessel at the Falkland Islands, &c., 1812–1816* (Syracuse: Syracuse University Press, 1986), 17; William Wade Hinshaw, *Encyclopedia of American Quaker Genealogy*, vol. III (Ann Arbor: Edwards Brothers, 1940), 26; *CHB*, 63; "United States Census, 1790," database with images, GenealogyBank (https://genealogybank.com/#), Valentine Barnard, Hudson, Columbia, New York, United States (original index: United States Census, 1790, FamilySearch, 2014); and "Portsmouth, Dec. 19," *Shipping News* (December 26, 1795). *Vital Records of Nantucket*, above, says that Valentine moved his family from Nantucket to Hudson in 1778, but the book also notes that the source for this information— the William C. Folger genealogical records in the possession of the Nantucket Historical Association—are suspect, and "should be received with caution." That, plus the fact that Hudson did not become Hudson until the mid-1780s, and that there is no evidence of folks from Nantucket leaving for upstate New York in the midst of the war, leads this author to conclude that Charles was born on Nantucket, and Valentine left for Hudson a few years later.

10 **Despite being . . . shipborne trade**: Margaret B. Schram, *Hudson's Merchants and Whalers: The Rise and Fall of a River Port, 1783–1850* (Hensonville, NY: Black Dome Press, 2004), 16–24.

12 **"emerged from a Dutch"**: Quoted in Stephen B. Miller, *Historical Sketches of Hudson* (Hudson, NY: Bryan & Webb, 1862), 103.

12 **Much of Hudson's**: Schram, *Hudson's Merchants*, 35–37.

12 **From an early age**: *CHB*, 10.

12 **Charles married**: "Married," *Weekly Museum* (March 24, 1804).

12 **"hireling priest"**: Dodge, *Marooned*, 21. See also Winshaw, *Encyclopedia of American Quaker Genealogy*, vol. III, 26.

12 **by his father, Valentine**: "United States Census, 1810," database with images, GenealogyBank (https://genealogybank.com/#), Valentine Barnard, New York Ward 2, New York, New York, United States. (Original index: United States Census, 1810, FamilySearch, 2014.)

13 **Charles quickly came . . . other men he engaged**: *CHB*, v–vi.

13 **At an auction . . . 10 feet 2 inches**: Ibid., v; "Pittsburgh, January 6," *Relfs Philadelphia Gazette* (January 13, 1804); "Public Sales," *New-York Gazette* (February 11, 1812); and "Register of Vessels" (April 3, 1812), *Manuscript Prize Appeal No. 889, HCA 42/474/889*, NA.

13 **"handsome"**: "Pittsburgh, January 7," *Chronicle Express* (January 19, 1804).

13 **"fast-sailing"**: "For Havanna," *Relfs Philadelphia Gazette* (May 8, 1809).

14 **built in Pittsburgh**: "Pittsburgh, January 6," *Relfs Philadelphia Gazette*.

14 **After its christening**: "Now Landing," *Relfs Philadelphia Gazette* (April 19, 1805); "Now Landing," *United States Gazette* (March 13, 1807); "Port of Philadelphia, June 29," *Mercantile Advertiser* (July 2, 1810); and "Green Coffee and Muscovado Sugar," *Relfs Philadelphia Gazette* (July 16, 1810).

CHAPTER 2: THE CREW

16 **Available records**: Bertrand, *Americans in Antarctica*, 31.

17 **Charles tapped . . . picked them up**: *CHB*, vi.

17 **Almost nothing is**: "British Inhumanity," *The Weekly Register, Supplement to Volume Five*, in The Weekly Register, ed. H. Niles (Baltimore: Franklin Press, 1814), 170; and "List of Officers and Men," April 3, 1812, *Manuscript Prize Appeal No. 889*.

17 **Captain Fanning . . . Oceans, China, etc.**: Betsy Tyler, "Edmund Fanning, I Presume: Or, How to Flesh Out a Life Through Local Records," *Historic Nantucket* (Spring 2004); Walter Frederic Brooks, *History of the Fanning Family*, vol. I (Worcester: Privately printed, 1905), 352; Edmund Fanning, *Voyages & Discoveries in the South Seas, 1792–1832* (Salem: The Southworth Press, 1924 (reproduction of original book prepared by The Marine Research Society of Salem)), iii–v; and Edmund Fanning, *Voyages Round The World; With Selected Sketches of Voyages to the South Seas, North and South Pacific Oceans, China, Etc.* (New York: Collins & Hannay, 1833).

17 **About thirty-eight-year-old**: The background for this section on Pease, and all the quotes, except for one, come from *BPJ*, Journal 1. See also, Harvey Sturm, "The Voyages of Barzillai Pease, American Seaman, 1789–1826," *Mariner's Mirror* (1989), 159–74.

19 **Like so many . . . a passing ship**: Sturm, "The Voyages of Barzillai Pease," 164–66.

20 **At one point**: Ibid., 166.

20 **"I took my leave"**: *BPJ*, Journal 13, March 31, 1812.1.

20 **When finding someone . . . sent home**: *CHB*, vii; *HID*, October 31, 1812; "Register of Vessels" (April 3, 1812), *Manuscript Prize Appeal No. 889*; and *BPJ*, Journal 13, insert in the middle of the journal, directly after protest given to Philip Rutter.

20 **Valentine was quite**: *BPJ*, Journal 13, p. 37.

20 **Besides the five . . . tip of Long Island**: *CHB*, 11; *BPJ*, Journal 13, April 9, 1812; "Sail-

ing Agreement," *Manuscript Prize Appeal No. 889;* and "List of Officers and Men *Nanina,*" *Manuscript Prize Appeal No. 889.*

20 **Henry Ingman Defrees:** *HID,* May 19, 1812.

CHAPTER 3: WAR INTERVENES

23 **By 1811:** George C. Daughan, *1812: The Navy's War* (New York: Basic Books, 2011), 1–22; and Robert P. Watson, *America's First Crisis: The War of 1812* (Albany: Excelsior Editions, 2014), 3–16. 60–62.

23 **Since 1800, Britain:** Alfred Thayer Mahan, *Sea Power in its Relations to the War of 1812,* vol. I (Boston: Little, Brown, 1905), 299–300.

23 **"war hawks . . . Sailors' Rights":** Quoted in Robert Leckie, *The Wars of America* (New York: Harper & Row, 1968), 232.

23 **Then, in May . . . war was declared:** Benjamin W. Labaree, William M. Fowler, Jr., Edward W. Sloan, John B. Hattendorf, Jeffrey J. Safford, and Andrew W. German, *America and the Sea: A Maritime History* (Mystic, CT: Mystic Seaport, 1998), 198, 212; Leckie, *The Wars of America,* 230–31; "Remarks (On Board the USS *President,* Commodore Rodgers) Made by M.C. Perry," in *Proceedings of the United States Naval Institute,* vol. XV (Annapolis, MD: United States Naval Institute, 1889), 339–42; and "From James Madison to Congress, 1 April 1812," *Founders Online,* National Archives.

24 **When they learned . . . Sandy Hook, New Jersey:** *CHB,* 10; *BPJ,* Journal 13, April 5, 1812; and *HID,* April 7, 1812.

25 **Seventy ships:** John Bach McMaster, *A History of the People of the United States: From the Revolution to the Civil War,* vol. III (New York: D. Appleton and Company, 1910), 451.

CHAPTER 4: VOYAGE TO THE FALKLANDS

26 **It took thirty-four . . . waterspout:** *BPJ,* Journal 13, April 12, 1812 to May 16, 1812.

26 **"one of the finest . . . mechanical shop":** Ibid., May 7, 1812.

26 **"the best in":** Ibid., May 19, 1812.

28 **"by his temerity":** *HID,* June 5 and June 14, 1812.

28 **"saucily on board":** *CHB,* 11; *BPJ,* Journal 13, June 22, 1812; *HID,* June 23, 1812. 16.

29 **"Neptune is, indeed":** *CHB,* 11.

29 **On July 4 . . . tempers cooled:** *HID,* July 4, 1812.

29 **In subsequent weeks:** *BPJ,* Journal 13, June 22 to September 6, 1812; and Dodge, *Marooned,* 218–20.

29 **No doubt contributing:** Ibid., August 9, 1812.

30 **"committed [the cat]":** *HID,* July 8, 1813.

CHAPTER 5: THE WINDSWEPT ISLES

32 **Powerful, nearly constant:** Met Office National Meteorological Archive, *South Atlantic Climate Brief,* Table 4.1 (London: Meteorological Office, 1990). See also Ian J. Strange, *The Falkland Islands* (London: David & Charles, 1972), 4.

32 **"the principal evil":** Robert Fitzroy, *Narrative of the Surveying Voyages of His Majesty's Ships Adventure and Beagle, between the Years 1826 and 1836,* vol. II (London: Henry Colburn, 1839), 243.

32 **When the wind . . . being knocked down:** Personal communication with Alison Barton, a former warden on New Island, September 28, 2022.

32 **During the Southern Hemisphere's . . . chills the bones:** Met Office, *South Atlantic Climate Brief,* Table 4.1. These averages are based on a dataset for temperatures in Stanley, the capital of the Falkland Islands, in the years 1962–1981, which is the most recent dataset available. An older dataset for 1874–1941 indicates that the aver-

age temperatures at Stanley were slightly lower than in the later period. See Met Office National Meteorological Archive, *Tables of temperature, relative humidity and precipitation for the world. Part 2 Central and South America, The West Indies and Bermuda—M.O. 617b* (London: Meteorological Office, 1978), 26–27.

33 **Despite speculation**: Kit M. Hamley et al., "Evidence of Prehistoric Human Activity in the Falkland Islands," *Science Advances* (October 27, 2021); and T. J. Clark, Jason Newton, and Ewan D. Wakefield, "Comment on 'Evidence of prehistoric human activity in the Falkland Islands'," *Science Advances* (April 29, 2022).

33 **Which Europeans deserve**: The background for this section on the discovery of the Falklands comes from a number of documents, including Robert Greenhow, "The Falkland Islands: A Memoir; Descriptive, Historical, and Political," *Hunt's Merchants' Magazine* (February 1842), 112; Lowell S. Gustafson, *The Sovereignty Dispute over the Falkland (Malvinas) Islands* (New York: Oxford University Press, 1988), 3–4; Barry Gough, *The Falkland Islands/Malvinas: The Contest for Empire in the South Atlantic* (London: The Athlone Press, 1992), 47–48; Rudolf Dozer, *The Territorial Status of the Falkland Islands (Malvinas): Past and Present* (New York: Oceana Publications, Inc., 1993), 1–29; Marcelo G. Kohen and Facundo D. Rodríguez, *The Malvinas/Falklands Between History and Law: Refutation of the British Pamphlet 'Getting It Right: The Real History of the Falklands/Malvinas'* (self-published, CreateSpace, 2017); Julius Goebel Jr., *The Struggle for the Falkland Islands: A Study in Legal and Diplomatic History* (New Haven: Yale University Press, 1927), 1–46; Angela Fordham, *Falkland Islands: A Bibliography of 50 Examples of Printed Maps Bearing Specific Reference to the Falkland Islands* (London: A. Wheaton and Co., 1964), 1–9; Mary Cawkell, *The Falkland Story, 1592–1982* (Shropshire, UK: Anthony Nelson, 1983), 1–16; Graham Pascoe and Peter Pepper, *Getting It Right: The Real History of the Falklands/Malvinas* (pamphlet published by the authors in 2008); Raphael Perl, *The Falkland Islands Dispute in International Law and Politics: A Documentary Sourcebook* (London: Oceana Publications, 1983), 4–6; and "History of the Falklands," *Britannica*.

33 **"[T]he records of"**: Goebel, *The Struggle for the Falkland Islands*, 2.

33 **Treaty of Tordesillas**: H. Michael Tarver and Emily Slape, "Overview Essay," in *The Spanish Empire: A Historical Encyclopedia*, vol. I, ed. H. Michael Tarver and Emily Slape (Santa Barbara: ABC-CLIO, 2016), 61–62.

34 **"fifty leagues"**: John Lane, "Cavendish—Last Voyage," in *Voyages of the Elizabethan Seamen to America, Select Narratives from the "Principal Navigations" of Hakluyt*, ed. Edward John Payne (Oxford: Clarendon Press, 1900), 145. See also Gough, *The Falkland Islands/Malvinas*, 3; and Strange, *The Falkland Islands*, 47–48.

34 **Things are clearer**: Background for this section on the settlement of the Falklands comes from Strange, *The Falkland Islands*, 51–55; Gough, *The Falkland Islands/Malvinas*, 8–27; Antoine-Joseph Pernety, *The History of a Voyage to the Malouine (or Falkland) Islands: Made in 1763 and 1764, Under the Command of M. de Bougainville, in Order to Form a Settlement There, and of Two Voyages to the Streights of Magellan, with an Account of the Patagonians* (London: T. Jefferys, 1771); Goebel, *The Struggle for the Falkland Islands*, 137, 226–410; and Paul Morrison, *The Falkland Islands* (Bourne End, Bucks., UK: Aston Publications, 1990), 4–6.

34 **In late January**: Morrison, *The Falkland Islands*, 4.

34 **"The inhabitants"**: V. F. Boyson, *The Falkland Islands* (Oxford: Clarendon Press, 1924), fn 30. See also Ibid., 30–31.

35 **By the mid-eighteenth**: "The Falkland Islands," *Hunt's Merchants Magazine*, 113.

35 **"prove extremely"**: George Anson, *A Voyage Round The World, in the Years 1740, 1741, 1742, 1743, 1744, by George Anson*, compiled by Richard Walter (London: John and Paul Knapton, 1748), 128.

35 **Despite Anson's boosterism**: G. T. Whitington, *The Falkland Islands* (London: Smith, Elder & Co., 1840), 5.

39 **"We found"**: Jedidiah Morse, *The American Universal Geography: Or A View of the*

Present State of All the Empires, Kingdoms, States and Republiks in the Known World, part first (Boston: J. T. Buckingham, 1805), 836.

39   **"[N]o inviting objects"**: Lewis de Bougainville, *A Voyage Round the World, Performed by Order of His Most Christian Majesty, In the Years 1766, 1767, 1768, and 1769*, trans. John Reinhold Forster (London: J. Nourse, 1772), 45.

39   **miserable . . . brown color"**: Charles Darwin, *Journal of Researches into the Natural History and Geology of the Countries Visited During the Voyage Round the World of H.M.S. Beagle*, vol. II (London: John Murray, 1873), 187.

39   **"The Falkland Islands are not"**: K. A. Patmore, "A Land of Derelicts," *Living Age* (July 3, 1897), 30.

39   **"It appeared to me"**: Delano, *A Narrative of Voyages and Travels*, 264.

40   **"With regard to"**: Laughlan Bellingham Mackinnon, *Atlantic and Transatlantic: Sketches Afloat and Ashore* (New York: Harper & Brothers, 1852), 264.

40   **"[T]he Falkland Islands"**: Townsend, "The Diary of Mr. Ebenezer Townsend, Jr.," 32.

40   **While the Falklands**: P. J. Stewart, "Trees for the Falkland Islands," *The Commonwealth Forestry Review* (September 1982), 219–25.

41   **"like a forest"**: "Notes From Books: The Tussock Grass of the Falkland Islands," *The Friend: A Religious and Literary Journal* (July 7, 1850), 125.

41   **The islands also**: Kew Botanic Gardens, "Falkland Islands," Witington, *The Falkland Islands*, 36–40; Phillip Parker King and Robert Fitzroy, *The South America Pilot* (London: Printed for the Hydrographic Office, Admiralty, 1860), 72; and Brewster, "Falkland Islands," *The Edinburgh Encyclopedia*, vol. IX (Edinburgh: Printed for William Blackwood, 1830), 271.

42   **"avoid kelp"**: "Soundings in the Atlantic," *The Nautical Magazine* (October 1832), 398. See also, Whitington, *The Falkland Islands*, 69.

42   **By dampening**: Townsend, "The Diary of Mr. Ebenezer Townsend, Jr.," 36.

43   **Not plentiful**: "The Warrah," Falkland Islands Museum and National Trust.

43   **The most important**: The background for these seals comes from Randall Reeves et al., Pieter Folkens, illustrator, *National Audubon Society Guide to Marine Mammals of the World* (New York: Knopf, 2002), 79–81, 106–9, 158–61; Townsend, "The Diary of Mr. Ebenezer Townsend, Jr.," 35–36; and W. H. B. Webster, *Narrative of a Voyage to the Southern Atlantic Ocean, in the Years 1828, 29, 30, Performed in H. M. Sloop Chanticleer*, vol. I (London: Richard Bentley, 1834), 104, 114.

44   **"like the flash"**: Webster, *Narrative of a Voyage to the Southern Atlantic Ocean*, 114; and Busch, *The War Against the Seals*, 6–7.

45   **"with outstretched neck"**: James Murie, "Report on the Eared Seals collected by the Society's Keeper François Lecomte in the Falkland Islands," *Proceedings of the Scientific Meetings of the Zoological Society of London for the Year 1869* (London: Longmans, Green, Reader, and Dyer, 1869), 106.

CHAPTER 6: THE KILLING BEGINS

48   **After so much time**: The background to this chapter comes from *BPJ*, Journal 13, September 7, 1812, to January 28, 1813; *HID*, September 7, 1812, to December 31, 1812; and *CHB*, 11–12.

48   **"A man might . . . a sea-beach"**: James Fenimore Cooper, *The Sea Lions; or, The Lost Sealers* (Paris: Baudry's European Library, 1849), 30.

50   **Although this was**: Delano, *A Narrative of Voyages and Travels*, 306.

50   **Once the drying . . . for years**: Townsend, "The Diary of Mr. Ebenezer Townsend, Jr.," 35–36; and Delano, *A Narrative of Voyages and Travels*, 306–7.

51   **Both men stripped**: *BPJ*, Journal 13, September 22, 1812; and *BPJ*, Journal 13, insert in the middle of the journal, directly after the protest given to Philip Rutter.

51   **At about the same**: *HID*, October 4, 1812.

51 **"have his heart's blood"**: *BPJ*, Journal 13, October 3, 1812.

54 **"blow [Fanning's]"**: *HID*, October 4, 1812. See also, *BPJ*, Journal, insert in the middle of the journal, directly after the protest given to Philip Rutter.

54 **Charles was angry... then stormed off**: *BPJ*, Journal 13, October 3, 1812; and *HID*, October 4, 1812.

54 **"to lay awake"**: *BPJ*, Journal 13, October 3, 1812.

54 **"mate, master, and owner"**: Ibid. See also, *BPJ*, Journal 13, insert in the middle of the journal, directly after the protest given to Philip Rutter.

54 **"a disposition to quarrel"**: *BPJ*, Journal 13, insert in the middle of the journal, directly after the protest given to Philip Rutter.

54 **"Collossean"**: *BPJ*, Journal 13, September 22 and October 3, 1812.

54 **"had always been"**: *BPJ*, Journal 1, 13.

54 **"surly"**: Ibid., 4.

55 **"I am sorry"**: *HID*, October 4, 1812.

55 **"hanging on his"**: Ibid.

55 **When the other... at the islands**: Ibid. and *HID*, October 31, 1812.

56 **"promised that he"**: *HID*, October 31, 1812.

57 **A few days after**: Ibid., November 2, 1812.

57 **A little more**: *BPJ*, Journal 13, November 25, 1812; and *HID*, November 25, 1812.

57 **During one**: *BPJ*, Journal 13, December 10, 1812.

CHAPTER 7: RIPPLES OF WAR

58 **On January 3, 1813**: *CHB*, 12; and *HID*, January 22, 1813.

59 **"null and void"**: *CHB*, 12.

60 **"[T]he time in"**: Ibid., 13. See also, *BPJ*, Journal 13, January 20 to January 25, 1812.

61 **"protected by four"**: *CHB*, 13.

CHAPTER 8: THE *ISABELLA*

62 **On a very hot**: Background on the *Isabella* comes from *JH*, vol. II, 230–24; The Archives Authority of New South Wales to Bertha S. Dodge, (April 22, 1974), in the MIT Archives Dodge Papers; *RL*, 282; Report of Richard Lundin to Manley Dixon, (September 13, 1813), *ADM* 1/21, NA; and David Miller, *The Wreck of the* Isabella (Annapolis: Naval Institute Press, 1995), 7–9.

62 **The *Isabella* had ten**: D. J. Cross to Bertha Dodge (April 22, 1974), in the Dodge Archive; and Miller, *The Wreck*, 8.

62 **Among them were**: Miller, *The Wreck*, 10–12.

62 **Durie was the senior**: "Government and General Orders," *The Sydney Gazette and New South Wales Advertiser* (November 7, 1812).

62 **Another Scottish**: "Governor Macquarie to Earl of Liverpool," *Historical Records of Australia*, series I, vol. VII (Sydney: The Library Committee of the Commonwealth Parliament, 1916), 617.

63 **Another passenger was**: Background for Richard Brooks comes from: Christine Maher, *Richard Brooks: From Convict Ship Captain to Pillar of Early Colonial Australia* (Kenthurst, Australia: Rosenberg Publishing, 2016); 9, 31–67. Vivienne Parsons, "Brooks, Richard (1765–1833)," *Australian Dictionary of Biography*, National Centre of Biography, Australian National University, https://adb.anu.edu.au/biography/brooks-richard-1830/text2103, published first in hardcopy 1966, accessed online October 22, 2022; Charles Bateson, *The Convict Ships: 1787–1868* (Glasgow: Brown, Son & Ferguson, 1959), 163–68.

63 **That was a death rate**: Maher, *Richard Brooks*, 55.

63 **"in a dreadfully"**: Bateson, *The Convict Ships*, 166.

64 **"the want of proper"**: "Examination Into the Conduct of Captain Brooks," *Historical*

Records of Australia, Series I, vol. III (Sydney: The Library Committee of the Commonwealth Parliament, 1915), 556.

64   **Britain's twenty-five-year-old**: Background for this policy comes from Robert Hughes, *The Fatal Shore: The Epic of Australia's Founding* (New York: Alfred A. Knopf, 1987), 40–77.

64   **Between 1718 and 1775**: Emily Salmon, "Convict Labor during the Colonial Period," Encyclopedia Virginia. Don Jordan and Michael Walsh, *White Cargo: The Forgotten History of Britain's White Slaves in America* (New York: New York University Press, 2008), 13–15; and Hughes, *The Fatal Shore*, 41.

65   **"venomous reptiles"**: "Felons and Rattlesnakes," *The Pennsylvania Gazette* (May 9, 1751).

65   **One well-known**: Background for this section on Holt comes from *JH*, vol. I, xii–xiv, 1–37, 314–27, 364–67; *JH*, vol. II, 23–25; and G. C. Bolton, "Holt, Joseph (1756–1826)," *Australian Dictionary of Biography*, National Centre of Biography, Australian National University, https://adb.anu.edu.au/biography/holt-joseph-2194/text2831, accessed October 21, 2022; Miller, *The Wreck*, 12–14; and "A Proclamation," *The Freeman's Journal* (September 25, 1798).

65   **ex-convict servants**: *JH*, vol. II, 320; and Miller, *The Wreck*, 15.

65   **"contented with"**: *JH*, vol. I, 15.

67   **"revenge"**: Ibid., 32.

67   **"sword, cane"**: Ibid., 27.

67   **"General Holt"**: Ibid., 206.

69   **To ensure that**: *JH*, vol. II, 320.

70   **Another infamous**: Background for this section on Hayes: Mary Pike and Ann Penrose, "The Case of Sir Henry Browne Hayes," *Historical Records of New South Wales*, vol. III, ed. F. M. Bladen (Sydney: Charles Potter, 1895), 281–83; John Philpot Currant, *The Speeches of The Right Honorable John Philpot Curran*, ed. Thomas Davis (Dublin: James Duffy, 1845), 462–82; *Trial of Sir Henry Browne Hayes, Knt, For Forcibly and Feloniously Taking Away Miss Mary Pike, on the Twenty-Second Day of July, 1797* (Cork, Ireland: James Haley, 1801); Charles Bertie, "Sir Henry Browne Hayes: A Stormy Petrel," *The Lone Hand* (January 1, 1910), 236–40; Charles H. Bertie, *Story of Vaucluse House and Sir Henry Browne Hayes* (Sydney: Vaucluse Park Trust, 1921); N. S. Lynravn, "Hayes, Sir Henry Browne (1762–1832)," *Australian Dictionary of Biography*, National Centre of Biography, Australian National University, https://adb.anu.edu.au/biography/hayes-sir-henry-browne-2172/text2787, accessed October 23, 2022; Miller, *The Wreck*, 15–16; "Kilkenny," *Finns Leinster Journal* (July 29, 1797); "Cork, Oct. 25," *The Freeman's Journal* (October 28, 1790); and "Lord Lieutenant and Council of Ireland, A Proclamation," *The Freeman's Journal* (October 5, 1797).

72   **Hayes paid . . . aboard the *Atlas***: Maher, *Richard Brooks*, 33–34.

72   **"stupid when sober"**: Ibid., 42.

72   **"Sir Harry"**: Miller, *The Wreck*, 16.

73   **Four others were**: Ibid., 19; and Maher, *Richard Brooks*, 107.

73   **One contemporary**: *CHB*, 154.

73   **Mattinson even took out**: "Advertisement," *Sydney Gazette and New South Wales Advertiser* (November 7, 1812).

73   **There were also**: *CHB*, 154; and W. E. May to Bertha Dodge (August 3, 1777), Dodge Archive.

74   **"The ship what"**: "On Nautical Superstition," *The United Service Journal and Naval and Military Magazine* (April 1838), 436.

74   **"[O]ur vessel was"**: *RL*, 282.

75   **Officer, Crew, and Passengers on the *Isabella***: *HID*, April 4, 1813; and Miller, *The Wreck*, 11.

CHAPTER 9: ON THE EDGE OF DISASTER

76 **Twelve days after leaving:** Background for this section on the *Isabella*'s near miss comes from *RL*, 282–84; Holt, vol. 2, 324–25; and "Report of Richard Lundin to Manley Dixon" (September 13, 1813).

76 **It was only a few:** Kenneth Panton, *Historical Dictionary of the British Empire* (Lanham, MD: Rowman & Littlefield, 2015), 106–7, 303–4.

77 **"Nothing could now be":** *RL*, 283.

78 **"were very much":** *JH*, vol. II, 325.

78 **"very hard set":** Ibid.

79 **"the deck to":** *RL*, 284.

79 **"[I]f the ship":** *JH*, vol. II, 326.

CHAPTER 10: GRIEF

80 **Around one in the morning:** *RL*, 284; and "Report of Richard Lundin to Manley Dixon" (September 13, 1813).

80 **"[R]ocks on one":** *JH*, vol. II, 327.

80 **"with dreadful":** *RL*, 284; and "Report of Richard Lundin to Manley Dixon" (September 13, 1813).

80 **"God's mercy":** *JH*, vol. II, 327.

82 **"[T]here is now":** Ibid., 328.

82 **"[W]e shall have":** *CHB*, 155.

83 **"rage and disappointment":** *RL*, 285.

83 **"effrontery, pleading . . . primary consideration":** Ibid., 286.

83 **"supported herself":** Ibid.

85 **Only Holt's third:** *JH*, vol. II, 329.

85 **"Never":** *RL*, 286.

85 **"sorrowful bank":** *JH*, vol. II, 330.

85 **"I will, Madam":** Ibid.

CHAPTER 11: FORLORN

86 **On the day after:** Background for this chapter is from "Report of Richard Lundin to Manley Dixon" (September 13, 1813); *JH*, vol. II, 330–42; and *RL*, 287–89.

87 **"Newtown Providence":** *JH*, vol. II, 368.

87 **"had it been":** *RL*, 287.

87 **"for he was":** *JH*, vol. II, 332.

88 **"First—That no man":** Ibid., 332–33.

89 **"bleak and barren":** *RL*, 286.

89 **"[Y]ou may rest":** *JH*, vol. II, 336.

90 **"good reason for":** Ibid., 335.

90 **"as fine indeed":** Ibid., 353.

90 **"spoke, and whistled . . . pretty polly":** Ibid., 355–56.

91 **"black rages":** Miller, *The Wreck*, 9.

91 **"in the agonies":** *CHB*, 156.

91 **"her hard lot":** *JH*, vol. II, 337.

91 **"endeavored to":** Ibid., 337–38.

92 **"a safe passage":** Ibid., 341.

92 **named Eliza Providence Durie:** Miller, *The Wreck*, 12.

92 **"drank very heartily":** *JH*, vol. II, 342.

92 **"it was only":** *RL*, 288.

CHAPTER 12: SEARCHING FOR SALVATION

94 **Unfortunately, the longboat:** Background for this section and all the quotes come
    from *RL*, 289–99.
99 **The first decision:** Background for this section about the voyage to Montevideo and
    all the quotes come from *RL*, 299–301.

CHAPTER 13: GETTING HELP

102 **Shortly after the six:** Background for this chapter and all of the quotes not otherwise
     cited come from *RL*, 302–7.
104 **"Nothing but the":** "April," *Edinburgh Annual Register* (1813), xxvii–xxviii; and
     "London News Continued," *Caledonian Mercury* (June 14, 1813).
105 **"Falkland Islands, Feb. 22":** "Robert Durie to Admiral De Courcy" (February 22,
     1813), Edward Tagart, *A Memoir of the Late Captain Peter Heywood, R.N.* (London:
     Effingham Wilson, Royal Exchange, 1832), 272.
106 **Heywood, at age fifteen:** For background on Heywood's involvement with the *Bounty*,
     the mutiny, and what followed, see Caroline Alexander, *The* Bounty: *The True Story of
     the Mutiny on the* Bounty (New York: Viking, 2003).
107 **After hearing . . . without delay:** Peter Heywood to Lt. D'Aranda (April 1, 1813), *ADM
     1/2855*, NA.
108 **The bottom line:** Miller, *The Wreck*, 90.
108 **took about a month to complete:** Miller, *The Wreck*, 78–79, 88–91; and "Notes about
     letter to Lieut. D'Aranda" (September 20, 1812), *ADM 50/98*, NA.
108 **Lundin volunteered:** "Report of Richard Lundin to Manley Dixon" (September 13,
     1813).
108 **Thus, his eagerness:** *CHB*, 27, 264.
108 **"utmost dispatch":** "D'Aranda's Log of the *Nancy*" April 10, 1813, *ADM 51/2601*, NA.
108 **The *Nancy* was also:** "Muster-Table of his Majesty's Brig the *Nancy*, between April 1
     and May 31, 1813," Nancy's Muster Table, *ADM 37/3851*, NA.
108 **Among the items:** "D'Aranda's Log of the *Nancy*," April 15, 1813.
109 **"As misfortune was one":** Tagart, *A Memoir of the Late Captain Peter Heywood, R.N.*,
     273–74.

CHAPTER 14: DISCOVERY

111 **The crew of the *Young Nanina*:** Background for this section on the discovery of the
     survivors comes from *CHB*, 15–22; and *JH*, vol. II, 356–58.
111 **Then, on March 30:** *HID*, March 30, 1813.
112 **This convinced him:** *CHB*, 18.
112 **"Among the latter":** Ibid., 18–19. See also *HID*, April 3, 181.
112 **"with as much ardor":** *CHB*, 19.
113 **"between hope and despair":** *JH*, vol. II, 356.
113 **"the most visionary":** *CHB*, 21.
113 **The boat had:** Ibid., 27.
113 **"change in their":** Ibid., 21.
115 **"of Captain Higton":** Ibid., 22.
115 **When they returned:** *RL*, 310.
115 **"We were so much":** *JH*, vol. II, 359.

CHAPTER 15: DEAL

116 **"the history of their":** *CHB*, 22–23.
116 **Since first constructing. . . food warm:** *JH*, vol. II, 347.

116 **The men had made:** *CHB*, fn 23.

116 **"chère amie . . . these desolate shores":** Ibid., 23.

118 **"conversed with . . . extent of our power":** *CHB*, 24–25.

118 **In fact, both Charles:** Valentine Barnard, Andrew Hunter, Barzillai Pease, and Edmund Fanning, "Protest to Philip Rutter" (September 6, 1813), *Manuscript Prize Appeal No. 889.*

118 **To convince them . . . opportunity for profit:** *CHB*, 25; *BPJ*, Journal, insert in the middle of the journal, directly after the protest given to Philip Rutter; Thomas Walker, "Appeal" (November 29, 1815), *Manuscript Prize Appeal No. 889*; and *HID*, April 5, 1813, NA.

118 **And that profit:** "Account of the Cargo," Document D, in Valentine Barnard, "Statement before Robert Sedgewick, Notary Public for the State of New York" (May 19, 1815), *Manuscript Prize Appeal No. 889*; *CHB*, 25; and "British Inhumanity," 170–71.

119 **Finally, the master:** "British Inhumanity," 171.

119 **"appeared surprised":** *CHB*, 25.

119 **"would use his":** Valentine Barnard and Barzillai Pease, "Statement before Robert Sedgewick, Notary Public for the State of New York" (May 19, 1815), *Manuscript Prize Appeal No. 889.*

119 **"Now you all have":** *JH*, vol. II, 361.

120 **With the agreement . . . three people:** Ibid., 362.

121 **When adding Charles:** *CHB*, 27; *JH*, vol. II, 362; *HID*, April 12, 1813; and "British Inhumanity," 171.

121 **Finally, with everyone:** *HID*, April 12, 1813.

CHAPTER 16: ROUGH PASSAGE

122 **While the *Young Nanina* was:** The background for this chapter and all the quotes, with one exception, come from *CHB*, 28–30. See also *HID*, April 13 to May 3, 1813; "British Inhumanity," 172; and *BPJ*, Journal 13, 33. (At about this point in his journal, Pease stops using daily entries and transitions to more of an essay, with dates thrown in periodically. The manuscript has penciled numbers for the pages at the top, and those are used instead of dates.)

124 **"farce":** *BPJ*, Journal 13, 32.

125 **The next day:** *BPJ*, Journal 13, September 22, 1812.

CHAPTER 17: PREPARATIONS

126 **Right after the *Young Nanina*:** The background for this section on preparations on Eagle Island comes from *JH*, vol. II, 362–65; and "British Inhumanity," 171.

127 **"lived merrily":** *JH*, vol. II, 364.

127 **Barnard's Harbor was:** Background for this section on preparations at Barnard's Harbor comes from *HID*, May 3–17, 1813; *CHB*, 30; and *BPJ*, Journal 13, May 16, 1813.

127 **"staunch as":** *CHB*, 30.

CHAPTER 18: D'ARANDA'S SURPRISE

129 **On April 17, 1813:** The background for this chapter comes from "Logbook of the Master," *ADM 52/4547*, NA; "D'Aranda's Log of the *Nancy*"; *RL*, 307–9; *JH*, vol. II, 365–67; "British Inhumanity," 171; Miller, *The Wreck*, 235; and "D'Aranda," in William R. O'Byrne, *A Naval Biographical Dictionary* (London: John Murray, 1849), 261.

129 **His postings had ranged:** Miller, *The Wreck*, 80–82.

129 **Although his Spanish-sounding . . . of the Falkland Islands:** Ibid., 235–38.

129 **"the weather was":** *RL*, 367.

129   **"tremendous seas"**: "Logbook of the Master" (April 28, 1813); and "D'Aranda's Log of the *Nancy*," (May 4, 1813).

129   **One wave swept:** "D'Aranda's Log of the *Nancy*" (April 28, 1813).

130   **"Sometimes the wind"**: *RL*, 367.

130   **With Britain at war . . . confronted the enemy**: "Logbook of the Master" (May 9, 1813).

130   **"Nothing could exceed"**: *RL*, 308.

131   **"Very well"**: *JH*, vol. II, 366.

131   **It was already apparent:** Ibid.

131   **D'Aranda's opinion:** *RL*, 311; "D'Aranda's Log of the *Nancy*" (May 19, 1813); "Logbook of the Master" (May 19, 1813).

131   **"I regretted that"**: *JH*, vol. II, 366.

131   **"[H]ad I attempted"**: Miller, *The Wreck*, 112–13.

131   **Having dealt . . . with his duties:** Miller, *The Wreck*, 113–14; "D'Aranda's Log of the *Nancy*," (May 21, 1813); "Logbook of the Master" (May 20, 21, 1813).

132   **At 5 a.m. on May 16:** Background for the remainder of this chapter from *HID*, May 16, 1813 to May 25, 1813; "D'Aranda's Log of the *Nancy*" (May 25 to June 15, 1813); "Logbook of the Master" (May 25 to June 15, 1813); *JH*, vol. II, 368; and Miller, *The Wreck*, 115–16.

132   **"damned rascal . . . or gentleman"**: *HID*, May 25, 1813. At this point, Defrees stopped making daily entries, and, after the May 25 entry, he concluded the journal with an extended essay, which detailed what happened after May 25 until the *Nanina*'s arrival in Rio de Janeiro. Subsequent references to the May 25 journal entry pertain to this essay.

CHAPTER 19: TREACHERY

134   **Charles's plan:** Background for this chapter comes from *BPJ*, Journal 13, June 1, 1813, to June 15, 1813, 34–36, and an insert in the middle of the journal, directly after the protest given to Philip Rutter: *CHB*, 30–32, 263; *HID*, May 25, 1813; "British Inhumanity," 172; and *HID*, May 25, 1813.

134   **hurled insults:** *BPJ*, Journal 13, May 18, 1813.

134   **"mutinous disposition"**: *CHB*, 30.

134   **To keep things . . . by a sentry:** *BPJ*, 34.

135   **On one of those:** *BPJ*, Journal 13, May 31, 1813, and 34–35.

135   **"fine ones"**: *CHB*, 64.

135   **"would rather wait"**: "British Inhumanity," 172; and Valentine Barnard et al., "Protest to Philip Rutter."

135   **When this plan:** *BPJ*, Journal, insert in the middle of the journal, directly after the protest given to Philip Rutter.

136   **The *Nanina*'s boat:** *CHB*, 136.

136   **"the most experienced"**: Ibid., fn 77.

137   **On June 13 . . . as soon as possible:** *BPJ*, Journal, insert in the middle of the journal, directly after the protest given to Philip Rutter, and 35.

137   **"had no objection . . . whatever happens"**: *BPJ*, Journal 13, June 13, 1813.

137   **"without sufficient"**: *RL*, 310.

138   **But when the *Nanina* . . . whether anyone appeared:** *BPJ*, Journal 13, June 14, 1813; Valentine Barnard et al., "Protest to Philip Rutter."

138   **"in the depth"**: *CHB*, 263.

CHAPTER 20: JUSTIFICATION

139   **At 9:13 a.m.:** Background for this chapter comes from *BPJ*, Journal 13, June 14 to July 27, 1813, and 36–37; "British Inhumanity," 171–72; *RL*, 311–13; *JH*, vol. II, 368; *HID*,

May 25, 1813; "D'Aranda's Log of the *Nancy*" (June 15 to July 27, 1813); "Logbook of the Master" (June 15 to July 27, 1813); and Miller, *The Wreck*, 115-20, 213-15.

139   **"with much hostility"**: *BPJ*, Journal 13, June 15, 1813, and 36.

140   **"Brought the *Nanina*"**: "D'Aranda's Log of the *Nancy*" (June 16, 1813).

140   **"Got intelligence"**: "Logbook of the Master" (June 16, 1813). See also Miller, *The Wreck*, 120.

140   **There was, however... from the Americans**: Miller, *The Wreck*, 120, 214-15.

141   **"late crew left"**: "D'Aranda's Log of the *Nancy*" (June 16, 1813).

141   **"I felt for... debt of gratitude"**: *JH*, vol. II, 370.

142   **"a shut mouth"**: Ibid., 368-69.

142   **"felt very sorry"**: Ibid., 371.

142   **"had it not been"**: *BPJ*, Journal 13, 37. See also Ibid., July 21, 1813.

142   **"was contrary"**: "British Inhumanity," 171.

142   **"would throw them"**: *BPJ*, Journal 13, July 17, 1813, and 37.

142   **"abusive language"**: Ibid., July 17, 1813.

143   **"public property"**: "British Inhumanity," 171; *HID*, May 25, 1813.

143   **The purloined property**: "Account of the Cargo," Document D in Barnard, "Statement before Robert Sedgewick."

143   **scattering all the feathers**: "British Inhumanity," 171.

143   **According to Valentine**: *CHB*, 264.

143   **Throughout all... completely cut off**: *JH*, vol. II, 372.

143   **"in consequence"**: "D'Aranda's Log of the *Nancy*" (July 11, 1813).

143   **Another all-too-common**: "D'Aranda's Log of the *Nancy*" (June 29, 1813).

144   **To rid the vessel**: S. B. Grubbs and B. E. Holsendorf, "Fumigation of Vessels for the Destruction of Rats," *Public Health Reports* (June 20, 1913), 1266-67; and Miller, *The Wreck*, 122.

144   **On July 10... the shallop returned**: *RL*, 113; "D'Aranda's Log of the *Nancy*" (July 10-13, 1813); *BPJ*, Journal 13, July 9-13, 1813.

145   **"was as destitute"**: "British Inhumanity," 172.

145   **"I think that"**: *JH*, vol. II, 370.

145   **After the sorting... from the *Nanina***: Miller, *The Wreck*, 125, 130; and "D'Aranda's Log of the *Nancy*" (July 23, 1813).

145   **"a common prostitute"**: *HID*, May 25, 1813. See also "British Inhumanity," 171-72.

CHAPTER 21: DESPERATE JOURNEYS

146   **On June 15**: Background for this chapter and all quotes (with one exception) come from *CHB*, 33-48.

151   **"The sailors who visit"**: *CHB*, fn 41-42. See also, Jonathan Meiburg, *A Most Remarkable Creature: The Hidden Life of the World's Smartest Birds of Prey* (New York: Alfred A. Knopf, 2021), 5-7.

CHAPTER 22: THE *NANCY* RETURNS

157   **D'Aranda's plan**: Background for this section is from *RL*, 113-14; "Logbook of the Master" (July 27 to August 19, 1813); "D'Aranda's Log of the *Nancy*" (July 27 to November 5, 1813); "Letter from William Bowles to Manley Dixon (August 20, 1813), *ADM* 1/21, NA; William D'Aranda, "Observations on the Qualities of His Majesty's Brig *Nancy*," *ADM* 95/48, NA; and Miller, *The Wreck*, 1-2, 124-27.

158   **"departed this life"**: "D'Aranda's Log of the *Nancy*" (August 19, 1813).

158   **"[I encountered] the most tempestuous"**: *The Times* (January 29, 1814).

159   **"We had suffered"**: Quoted in Miller, *The Wreck*, 211.

159   **"[T]here seems to be no"**: Ibid.

160   **The *Nanina*'s voyage**: Background for the *Nanina*'s voyage from the Falklands to Rio comes from "Letter from Lundin to Manley Dixon" (September 13, 1813); *RL*, 313–14; *BPJ*, Journal 13, July 27–August 23, 1813, and 37–38; and *HID*, May 25, 1813.

160   **"a most miserable"**: *RL*, 313.

160   **"as much spare"**: *JH*, vol. II, 373.

160   **Part of the reason . . . benefit the *Nancy***: *BPJ*, Journal 13, July 25, 1813.

161   **"a complete shell"**: *HID*, May 25, 1813.

161   **"[O]ur decks [were]"**: *BPJ*, Journal 13, 37.

161   **"Botany Bay convicts"**: Ibid., July 29, 1813.

161   **"as poor a set"**: Ibid., 38.

161   **To top**: *JH*, vol. II, 373.

161   **Their help was**: *RL*, 314. See also *BPJ*, Journal 13, July 29, 1813, and 38; and "British Inhumanity," 172.

161   **"On the fourteenth"**: *JH*, vol. II, 374.

163   **Having reached Rio**: Background for this chapter comes from *JH*, vol. II, 375–85; and *BPJ*, Journal 13, August 23 to October 8, 1813.

163   **Holt went to . . . get involved**: Barnard, "Statement before Robert Sedgewick"; and Miller, *The Wreck*, 133.

163   **Five days after**: Barnard, "Statement before Robert Sedgewick."

164   **"bad job . . . so many lives"**: *JH*, vol. II, 377.

164   **"The Americans generously"**: Ibid., 378.

164   **Next stop for the captains**: Valentine Barnard et al., "Protest to Philip Rutter."

164   **"damages, losses"**: "British Inhumanity," 170–73.

164   **About a month**: *BPJ*, Journal 13, 38, and October 7 and 8, 1813.

164   **A few Americans**: Ibid., October 7, 1813.

165   **"Such are the particulars"**: "An Infamous Transaction," *The Evening Post* (December 10, 1813); "An Infamous Transaction," *The New York Gazette* (December 11, 1813); and "An Infamous Transaction," *The Palladium of Liberty* (December 16, 1813).

165   **"We request the"**: "British Inhumanity," in *The Weekly Register*, 170. See also: "From the *Hudson Bee*, British Inhumanity," *Washington City Gazette* (February 9, 1814).

165   **He was greatly**: "Letter from Lundin to Manley Dixon" (September 13, 1813).

166   **On October 14**: Barnard, "Statement before Robert Sedgewick."

166   **Valentine replied**: Ibid.; and *BPJ*, Journal 13, insert between entries for July 29 and July 30, 1813.

166   **The same day**: Valentine Barnard to Admiral Dixon (October 14, 1813), in Barnard, "Statement before Robert Sedgewick."

166   **"as she now stands"**: Manly Dixon to Valentine Barnard (October 16, 1813), Document B, Barnard, "Statement before Robert Sedgewick"; and Valentine Barnard to Admiral Dixon (October 19, 1813), "Statement before Robert Sedgewick."

166   **"a future claim"**: Barnard, "Statement before Robert Sedgewick."

167   **After relinquishing**: Background for this section is from Barnard, "Statement before Robert Sedgewick."; and Miller, *The Wreck*, 134–40.

168   **"promptly declined"**: Barnard, "Statement before Robert Sedgewick." See also *BPJ*, Journal 13, insert between entries for July 29 and July 30, 1813.

168   **"contrary to"**: Barnard, "Statement before Robert Sedgewick."

168   **"of the most"**: Miller, *The Wreck*, 138.

169 As for D'Aranda ... go home to London: Ibid., 137–39.
169 "[I]f you hit": Ibid., 135. See also "Greenock, May 25," *Caledonian Mercury* (May 28, 1814).
169 mutinous conduct: Miller, *The Wreck*, 135–36.
169 "after much vexation": Barnard, "Statement before Robert Sedgewick."
169 He arrived in Thomaston, Maine: Barnard, "Statement before Robert Sedgewick."

CHAPTER 26: ROUTINE, THEN DECEIT

171 Soon after Barnard: Background for this chapter, and all quotes, with exceptions noted: *CHB*, 48–57, 91.
173 Finally, Charles took ... as his stylus: Ibid., 115; and Dodge, *Marooned*, 35.
177 The species they: "Black-browed albatross," Falklands Conservation.
177 The Falkland Islands currently: Ibid.
178 "To stand at a": Delano, *A Narrative of Voyages and Travels*, 264.

CHAPTER 27: ALONE

181 After tending to the: Background for this chapter, and all quotes, except as noted: *CHB*, 58–72.
185 "I am monarch": William Cowper, "Verses Supposed to be Written by Alexander Selkirk, During His Solitary Abode on the Island of Juan Fernandez," *The Poems of William Cowper*, vol. II (Chiswick, UK: C. Whittingham, 1822), 196.
187 Charles's claim ... as a mutineer: Diana Souhami, *Selkirk's Island: The True and Strange Adventures of the Real Robinson Crusoe* (New York: Harcourt, Inc., 2001), 82–92, 100–101.

CHAPTER 28: RECONCILIATION

192 The boat landed: Background for this chapter, and all quotes: *CHB*, 73–76.

CHAPTER 29: EXPLANATION

196 Charles had long: Background for this chapter, and all quotes: *CHB*, 76–80.

CHAPTER 30: REPRIEVE, RELAPSE, AND RETURN TO EAGLE ISLAND

199 That night, Green: Background for this chapter, and all quotes: *CHB*, 80–92, 272.

CHAPTER 31: FORGIVENESS

206 A little more than: Background for this chapter, and all quotes: *CHB*, 92–96.

CHAPTER 32: TO SEA DOG ISLAND AND BACK

210 There being no: Background for this chapter, and all quotes: *CHB*, 97–99.

CHAPTER 33: BUILDING, HUNTING, AND SKINNING

213 Back on New Island: Background for this chapter, and all quotes: *CHB*, 67, 99–104.

CHAPTER 34: RETURN TO HOOK CAMP

217 Since young fur seals: Background for this chapter, and all quotes: *CHB*, 104–8.

CHAPTER 35: NEAR DISASTER

222   **Over the next**: Background for this chapter, and all quotes: *CHB*, 108–10.

CHAPTER 36: A LONG WAIT

225   **Weeks turned into**: Background for this chapter, and all quotes: *CHB*, 111–17.

CHAPTER 37: "TWO SHIPS, TWO SHIPS!"

227   **During the next**: Background for this chapter: *CHB*, 114–17, 270.
228   **Balsam bog**: James Clark Ross, *A Voyage of Discovery and Research in the Southern and Antarctic Regions, During the Years 1839–43*, vol. II (London: John Murray, 1847), 263.

CHAPTER 38: DELIVERANCE

230   **For a few minutes**: Background for this chapter, and all quotes, with noted exceptions: *CHB*, 118–23.
233   **In fact, Captain David Porter**: Background for Porter's exploits comes from Eric Jay Dolin, *Leviathan: The History of Whaling in America* (New York: W. W. Norton, 2007), 188–202.
233   **"fall an easy"**: Captain David Porter, *Journal of a Cruise Made to the Pacific Ocean by Captain David Porter*, vol. I (Philadelphia: Bradford and Inskeep, 1815), 111.
233   **"it was an unprecedented"**: Theodore Roosevelt, *The Naval War of 1812* (New York: Da Capo Press, 1999; originally published 1882), 166.
234   **"had burnt"**: Thomas Hart Benton, *Thirty Years' View; Or, A History of the Working of the American Government for Thirty Years From 1820 to 1850*, vol. II (New York: D. Appleton and Company, 1857), 498.
235   **"They had built"**: James Choyce, *The Log of a Jack Tar; or, The Life of James Choyce, Master Mariner* (London: T. Fisher Unwin, 1891), 203–4.

CHAPTER 39: PRIZE

237   **To keep his . . . the brig was offloaded**: "William D'Aranda In the High Court of Admiralty" (June 1, 1814), *Manuscript Prize Appeal No. 889*; "Nanina-Barnard, Commission of Unilevery" (June 2, 1814), *HCA 30/215*, NA; and Miller, *The Wreck*, 191.
237   **Given all of this**: "Nanina" (November 29, 1814), *HCA 8/155*, NA; and "Motion from Prize Court calling for parties to appear in the case of the *Nanina* (June 2, 1814)," *Manuscript Prize Appeal No. 889*.
238   **Peace made it**: "Letter from John B. Murray and Son to Secretary of State James Monroe" (May 18, 1815), Record Group 59, General Records of the Department of State, US National Archives.
238   **In the meantime**: "Gosport, For Sale by Public Auction," *Hampshire Chronicle* (January 9, 1815); and "Motion to bring in account" (December 9, 1815), *Manuscript Prize Appeal No. 889*.
238   **"appeal instantly . . . have been made"**: Quoted in Miller, *The Wreck*, 193.
238   **Appeal Murray did . . . have run out**: George Jenner, "Appeal" (November 28, 1815), *Manuscript Prize Appeal No. 889*; Thomas Walker, "Appeal" (November 29, 1815), *Manuscript Prize Appeal No. 889*; "Nanina Appeal" (November 29, 1815), *HCA 44/80*, NA; "Decree, High Court of Delegates" (December 9, 1815), *Manuscript Prize Appeal No. 889*; "Letter from John B. Murray and Son to Secretary of State James Monroe" (May 18, 1815); and Miller, *The Wreck*, 192–93.
238   **"It would appear"**: "Richard Rush to British Ambassador" (April 15, 1817), *FO 5/122*, NA.

239 **"The infamous . . . unpardonable"**: Miller, *The Wreck*, 212.
240 **Finally, on February 5 . . . Murrays**: Miller, *The Wreck*, 194.

CHAPTER 40: LONG, STRANGE TRIP HOME

241 **Charles's journey back**: Background for this section, and all quotes: *CHB*, 123–51, 166–259.

EPILOGUE

250 **As for the British**: *JH*, vol. II, 426–32; and *The Freeman's Journal* (April 7, 1814).
250 **"The insurrectionary"**: S.J.L., "Joseph Holt," *Irish Press* (May 16, 1973).
250 **Richard Brooks**: Parsons, "Brooks, Richard (1765–1833)"; *Australian Men of Mark*, vol. 1 (Melbourne: Charles F. Maxwell, 1889), 34; "Died," *The Sydney Herald* (October 24, 1833); and Maher, *Richard Brooks*, 208.
250 **Robert Durie . . . died in 1835**: Miller, *The Wreck*, 198–200, 240–42; and Personal communication with Bruce Durie, November 27, 2022.
250 **"meritorious . . . so much indebted"**: Quoted in Miller, *The Wreck*, 199.
250 **Sir Henry Browne**: Charles H. Bertie, *Story of Vaucluse House and Sir Henry Browne Hayes*, 22.
251 **Coincidentally, that same**: Turlough O'Riordan, "Pike, Mary," *Dictionary of Irish Biography*.
251 **William D'Aranda . . . at the age of eighty-four**: Miller, *The Wreck*, 196–98 (quote from this source); "D'Aranda," *A Naval Biographical Dictionary*, 261–62; and *CHB*, 177.
251 **"his active and persevering"**: "Rear Admiral Manley Dixon to John Wilson Crocker (September 13, 1813), in Dodge, *Marooned*, Appendix 1, 248–49. See also "Letter from Lundin to Manley Dixon" (September 13, 1813).
251 **Edmund Fanning . . . he had accrued**: Tyler, "Edmund Fanning, I Presume," 11–15.
252 **Henry Ingman Defrees**: Background for Defrees comes from "Port of Boston," *Columbian Centinel* (February 8, 1817); "Old Sherry Wine," *Nantucket Inquirer* (August 10, 1836); "For Sale," *Nantucket Inquirer* (July 26, 1837); "For Sale," *Nantucket Inquirer* (January 10, 1825); "For St. Salvador," *Nantucket Inquirer* (November 1, 1823); personal communication with Michael R. Harrison, Chief Curator and Obed Macy Research Chair, Nantucket Historical Association; *HID*, July 4 and December 8, 1815, and May 2, 1816; and "Died," *The Inquirer and Mirror* (November 25, 1871).
252 **When Barzillai Pease**: "Died": *Northern Whig* (October 12, 1813); and *BPJ*, Journal 13, 46.
252 **Near the end**: Anthony Slosek, "Captain Pease Moves an Army," *Oswego County Messenger* (February 13, 1984); and *BPJ*, Journal 13, 47.
252 **"insolvent debtor"**: "By order of Ambrose L. Jordan," *Albany Argus* (April 30, 1824). See also *BPJ*, Journal 13, 53–54.
252 **"performed a certain"**: *BPJ*, Journal 19, June 3, 1826.
252 **"so shabby"**: Ibid., June 11, 1826.
252 **"[M]y voyage at"**: Ibid., July 2, 1826.
253 **"could not find"**: Ibid., August 12, 1826.
253 **Valentine Barnard never**: "Died," *The Long-Island Star* (December 25, 1823).
253 **"Fourteen armed . . . chicken-hearted"**: *CHB*, 153.
253 **"But this contemptible . . . pity or fear"**: Ibid.
254 **"After an absence"**: Ibid., 261.
254 **"an insolvent"**: Advertisement, *The Columbian* (November 27, 1816).
255 **New York brig *Charity***: Edouard A. Stackpole, *The Voyage of The Huron and the Huntress: The American Sealers and the Discovery of the Continent of Antarctica* (Mystic, CT: The Marine Historical Association, 1955), 16.

255 **"greedily devoured . . . Robinson Crusoe":** James Weddell, *A Voyage Towards The South Pole, Performed in the Years 1822–24* (London: Longman, Hurst, Rees, Orme, Brown, and Green, 1825), 90–91.

256 **"I now . . . inhospitable island":** *CHB*, 261.

256 **Reflecting on his . . . and rescue them:** *CHB*, 261–62.

258 **"iron-hearted captain":** Ibid., 262.

258 **"May the sufferings":** Ibid., 265–66.

258 **"[T]he book is not":** "Barnard's Narrative," *New-York Mirror and Ladies' Literary Gazette* (August 1, 1829).

258 **"is said to be":** Miscellaneous, *Georgian* (August 1, 1829).

258 **Beyond captaining . . . in relative obscurity:** Miscellaneous, *Georgian* (August 1, 1929); Miscellaneous, *Daily Chronicle* (March 18, 1831); "Appointments Made," *Evening Post* (March 26, 1833); "Appointments by the Governor and Senate," *Evening Post* (March 10, 1835); "Rejections of the Nominations of the Governor (May 3, 1839)," *Commercial Advertiser* (May 10, 1839); "At a meeting of," *Evening Post* (January 10, 1837); Dodge, *Marooned*, 21; and "Died," *New York Herald* (November 17, 1863).

ILLUSTRATION CREDITS

═══

page 4: Wikimedia

page 5: George Henry Mason, *The Costume of China: Illustrated by Sixty Engravings; with Explanations in English and French* (London: W. Miller, 1800)

page 6: John James Audubon and John Bachman, *The Quadrupeds of North America*, vol. III (New York: V. G. Audubon, 1854)

page 8: William Jardine, *The Naturalist's Library*, vol. XXV (London: Henry G. Bohn, 1860)

page 9: Courtesy Alison Barton

page 10: William Jardine, *The Naturalist's Library*, vol. XXV (London: Henry G. Bohn, 1860)

page 11: Courtesy David Rumsey Map Collection, David Rumsey Map Center, Stanford Libraries

page 12: Courtesy Library of Congress

page 13: Courtesy Naval History and Heritage Command

page 16: Courtesy Library of Congress

page 19: *The Progressive Drawing-Book* (London: Henry G. Bohn, 1853)

page 24: Wikimedia

page 25: Courtesy Library of Congress

page 27: (waterspout) Courtesy Geography: waterspouts at sea. Engraving by C. Heath after H. Salt. Wellcome Collection. Public Domain Mark

page 27: (Cape Verde islands map) Courtesy David Rumsey Map Collection, David Rumsey Map Center, Stanford Libraries

page 28: Boyd Horsbrugh, *The Game-Birds & Water-Fowl of South Africa* (London: Witherby & Co., 1912)

page 32: Courtesy David Rumsey Map Collection, David Rumsey Map Center, Stanford Libraries

page 35: Courtesy Alison Barton

page 36: Courtesy New York Public Library, Public Domain Library

page 37: Courtesy David Rumsey Map Collection, David Rumsey Map Center, Stanford Libraries

page 38: (Falkland Islands map) Courtesy John Carter Brown Library, Brown University

page 38: (Fort St. Louis) Courtesy John Carter Brown Library, Brown University

page 40: W. J. Hooker, *Notes on the Botany of the Antarctic Voyage, Conducted by Captain James Clark Ross, R.N., F.R.S., in Her Majesty's Discovery Ships* Erebus *and* Terror; *with Observations on the Tussac Grass of the Falkland Islands* (London: H. Bailliere, 1843)

page 41: (Falkland Strawberry) E. F. Vallentin, *Illustrations of the Flowering Plants and Ferns of the Falkland Islands* (London: L. Reeve & Co., 1921)

page 41: (scurvy grass) E. F. Vallentin, *Illustrations of the Flowering Plants and Ferns of the Falkland Islands* (London: L. Reeve & Co., 1921) page 42: Henry Johnson, *Johnson's Household Book of Nature*, ed. Hugh Craig (New York: Henry J. Johnson, 1880)

page 43: Courtesy John Carter Brown Library, Brown University

page 44: Courtesy John Carter Brown Library, Brown University

page 45: Henry Johnson, *Johnson's Household Book of Nature*, ed. Hugh Craig (New York: Henry J. Johnson, 1880)

page 46: (sea lion engraving) William Jardine, *The Naturalist's Library*, vol. XXV (London: Henry G. Bohn, 1860)

page 46: (elephant seals) Courtesy Alison Barton

page 49: (goose) Courtesy Nick Morton licensed under CC BY 4.0

page 49: (sealers) Edmund Fanning, *Voyages Round the World* (London: O. Rich, 1834)

page 50: Edmund Fanning, *Voyages Round the World* (London: O. Rich, 1834)

page 52: Charles H. Barnard, *A Narrative of the Sufferings and Adventures of Capt. Charles H. Barnard, in a Voyage Round the World, During the Years 1812, 1813, 1814, 1815, & 1816; Embracing an Account of the Seizure of His Vessel at the Falkland Islands, by an English Crew Whom He Had Rescued from the Horrors of Shipwreck; and of Their Abandoning Him on an Uninhabited Island, Where He Resided Nearly Two Years* (New York: J. Lindon, 1829)

page 56: Courtesy Alison Barton

page 59: Courtesy Alison Barton

page 60: Courtesy Georgina Strange, Design In Nature

page 63: (Sydney) Courtesy David Rumsey Map Collection, David Rumsey Map Center, Stanford Libraries

page 63: (Captain Robert Durie) Courtesy Andrew Maule Dewar Durie of Durie and Christian Frances Dewar Durie

page 64: *Australian Men of Mark*, vol. 1 (Melbourne: Charles F. Maxwell, 1889)

page 65: Courtesy Dixson Library, State Library of New South Wales

page 66: (convict transports) Courtesy Mitchell Library, State Library of New South Wales

page 66: (convicts embarking) Courtesy Mitchell Library, State Library of New South Wales

page 67: Wikimedia

page 68: Joseph Holt, *The Memoirs of Joseph Holt, General of the Irish Rebels, in 1798*, vol. II, ed. T. Crofton Croker (London: Henry Colburn, 1838)

page 69: Wikimedia

page 70: Courtesy Vaucluse House Collection, Sydney Living Museums

page 71: Charles Bertie, "Sir Henry Brown Hayes: A Stormy Petrel," *The Lone Hand* (January 1, 1910)

page 73: Charles Bertie, "Sir Henry Brown Hayes: A Stormy Petrel," *The Lone Hand* (January 1, 1910)

page 74: Caroline Simpson Library, Museums of History NSW

page 77: Courtesy David Rumsey Map Collection, David Rumsey Map Center, Stanford Libraries

page 79: Courtesy Library of Congress

page 82: Chris and Lindsey May, current owners of Speedwell Island

page 84: (beach) Chris and Lindsey May, current owners of Speedwell Island

page 84: (anchor) Chris and Lindsey May, current owners of Speedwell Island

page 85: Chris and Lindsey May, current owners of Speedwell Island

page 86: Chris and Lindsey May, current owners of Speedwell Island

page 87: Courtesy Jennifer Sol, Falklands Conservation

page 88: Chris and Lindsey May, current owners of Speedwell Island

page 95: George R. Waterhouse, *The Zoology of the Voyage of H.M.S. Beagle. Part II, Mammalia* (London: Smith, Elder and Co., 1839)

page 101: Courtesy David Rumsey Map Collection, David Rumsey Map Center, Stanford Libraries

page 103: Wikimedia

page 105: © National Maritime Museum, Greenwich, London

page 106: Wikimedia

page 114: Charles H. Barnard, *A Narrative of the Sufferings and Adventures of Capt. Charles H. Barnard, in a Voyage Round the World, During the Years 1812, 1813, 1814, 1815, & 1816; Embracing an Account of the Seizure of His Vessel at the Falkland Islands, by an English Crew Whom He Had Rescued from the Horrors of Shipwreck; and of Their Abandoning Him on an Uninhabited Island, Where He Resided Nearly Two Years* (New York: J. Lindon, 1829)

page 120: Chris and Lindsey May, current owners of Speedwell Island

page 162: William Hadfield, *Brazil, The River Plate, and the Falkland Islands* (London: Longman, Brown, Green, and Longmans, 1854)

page 172: Charles Ellms, *Robinson Crusoe's Own Book; or, The Voice of Adventure, from the Civilized Man Cut Off from His Fellows, by Force, Accident, or Inclination, and from the Wanderer in Strange Seas and Lands* (Boston: William C. Perry, 1843)

page 175: Charles Ellms, *Robinson Crusoe's Own Book; or, The Voice of Adventure, from the Civilized Man Cut Off from His Fellows, by Force, Accident, or Inclination, and from the Wanderer in Strange Seas and Lands* (Boston: William C. Perry, 1843)

page 176: John James Audubon and John Bachman, *The Quadrupeds of North America*, vol. II (New York: V. G. Audubon, 1854)

page 177: Courtesy Alison Barton

page 178: (albatross) Courtesy Falkland Islands Tourist Board

page 178: (albatross roockery) Courtesy David Stanley

page 182: Charles Ellms, *Robinson Crusoe's Own Book; or, The Voice of Adventure, from the Civilized Man Cut Off from His Fellows, by Force, Accident, or Inclination, and from the Wanderer in Strange Seas and Lands* (Boston: William C. Perry, 1843).

page 184: Courtesy Georgina Strange, Design In Nature

page 186: Courtesy John Carter Brown Library, Brown University

page 189: Courtesy Georgina Strange, Design In Nature

page 193: Charles H. Barnard, *A Narrative of the Sufferings and Adventures of Capt. Charles H. Barnard, in a Voyage Round the World, During the Years 1812, 1813, 1814, 1815, & 1816; Embracing an Account of the Seizure of His Vessel at the Falkland Islands, by an English Crew Whom He Had Rescued from the Horrors of Shipwreck; and of their Abandoning Him on an Uninhabited Island, Where He Resided Nearly Two Years* (New York: J. Lindon, 1829)

page 194: Courtesy Alison Barton

page 201: Charles H. Barnard, *A Narrative of the Sufferings and Adventures of Capt. Charles H. Barnard, in a Voyage Round the World, During the Years 1812, 1813, 1814, 1815, & 1816; Embracing an Account of the Seizure of His Vessel at the Falkland Islands, by an English Crew Whom He Had Rescued from the Horrors of Shipwreck; and of their Abandoning Him on an Uninhabited Island, Where He Resided Nearly Two Years* (New York: J. Lindon, 1829)

page 214: Charles Ellms, *Robinson Crusoe's Own Book; or, The Voice of Adventure, from the Civilized Man Cut Off from His Fellows, by Force, Accident, or Inclination, and from the Wanderer in Strange Seas and Lands* (Boston: William C. Perry, 1843)

page 220: Charles Ellms, *Robinson Crusoe's Own Book; or, The Voice of Adventure, from the Civilized Man Cut Off from His Fellows, by Force, Accident, or Inclination, and from the Wanderer in Strange Seas and Lands* (Boston: William C. Perry, 1843)

page 228: Courtesy Alison Barton

page 229: Charles H. Barnard, *A Narrative of the Sufferings and Adventures of Capt. Charles H. Barnard, in a Voyage Round the World During the Years 1812, 1813, 1814, 1815, & 1816; Embracing an Account of the Seizure of His Vessel at the Falkland Islands, by an English Crew Whom He Had Rescued from the Horrors of Shipwreck; and of Their Abandoning Him on an Uninhabited Island, Where He Resided Nearly Two Years* (New York: J. Lindon, 1829)

page 234: Courtesy Naval History and Heritage Command

page 235: Courtesy Library of Congress

page 239: Rudolph Ackermann, *The Microcosm of London; or London in Miniature*, vol. I (London: Bensley, 1815)

page 243: Charles H. Barnard, *A Narrative of the Sufferings and Adventures of Capt. Charles H. Barnard, in a Voyage Round the World, During the Years 1812, 1813, 1814, 1815, & 1816; Embracing an Account of the Seizure of His Vessel at the Falkland Islands, by an English Crew Whom He Had Rescued from the Horrors of Shipwreck; and of Their Abandoning Him on an Uninhabited Island, Where He Resided Nearly Two Years* (New York: J. Lindon, 1829)

page 246: (Más Afuera Island) Courtesy John Carter Brown Library, Brown University

page 246: (*Millwood* arrival) Charles H. Barnard, *A Narrative of the Sufferings and Adventures of Capt. Charles H. Barnard, in a Voyage Round the World, During the Years 1812, 1813, 1814, 1815, & 1816; Embracing an Account of the Seizure of His Vessel at the Falkland Islands, by an English Crew Whom He Had Rescued from the Horrors of Shipwreck; and of Their Abandoning Him on an Uninhabited Island, Where He Resided Nearly Two Years* (New York: J. Lindon, 1829)

page 248: Charles Ellms, *Robinson Crusoe's Own Book; or, The Voice of Adventure, from the Civilized Man Cut Off from His Fellows, by Force, Accident, or Inclination, and from the Wanderer in Strange Seas and Lands* (Boston: William C. Perry, 1843).

page 255: James Weddell, *A Voyage Towards the South Pole, Performed in the Years 1822–24* (London: Longman, Hurst, Rees, Orme, Brown, and Green, 1825).

page 257: Courtesy Phillips Library, Peabody Essex Museum, Rowley, MA

page 259: Courtesy Alison Barton

page 260: (settlement) Courtesy Alison Barton

page 260: (Barnard Museum) Courtesy Alison Barton

All images in the insert: Courtesy Georgina Strange, Design In Nature

INDEX

===

Page numbers in *italics* refer to illustrations. Page numbers after 262 refer to endnotes.

ABOUT THE AUTHOR

═

ERIC JAY DOLIN is the author of sixteen books, including *Leviathan: The History of Whaling in America*, which was chosen as one of the best nonfiction books of 2007 by the *Los Angeles Times* and the *Boston Globe*, was an "Editor's Choice" selection by the *New York Times Book Review*, and also won the 2007 John Lyman Award for US Maritime History; and *Black Flags, Blue Waters: The Epic History of America's Most Notorious Pirates*, which was chosen as a "Must-Read" book by the Massachusetts Center for the Book. Other books include *A Furious Sky: The Five-Hundred-Year History of America's Hurricanes*, which won the Atmospheric Science Librarians International Choice Award for History, and was chosen by the *Washington Post* as one of 50 Notable Works of Nonfiction in 2020, by *Kirkus Reviews* as one of the Best Nonfiction Books of 2020 (in addition to being a Kirkus Prize finalist), by the *Library Journal* and *Booklist* as one of the Best Science & Technology Books of 2020, and by the *New York Times Book Review* as an "Editors' Choice"; *Fur, Fortune, and Empire: The Epic History of the Fur Trade in America*, which was chosen by the *Seattle Times* as one of the best nonfiction books of 2010, and also won the James P. Hanlan Book Award, given by the New England Historical Association; *When America First Met China: An Exotic History of Tea, Drugs, and Money in the Age of Sail*, which was chosen by *Kirkus Reviews* as one of the 100 best nonfiction books of 2012 and was a finalist for the New England Society in the City of New York Book Award; and *Brilliant Beacons: A History of the American Lighthouse*, which was chosen by the website gCaptain and by *Classic Boat* magazine as one of the best nautical books of 2016 and was selected as a "Must-Read" book. His most recent book prior to *Left for Dead* was *Rebels at Sea: Privateering in the American Revolution*, which won the Fraunces Tavern Museum Book Award for 2023 and the Samuel Eliot Morison Book Award for Naval Literature. It was also selected as a "Must-Read" book and was a finalist for both the Boston Authors Club Julia Ward Howe Award for nonfiction and the New England Society Book Award. A graduate of Brown, Yale, and MIT, where he received his PhD in environmental policy, Dolin lives in Marblehead, Massachusetts, with his family. For more information on his background and books, visit his website, ericjaydolin.com. You can also follow Dolin's posts on his professional Facebook page, @Ericjaydolin.

MORE FROM
Eric Jay Dolin

"Dolin convincingly contends that the underappreciated 'militia of the sea' played a critical role in the colonies winning their independence."

—Gerard Helferich,
Wall Street Journal

"Rumbustious enough for the adventure-hungry. . . . [I]t draws the pirate in a clear light."

—Peter Lewis,
San Francisco Chronicle

"[A] lively chronicle of five tempestuous centuries."

—Elizabeth Kolbert,
New York Times Book Review

"*Leviathan* is an exhaustive, richly detailed history of industrial American whaling."

—Bruce Barcott,
New York Times

Liveright Publishing Corporation

A Division of W. W. Norton & Company
Independent Publishers Since 1923